Identity and social interaction in a multi-ethnic classroom

the Tufnell Press,
London,
United Kingdom

www.tufnellpress.co.uk

email contact@tufnellpress.co.uk

British Library Cataloguing-in-Publication Data
A catalogue record for this book is
available from the British Library

paperback ISBN *1872767346*
ISBN-13 *978-1-872767-34-5*

Kindle *978-1-872767-39-7*

Printed in England and U.S.A. by Lightning Source

Identity and social interaction in a multi-ethnic classroom

by

Ruth Barley

Ethnography and Education

The Ethnography and Education book series aims to publish a range of authored and edited collections including both substantive research projects and methodological texts and in particular we hope to include recent PhDs. Our priority is for ethnographies that prioritise the experiences and perspectives of those involved and that also reflect a sociological perspective with international significance. We are particularly interested in those ethnographies that explicate and challenge the effects of educational policies and practices and interrogate and develop theories about educational structures, policies and experiences. We value ethnographic methodology that involves long-term engagement with those studied in order to understand their cultures, that use multiple methods of generating data and that recognise the centrality of the researcher in the research process.

www.ethnographyandeducation.org

The editors welcome substantive proposals that seek to:

explicate and challenge the effects of educational policies and practices and interrogate and develop theories about educational structures, policies and experiences,

highlight the agency of educational actors,

provide accounts of how the everyday practices of those engaged in education are instrumental in social reproduction.

Contents

Dedication

Many thanks must go to all those who have supported me in designing, conducting and writing this book and the doctoral thesis that it is based on.

Specifically I would like to thank my editor Prof. Geoffrey Walford and my doctoral supervisory team Prof. Guy Merchant, Dr. Caroline Bath and Prof. Sarah Salway for their invaluable feedback, guidance and support. Further, I would like to thank Dr. Jenny Blain and Dr. Ros Garrick who examined initial stages of this study and offered an insight into how the study might progress. Thanks must further go to Dr. Ros Garrick for her reading of, and feedback on, this full monograph.

Special thanks must also go to my two proof-readers: my Mum, Jane Barley, who proof-read initial versions of the following chapters and my good friend, Nadia Lipsey, who proof-read a near final version. Their comments have helped to produce this polished version of my work.

Further thanks must go to my partner, parents, friends and colleagues who offered their support through the ups and downs of this project as well as welcome distractions when I needed a short break from this work.

Lastly, but most importantly, I must thank the children, staff and families whose stories are told in this book. Without you none of this would have been possible. By telling your stories I hope to give something back to you just as you gave me a thirst for knowledge and reinvigorated my passion to fight against social injustice.

This study is dedicated to the memory of my Gran, Mary Moore, whose stories of her world travels created in me a thirst to explore the world, meet new people and challenge global inequalities.

Chapter 1

Setting the scene: Introduction

'The distinctness of a group is neither a fiction nor an essence' (Modood, 2007: 115).

Focus and rationale for the study

It is early June and I am sitting with Annakiya as she draws a picture.[1] Annakiya, who is now five years old, arrived in the UK with her immediate family, nine months earlier, from West Africa. She has attended Sunnyside School since the start of the academic year in September. Annakiya begins to draw a picture of her future self as a princess, chatting to me as she does so. As she begins to colour in her picture she recites to me the different colours that she is using to create her rainbow dress, her pink shoes, her brown hair and her golden tiara. After she finishes colouring in these parts of the princess, she pauses and looks at the picture before telling me 'I'm not gunna colour my face because this is when I'm grown up. My hair is curly, I'm a princess and I am light, like you.' I ask her why she wants to be light when she is older. 'Now I'm dark and you are light' she continues. 'When I'm grown up I'm gunna be light, like you, and like my mum. My mum's light too.' As I reflect on this last statement I recall that Annakiya's mum's skin colour is much lighter than her dad's. I tell Annakiya that I like the colour of her skin as it is now, saying that it is very pretty. She ponders this for a while, as she continues to colour in her picture, before saying 'It's OK to be different, like *Elmer*,[2] but really I wanna be like you.'

This study unearths how a group of young children (4-5 year-olds) explore difference and identity in their peer interactions thereby raising questions for how policy and practice can begin to break down the barriers of fear that so often pervade these discourses. The conversation is just one example of how children at Sunnyside understand difference, in relation to their own identity, as being hierarchical; in this instance, 'light' skin colour being viewed as better than 'dark' skin colour. As will be seen throughout this book, children at Sunnyside regularly discuss diversity relating to ethnicity, religion and gender within the context of

1. Pseudonyms are used throughout.
2. The class project at this time focused on the story of *Elmer*, the brightly coloured patchwork elephant who discovers that 'It is OK to be different' when the other elephants in his troop accept him for who he is (McKee, 1989).

identity maintenance and (re)negotiation amongst themselves as well as with me. Within these conversations, children often use 'being ...' phrases to describe themselves and others. Phrases such as 'being a girl' and 'being a boy', 'being Muslim' and 'being Christian' regularly feature in their daily social interactions. 'Being' phrases are also used by children to discuss the more abstract concept of 'being different.' Within these everyday conversations, children conceptualise and operationalise social abstractions of difference, discourses of discrimination and hierarchies of difference relating to their ethnic, religious and gendered identities. In doing this they employ both bodily and material markers of difference as they explore the performative, situated and dialectical nature of identity. Both social structure and social agency are salient in children's daily identity (re)negotiations amongst their school peers. All of these aspects will be explored in more detail in later chapters of this book.

Children's discussions about difference and identity are not constructed in isolation from wider social discourses but, as this study reveals, discourses and social structures that are dominant in both mainstream popular and minority cultures, and embedded across time and space, are foundational in children's own constructions of self and others. Consequently, as Hall (2000: 4) points out, identities can be understood as being 'constructed within, not outside [of], discourse'. Discourses of difference, and particularly fear or disdain of the so-called 'other', are prevalent in all aspects of life. From classical Western children's stories, such as Burnett's *The Secret Garden* and Twain's *The Adventures of Huckleberry Finn*, to popular culture and science fiction, like *Battlestar Galactica*, discourses of difference are promoted, perpetuated and, at times, challenged. The recent rise of right wing politics across Western Europe, which perpetuates a fear of migrants stealing local jobs, the threat of global terrorism and the onslaught of non-Western cultural values, further entrenches discourses of difference and discrimination (Lowles and Painter, 2011). Segregated social systems in many of the countries, where children at Sunnyside have recently arrived from, create an artificial distance between communities, discouraging interaction and encouraging fear of 'the other', resulting in the prominence of systematic inequality and at times tribal factions and civil war (United Nations Human Rights Council [UNHRC], 2010). Media advertising that uses digital technology to lighten celebrities' skin colour and promotes skin lightening creams to minority communities adds to this, by creating a hierarchy of difference that views the ideal body image and so-called beauty (particularly of girls and women) as being linked to a specific ethnic identity (Glenn, 2008). Disdain of 'the other' and dominant views of what is best consequently become part of wider social discourses with language such as 'us' and 'them' peppering everyday conversations. Consequently, identity becomes a salient feature of social interaction. While, as this study reveals, identity and social divisions, such as ethnicity and gender, are socially constructed, associated forms of discrimination, such as racism and sexism, are very real and can have a profound impact on an individual's life. As Modood (2007: 115) states, groups and collective identities should not be considered to be 'a fiction nor an essence' as the impact of social discourses leaves a very real mark on individuals' and communities' sense of self.

The prevalence of such discourses raise a range of questions about the social world: What unites and divides individuals? Why do we fear difference? Why do we feel a need to protect our own against 'the other'? Why does inequality and discrimination pervade all aspects of society? The answers to these and other similar questions are too big for this book. However, this study will begin to address how a group of young children explore identity and diversity in their peer interactions thereby raising questions for how policy and practice can begin to break down the barriers of fear that so often pervade these discourses. In doing so, this study begins to illuminate how and why young children are influenced by wider social structures of difference and fear or disdain of 'the other.'

Previous research that identifies young children's understanding of difference as a hierarchical social construction, in which certain identities are considered to be more valid than others, forms the foundation of this research. Earlier studies show that some young children try to deny aspects of their own identity because of this wish to have an externally validated identity and feel that they 'belong', for example in wanting to be considered 'white' (Holmes, 1995; Nayak, 2009). These views reveal underlying structural inequalities in society that commonly view 'white as better' and majority forms of capital as more valid than minority capital (Lin, 2000). When taken to an extreme, these views can lead to racial and/or ethnic segregation but more commonly impact on a daily basis on an individual's social interactions; such as their friendship groups and social networks (Holmes, 1995). This patterning of social capital impacts directly on an individual's access to resources and services, such as education and healthcare. As the UK is a multi-ethnic society with a continually diversifying population (Nazroo, 2006; Vertovec, 2007), research, such as the current study, and policies that address the inequalities that ethnic minorities face, and aim to bring some form of social justice, are becoming more and more important.

Building on this foundation, this study fills a gap in the current literature by exploring the experiences of young children from North and Sub-Saharan African families. The rationale for this focus stems from the prevalence of research in the UK that focuses on children from South Asian families and fails to uncover the experiences of children from other backgrounds. Adding to this, previous studies that have explored notions of difference with young children have tended to frame this within a discussion about bodily markers of difference failing to unearth how children understand material markers of difference. Addressing these gaps in the literature, my study uncovers how children from a diverse range of backgrounds conceptualise and operationalise a range of identity markers in a dynamic social world, over a specific period of time.

Aim and objectives

Building on the rationale outlined above the central aim of this study was *to uncover and improve understanding of how cultural minority children explore identity and social interaction in a multi-ethnic Early Years classroom.*

To achieve this, an ethnography was undertaken to explore young children's identities and peer interactions through sharing their stories and co-constructing an interpretation of their social meaning. Within this framework, children are understood as being 'rich', competent social actors (Moss et al., 2000). Previous ethnographies also adopting this framework, such as van Ausdale and Feagin's (2001) work in America and Connolly's (2003) in Ireland, discovered that young children actively understand and employ 'conventional' markers of difference and apply social meaning to abstract social discourses. Further to this, these studies have also revealed that children are aware of, and at times actively perpetuate, wider social discourses of discrimination and hierarchies of difference. Each of these aspects are also unearthed in the current study.

As Malinowski (1922) advocates, I entered the field with a clear but unrestrictive aim and an open mind as to how the ethnography would unfold. Once in the field, the project began to take shape as the children participated in the ongoing design of the study and highlighted the aspects of identity and diversity that were important to them. Based on my initial observations in the field, conversations with children and staff as well as an initial review of related literature I devised the following six research objectives:

1. To determine how young children conceptualise and operationalise identity.
2. To discover how young children view difference.

3 To uncover what part these aspects play in how patterns of interaction are formed in a multi-ethnic context.

4 To develop an interdisciplinary theoretical framework to explore the concept of identity.

5 To explore how ethnography can support and develop educational research methodology and vice versa.

6 To raise questions for consideration in policy and practice.

My initial review of the literature, highlighted a number of aspects that we already know about the nature of identity, diversity and difference as well as how young children conceptualise and operationalise these concepts. To briefly summarise this, previous theoretical and empirical research has revealed that:

identity is performative, situated and dialectical in nature;

'strong structuration' is a useful concept that allows researchers to uncover and understand social relations and practices;

research with young children predominantly adopts a developmental approach that views identity as asocial;

children are competent and capable social actors who hold important perspectives on social life that need to be heard and valued;

young children are aware of abstract concepts such as identity, racism etc.;

young children can, and do, apply 'conventional meaning' to abstract concepts.

Building on this foundational knowledge, this ethnography uncovers a group of young children's experiences of identity, diversity and inequality. In this way, it can be seen as a vehicle guiding the way in which we currently understand young children, as it seeks to influence current educational practice in an ever diversifying social world. In exploring how children from North and Sub-Saharan African families conceptualise and operationalise difference in relation to bodily and material markers this study unearths theoretical, methodological and representational insights as it:

draws together and critiques different identity theories within a 'strong structuration' framework;

adds to the growing body of literature that applies 'strong structuration' to empirical contexts and by doing so helps to develop the ongoing critique of this concept;

develops the related concepts of bodily and material markers of difference;

highlights how educational research methodology can learn from ethnography and vice versa;

shows how young children conceptualise and operationalise a complex understanding of identity in their everyday lives;

highlights the salience of identity for young children;

reveals the lived experiences of young children's experiences of identity and inequality;

uncovers the details and prominence of children's daily negotiations about identity and diversity;

illustrates how children's collective experiences can and do link global (macro) and local (micro) contexts.

The way in which this study uncovers each of these aspects will be explored in later chapters of this book.

The field location for this ethnography was a Reception class (aged 4-5) in a culturally diverse primary school, Sunnyside, in the North of England, where the majority of children are from North or Sub-Saharan African families. The rationale for selecting Sunnyside as the field location was based on advice from research colleagues, two locally based English as Additional Language Coordinators (employed by the Council), and also through reviewing recent Ofsted reports for basic school demographics relating to the minority cultural (and language) make-up of children at the school. Access was then negotiated via a colleague.

Data about the school's demographics have been compiled from recent Ofsted reports, national school level census statistics and the school's own data. To protect the identity of the school references for these documents are not given below.

Two-hundred and ten children attended the school during my fieldwork period (DfE, 2011). A number of pupils are perceived as being from deprived backgrounds as is reflected in the forty-one per cent that are entitled to free school meals , a measure described by Gillborn and Youdell (2000: 10) as 'a crude proxy of poverty'. The national average across all state-funded primary schools for the same year was nineteen per cent.

The majority of pupils, in Ofsted's words, are from cultural minority 'groups' and in 2005 (i.e. during the last Ofsted inspection before I started my fieldwork) it was reported that there were at least fifteen different home languages spoken. Many pupils are new to the UK when they first arrive at Sunnyside and have a limited grasp of the English language. The majority of children from cultural minority families fall into two broad categories: refugees or asylum seekers, and children of international students studying at post-graduate level at the nearby university.

Sunnyside works hard to celebrate the diversity and cultural capital that each child brings to the school. They do this via whole school projects, school assemblies and class-based activities. Sunnyside has also teamed up with the initiative *Our Languages* that aims to promote the use of community languages in schools across England. As part of this initiative, Sunnyside is teaching Somali, which is one of the most common community languages within the school, to all Year-3 children and staff. By promoting the Somali language, Sunnyside hopes to support Somali parents in encouraging their children to speak Somali at home, promote self-esteem amongst Somali children and raise the status of the language amongst the whole school community. As Chapter 6 reveals, Somali families are less likely to value their own linguistic capital than other minority families in the school (particularly Arabic speakers). Therefore this is an important initiative that can help families see the importance of their own minority linguistic capital.

Building on this whole school initiative of celebrating diversity and each individual's cultural capital, the Reception class incorporates these principles into the everyday fabric of the classroom, most notably through using multilingual and multi-ethnic resources and topic work, such as multilingual signage and reading books, toys that reflect the ethnic and religious diversity of the children in the class, and anti-discriminatory topic work such as the story of *Elmer*, the patchwork elephant (McKee, 1989).

In 2011/12 (the academic year in which my fieldwork was conducted) the Reception class at Sunnyside was staffed by a classroom teacher (Mary), teaching assistant (Susan) and were scheduled to be supported for two half day sessions by multilingual support workers. At Sunnyside children call staff in the early years by their first names. I was therefore automatically known to the children as Ruth. Throughout the course of the year a number of college students were placed in the class. In January a final year teaching student conducted her final placement there.

Owing to pressures throughout the school, multilingual support workers were often required elsewhere meaning that the Reception class regularly did not receive the multilingual support that they had been timetabled for. According to the senior leadership team (SLT), financial constraints mean that the school as a whole is understaffed in this area. When language support workers are required elsewhere on a regular basis, lack of support for a particular class can have a profound impact on the learning of children with little English, as well as their social interaction with peers across languages.

Arabic and Somali were the two key languages, other than English, that were spoken in the class. Most children took part in the study in English though the school's multilingual and bilingual support workers were used as translators when appropriate. Peer translators were also used as and when children required. In our conversations some children interspersed English with an Arabic or Somali term, such as *Aljana* (Arabic for heaven) or *Ayeeyo* (Somali for grandmother). Children's own (emic) terms have been used throughout this written ethnography.

The class had two intakes during the course of the year, the first in September and the second in January. In September there were nineteen children in the class: ten girls and nine boys. In January an additional ten children joined the class: five girls and five boys. Due to ongoing migration, two children left the school over the course of the year and two new children joined the class. A total of thirty-one children therefore took part in the study.

On starting school, Sunnyside collected registration data for all children. This data refers to all thirty-one children who were in the class during the course of the year. Additionally data pertaining to the children who joined the class in the second term is included in the January starter data to further protect their anonymity. Key points of interest are highlighted below.

Registration data

The ethnic categories given on the registration form were as follows: Black Somali; Other Black African; Yemeni; Bangladeshi; Other Asian; White British; Other ethnic group.

It should be noted the information in Figure 1.1 relating to ethnicity was provided by families and does not always reflect the child's self-definition of their ethnic background. As Russell (2011) highlights family-defined ethnicity, such as this, can conflict with children's individual ethnic identification. This was at times the case in the present study. Children's views on their ethnic identity were explored as part of the project and are described in later chapters.

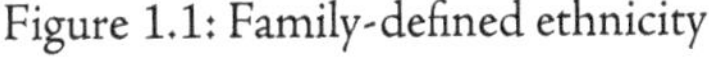
Figure 1.1: Family-defined ethnicity

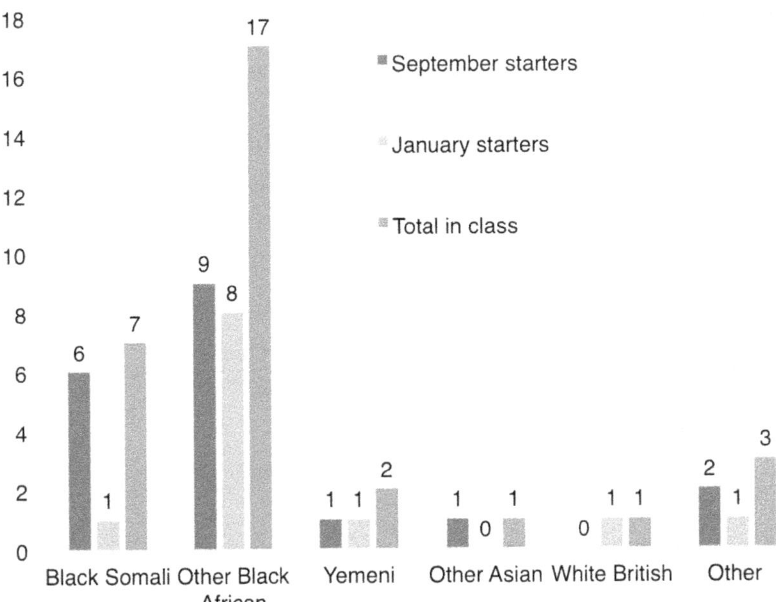

As can be seen from the above figure it is notable that there were (according to the school's official records) no White British children in the September intake. However, what is not clear from this data is that the three children (two September and one January starter) in the 'other category' are both from a mixed heritage with one white English parent.

Additionally it should be noted that categories that are used in this figure were supplied by the school and are problematic, as they mix both national and ethnic categories and also inappropriately include a number of umbrella terms. Umbrella terms, such as Black, can be effectively employed when discussing the politicised nature of ethnic identity i.e. as a term to refer to minority status and inequality. This, however, is not the way in which this term was employed in Sunnyside's school registration data.

The category 'Other black African' is particularly problematic as families from a number of North African countries, e.g. Egypt and Libya, are included here with families from Sub-Saharan Africa. Some children included in this category adamantly self-defined as 'being White' in our research activities.

Within each of these nationalities, families are also from a range of diverse ethnic and cultural 'groups'. Across the whole school, 98% of pupils are from an ethnic minority group. These figures are in stark contrast to the national picture where only 13% of school pupils in state funded primary schools in England are from an ethnic minority group (DfE, 2011).

As can be seen from Figure 1.2, the majority of children in the class speak Arabic as their first language. Within the class children speak four different first languages. This is in stark contrast to the fifteen languages that Ofsted identified across the school.

Figure 1.2: First language profile

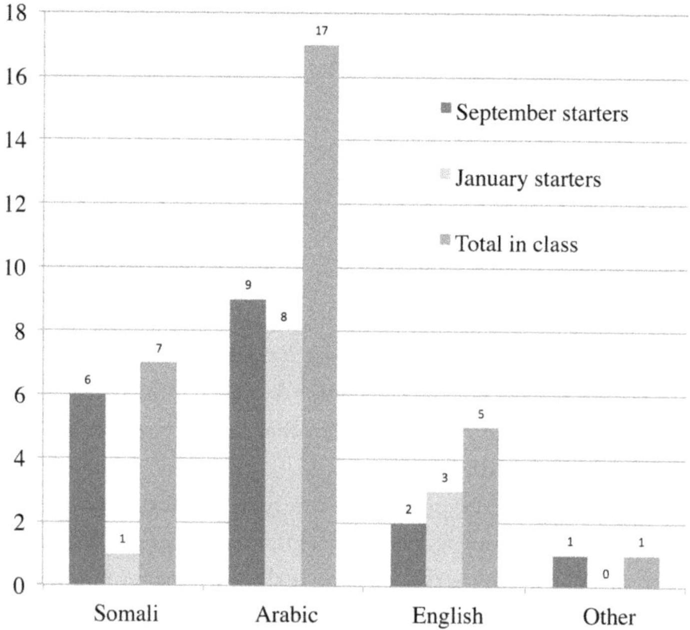

Within the class there were twenty six children who spoke English as an additional language (EAL). Notably, 84% of children in the class spoke a first language other than English compared to the whole school average of 88% and the national average of 17% (DfE, 2011). This figure relates to state funded primary schools in England. Out of the September starters, four children had no (or very little) English at the start of the school year. In January, eight of the January starters also had no (or very little) English. These twelve children received extra language support throughout the course of the year.

Additionally 26% (n=8) of the total number of children in the class were entitled to free school meals. While this figure is considerably lower than the school's overall figure of 43% (n=88) it is considerably higher than the national average where 14% of children under the age of five years old and 18% of all primary aged children are eligible for free school meals (DfE, 2011). These figures relate to maintained nurseries and state funded primary schools in England respectively.

Key definitions

Before outlining the structure of this book I will first define the key terms that are used throughout this study. As some of these terms are debated and disputed it is important to outline the way in which I use them. Key terms are listed in alphabetical order below.

Culture: Building on Geertz' (1973) work, culture is understood as being *the lens through which an individual interprets their social world.* This interpretation stems from an individual's identity, which can incorporate their gendered, national, ethnic, religious, class, educational, positioning in their social context. Aspects of identity such as gender, ethnicity and religion are therefore not purely understood as variables of analysis but rather as social attributes that qualitatively affect how an individual conceptualises and operationalises their identity. The intersecting nature of an individual's identity consequently reveals that the different identities that an individual subscribes to means that their overall worldview may share aspects of another's worldview based on a common identity (e.g. religion) but at the same time may differ based on another aspect of identity (e.g. gender). Additionally an individual's life experiences [as described by Denzin and Lincoln (2003)] such as experience of (in)equality, belonging, community and so on, also has a part to play in how an individual interprets their social world.

Discourse: Adopting Connolly's (1998: 26) definition, discourse can be interpreted as *the way in which we think about the social world.* In order to make sense of the social world discourses employ labels and categories to delineate socially accepted ways of thinking and behaving. Discourses, consequently, 'influence and shape the way in which the social world is structured' while also 'underpin[ning] our knowledge of ... the social world.' Discourses, as this study highlights, are fundamental in the development and maintenance of identity.

Ethnicity: As Salway et al. (2009a: 2) highlight, 'the term 'ethnicity' is employed in diverse and contradictory ways in social research as well as in wider societal discourse'. It can refer to shared origins and ancestry, cultural values and beliefs, geographical origins, biological features and socio-political dimensions. For the purposes of this study *ethnicity is understood as being socially constructed.* Children's own definitions of the significance of ethnicity are employed when uncovering their emic perspectives. Some children employ shared origins while others refer to cultural values, biological features or socio-political dimensions in their conceptualisations of ethnic identity. The multi-faceted and fluid nature of ethnicity and ethnic identity is therefore integral to this study. The term ethnicity is employed throughout instead of the term race due to the latter's common association with genetic stratification.

Gender: Like ethnicity, *gender is also viewed as being socially constructed.* However, the prevalence of the male-female binary as a central component of dominant gender discourses is also acknowledged (Davies, 2003) as is its incorrigible prevalence in the discourses that were employed by children at Sunnyside. Within this binary relationship, gender and gendered interactions can be heavily sexualised (Walter, 2010).

North Africa: The United Nations (UN) includes seven countries in its geopolitical definition of North Africa: Algeria, Egypt, Libya, Morocco, Sudan, Tunisia and Western Sahara. North Africa is considered to be part of the Arab World. There were children from Egypt, Libya and Morocco in the reception class at Sunnyside.

Operationalise: The term operationalise refers to the ways in which individual's perform and embody aspects of their identity. This concept depicts the fluid ways in which identity can be enacted and incorporates the way in which social structures can influence and constrain identity (re)negotiation as well as the role that social agency has in how individuals replay and reinvent their identity as a form of agentive borderwork.

Patterns of interaction: Due to the challenges of defining friendship with young children the term patterns of interaction will be used throughout. It should be noted though that when discussing with children who they like to play with the term 'friend' was often used by them and subsequently was also used by me when employing research activities.

Religion: The concept of religion and associated concepts of religious belief and identity are defined by Durkheim (1912) as *a collection of cultural belief systems or worldviews* that manifest themselves in a collective identity. This collective role of religion was also expressed by children at Sunnyside as a way of uniting themselves with, or separating themselves from, their peers.

Sub-Saharan Africa: Sub-Saharan Africa refers to all countries that lie (either partially or fully) south of the Sahara desert. Geopolitically Sub-Saharan Africa contrasts with the Islamic countries in North Africa. In the reception class at Sunnyside there were children from two countries in Sub-Saharan Africa: Nigeria and Somalia.

Rationale for book structure

Following on from this introductory chapter Chapter 2 *Being in the field* discusses my methodological approach and justification before shedding further light on my fieldwork location, sampling strategy, research methods, collaborative analysis, ethics and researcher positionality.

As Wolcott (1995; 1999) advocates, a full ethnography in terms of its focus, process and output was adopted throughout this study. Consequently, the main body of this book has been constructed as a written ethnographic account where literature, data and reflections are inter-woven to create an overall narrative that elicits children's emic perspectives of diversity and identity. Therefore Chapters 2-6 all deal with a theme or set of related themes that have emerged from my data. The narrative in these chapters is presented in an inductive-deductive circular approach. The titles of these chapters incorporate a 'being ... ' phrase that the children at Sunnyside used in their conversations about identity and diversity.

Chapter 3, *Being me* introduces children's narratives about their own and others' identity, while also laying the theoretical framework on which these encounters will be built through examining the concept of identity itself. By using Mill's (1959) concept of the *sociological imagination* and Stones' (2005) notion of *strong structuration*, this chapter shows why identity is important, before moving on to discuss the roots of the term and its fundamental notions of similarity and difference. Goffman's (1959) theory of *dramaturgical analysis* is used to reveal the agentive nature of identity before Hughes' (1945) *master status theory* [sic] highlights the structural discourses that can constrain an individual's social agency. Jenkins' (1996; 2008) work then shows how *the duality of structure* is important within this discussion through interpreting identity as a dialectical process.

Chapter 4, *Being all of me* reveals how children conceptualise and operationalise the complex ways in which aspects of their identities intersect. The concept of intersectionality grounds these narratives in a theoretical framework. This chapter then explores how children at Sunnyside operationalise their intersecting identities through symbolic mediation. Building on Goffman's

(1959) theory of dramaturgical analysis, this chapter explores the concept of symbolic interactionism (Blumer, 1962) as well as how dynamic aspects of identity play out in the lived experience of children at Sunnyside.

Chapter 5, *Being different* explores in more detail how Sunnyside's children view difference and conceptualise and operationalise their identities amongst their school peers. The chapter starts by discussing how children understand notions of self and others before moving on to discuss how wider social discourses of discrimination and hierarchies of difference play a part in how children understand ethnic, religious and gender diversity. This chapter then moves on to reveal how children discuss identity in their peer conversations before showing how children used imaginative play to operationalise their identities at Sunnyside.

Chapter 6, *Being friends* initially explores the relationship between language, identity and patterns of interaction. Building on previous chapters, it will then uncover how children at Sunnyside negotiate their patterns of peer interaction both at and outside school in relation to how they conceptualise and operationalise their identities.

Chapter 7, *The story so far* summarises the key arguments in the book and discusses how some children actively challenge structural discourses of discrimination (both *external* and *internal*) at Sunnyside and in the process reveals how children can unlearn discrimination, highlighting the role that educational settings can play in this process. In doing this, this concluding chapter will raise questions relating to how policy, practice and future research can respond to the key findings in this study.

Chapter 2

Being in the field: Methodological approach and justification

'Doing ethnography is like trying to read a manuscript—foreign, faded, full of ellipses, incoherencies, suspicious emendations, and tendentious commentaries, but written not in conventionalized graphs of sound but in transient examples of shaped behaviour' (Geertz, 1973: 10).

Being at Sunnyside

My edited fieldnotes of Thursday, 18th November highlight how the children typically interacted with each other throughout the different stages of the school day. These, and my other fieldnotes, were produced by scribbling down rough notes of what I saw in the field as events were unfolding. These rough notes were then written up as full fieldnotes on the next day. These fieldnotes have since been edited to include pseudonyms and, where necessary, other anonymising features.

> I arrive at the school at 8.35am and notice a new Eid display in the school entrance. The display has books about Eid and pilgrimages as well as Eid cards, sweet bowls and beads. Before the children arrive I chat with the classroom teacher, Mary, about the week so far. She mentions that it had been a funny week. Tuesday and Wednesday have been quiet because a lot of children had taken time off for Eid. Most are expected back today though Mary mentions that one or two might not come if they have extended family visiting for the holiday. As Eid isn't a public holiday the school can't officially close but has to open as normal. Only a handful of children came though earlier in the week—ten in the nursery/reception combined class. The school's policy is to recognise absences for religious reasons and not follow them up as unexplained. Mary mentions, though, that some other schools with high Muslim populations plan in service days over Eid as a way of minimising disruption to the children's learning.
>
> When the children arrive I notice that Fariido is wearing hijab.[3] This is the first time I've noticed this, though her sister regularly wore hijab last year when

3. In line with the children's emic definitions throughout this study, hijab is understood to refer to a headscarf rather than the more general Arabic translation of (unspecified) modest clothing.

she was in the reception class. When I later mention to Mary that today is the first time I have seen Fariido wear hijab, Mary tells me that while Fariido doesn't wear hijab every day she does on occasion wear hijab to school.

I go to sit at the red group's writing table as the children are practicing to write their names. Mubarak and Barak sit down with me and Mubarak tells me about his journey to school that morning. Kareem joins us. After a few minutes Amir arrives and sits down at his table to write his name. When setting out the name cards the school staff regularly split up *the gang* (see p. 26). Amir and Mubarak chat loudly to each other over the other children's heads while writing their names at their separate tables. Daud, the third member of *the gang*, hasn't arrived yet. The older girls' sit at two separate tables writing their names and chatting in small groups.

At 9.05 Mary rings the tambourine to call the children to come and sit on the carpet area. She takes the register. Nasra and Fazia are absent. Gamal put his hand up to speak when Mary has finished. He tells her in broken English that over the last few days he and Daud played together outside Gamal's house. The two boys live close to each other.

Jabir, is the Star of the Day, i.e. the child who was deemed to have completed the 'best work' on the last day at school. Amongst the children this is a highly coveted status as the day after they have received their award 'the star' gets to sit on a special chair during formal learning sessions while the other children sit on the carpet. Sitting in his chair Jabir proudly tells the other children 'That's my Eid clothes' as he points to his new shirt. 'And I've got a new belt. It's a yellow belt.'

At 9.15 the children do their phonetics lesson. Mary brings out the puppet who is hiding the new sound 'th'. The puppet has been staying with one of the children for Eid She was asleep when Mary took her out of her bag. 'She's tired', Mary tells the class, 'because she's been having fun at Eid.' The children laugh at this.

After introducing the new sound 'th', Susan, the classroom assistant, takes the yellow and red groups (i.e. the two lowest literacy sets) to the break out area to do a guided task learning the new sound. Mary does a guided writing task with the other children on the carpet writing 'th' words. Amir, who often gets bored when doing guided learning, is engaged in the task and concentrating well. Mary asks him to 'be teacher' and write on the interactive board. He relishes this role and responds well to Mary's praise at his writing skills.

At 9.55 the children in the classroom can choose an activity to do from the activity stations. Susan is still working with the red and yellow groups in the break out area. After a short break Mary takes the children in small groups to do a guided writing tasks about what they did during Eid.

I sit next to the computer and watch the children play. Fariido sits at the writing table and says to me 'I'm playing with Dahlia.' Amir sits down next to them. Annakiya goes to the interactive white board and draws a picture of Aafia. Aniso plays next to her with the other white board. They occasionally chat while drawing their separate pictures. The other older girls are in the break out area with Susan.

Daud and Barak play in the small world area. After a few minutes Amir goes over to them, chats to Daud and then goes back to his drawing. Mubarak, the third gang member, is in the break out area with Susan.

Annakiya and Aniso swap white boards and start to chat about which colours they will draw with. Daud goes over to them briefly and watches them draw. Amir finishes his picture (of the queen and her castle) and shows it to Mary. He then goes over to the construction area where Daud and Barak have migrated to. They all play together.

Looking behind me I realise that no-one has gone to the role play area, which has been turned into the woods over half term. I then realise that I am part blocking the entrance to it so move to the other side of the computer. After a few minutes Daud goes into the area and plays with the bear masks on his own. Amir soon joins him and shortly after Barak also goes into the woods. All three play together with the bear masks.

As the boys leave the construction area Annakiya and Anisa go to it and watch the boys playing in the woods. After a few minutes the boys leave the woods and the girls enter. It is now 10.10. Aniso plays in the woods for a few minutes before wandering to the other side of the classroom. Annakiya calls to me and asks me to play with her. She tells me that Goldilocks, i.e. herself, isn't feeling well and asks me to be the doctor. We role play this scenario.

At 10.15 Susan comes back to the classroom with the red and yellow groups. Mubarak and Gamal head straight to the woods with Amir. The boys play for a few minutes with the masks and then move *en masse* to another area. Just after they have left Kareem, who was working with Susan, comes in and picks up the Goldilocks mask. He comes up to me and says hello with the mask. Annakiya turns to him and says 'You can't be Goldilocks. She is a girl.' He smiles at her (uncomprehendingly) and carries on playing with the mask. Annakiya starts to make dinner for the Goldilocks doll. Kareem copies her and makes some food for Goldilocks too.

At 10.35 Mary calls for tidy up time. Sitting on the carpet at 10.40 Mary reads to the class the guided writing that some of the children have been doing about

Eid. Amir gets his name on the board for talking, i.e. he gets his first warning for perceived inappropriate behaviour.

At 10.45 we go outside. The nursery class are already in the outside area. It is a very cold day. Deka puts on her hijab to go outside telling me that it will help to keep her warm.

When we get outside Annakiya picks up a ball and asks me to play with her. Fariido comes up and asks to play. The two girls throw the ball to each other. Kareem joins us. I throw another ball back and forth with him while the girls play together.

The class start to play a mass chasing game where *the gang*, i.e. the monsters, chase 'the older girls'. We stop our ball throwing game to watch. Fariido runs over to join the other girls being chased while Annakiya joins in as a monster. Kareem watches for a few minutes before joining the group of girls being chased. Annakiya is the only girl who chases the other children. Kareem is the only boy being chased.

At 11.10 we line up to go back inside. While we are taking off our jackets Deka also takes off her headscarf. She turns to Fariido and asks 'Are you keeping yours?' Fariido looks at her, shakes her head and then also takes her headscarf off.

The children go back into the classroom and wash their hands in preparation for lunch. The lunchtime supervisors come to take the children to the dining room. Mary and I eat our lunch in the classroom and chat about the morning's activities. The nursery teacher joins us.

The children come back in at 12.40. Mubarak comes up to the table where I am sitting with Mary and the nursery teacher. The nursery teacher asks him 'Are those your new Eid clothes?' He nods and smiles.

Mary takes the register and gets the 'write and tell' writing off the wall in the Early Years entrance area to share with the class. This is a new item that parents are encouraged to complete with children when they drop them off at school or pick them up. Amir has written about being good at home. After sharing his piece Mary reminds the students about the circle time activity last week about being good at home and listening to adults as they do at school. Today Amir, Mustafe, Fariido and Dahlia have all written something on the board.

Mary then takes a maths session with the whole class on the carpet about sizing objects. Kareem sits at the side of the group away from the others.

At 1.05 the blue group do a maths activity with Susan while the others choose. I go and sit at the creative table where Eid card templates are set out. Mubarak comes over and sits down saying 'Write with me.' He then writes his name on one of the Eid cards. Daud, Jabir and Kareem come and sit at the nearby snack table. Amir is with Susan doing the maths activity. Daud chats with me while eating his banana and tells me that at lunch time he played outside with Amir, Mubarak and Barak.

Annakiya comes over to the snack table and opens a banana that has gone black and squishy. She gets it on her hands and goes to wash them handing me the bruised banana. She comes back over and touches me with her cold hands. I tell her that her hands are really cold! She says that she has just washed them in cold water. Mubarak and Barak both reach out to touch them. Barak then screams and jumps back in mock horror. Mubarak turns to him and says 'Don't scream like a girl!' Barak touches Annakiya's hand again, 'screams' in a much a deeper voice and laughs. Annakiya and Mubarak laugh with him. Mubarak moves over to the sand where Gamal and Jabir are playing. Daud soon follows them.

Kareem, who has been playing on his own at the play dough table, comes over to me and says, 'Come.' I follow him back to the play dough table and he shows me the model he has made with the dough. Aafia walks past and sits at the creative table. Kareem says to her in English 'Look Aafia.' She smiles at him. Kareem then moves over to the white board and I go back to the creative table.

Amir finishes his maths task with Susan and heads to the whiteboard where Kareem is playing on his own. Mubarak who is still at the sand pit shouts over to him 'Amir—a birthday cake for you.' Amir runs over from the white board looks into the sand pit and then runs back to the white board. After a few more minutes he goes to the woods with Jabir. They play there with Deka who has previously been there on her own.

Mustafe comes over to where I am sitting at the creative table and starts to make a model. He asks me to cut tape for him. Ferran comes over and also asks me to cut tape for him. Barak comes to the nearby snack table and tells me that he has being playing with the cars (in the small world area). 'We killed them' he informs me. 'Who?' I ask. 'Me, Amir, Daud and Mubarak,' he replies. As I enquire further Barak goes onto explain to me that he and the other boys killed the cars by crashing them into things.

At 2.15 it is time to tidy up. As it is very cold today we don't go back outside for the normal choose session. At 2.25 the children settle on the carpet for a number writing session. Again Kareem sits at the side, on his own, away from the group but this time Mary asks him to join the group which he does. Some children write their numbers from right to left. Susan helps them to write from left to right explaining that 'we write differently in English.'

At 2.55 the children's drawings and pictures from the home drawer are handed out and it is time to go home. After the children leave I talk to Mary about the day's events while helping her set up the classroom for tomorrow.

The school day

For the reception children the day started at 8.55 a.m. and finished at 3.10 p.m. Lunch was for an hour and ten minutes from 11.30 a.m. until 12.40 p.m. Two lunchtime supervisors collected the children and took them to the dinner hall. They then took them outside and supervised them in the outdoor play area until the afternoon session started. There were no other breaks during the school day though the outdoor play area was also used for outdoor learning during both morning and afternoon sessions.

The school day was divided between two areas of learning: indoors and outdoors. Formal learning mostly took place in the indoor area (on the carpet) though at times during the third term (after Easter) these sessions also took place outside. There were normally two short (twenty minutes) formal whole class sessions per day. The indoor area also contained thirteen activity stations, e.g. the role play area, the construction area etc., where children could choose which activity they wanted to work on during 'choose sessions' (i.e. continuous provision). During these sessions children had to choose an activity station to work at from the available locations on the choose board. Each activity station had a maximum number of children who could be there at one time depending on the type of activity and available space. During 'choose sessions' the class teacher and/or teaching assistant normally took a small group of children for a guided activity e.g. guided reading and writing.

Like the indoor area the outdoor area was split into activity sessions e.g. the sand pit, the den etc. When outside the children were able to move from one activity to another with more freedom than in the indoor area as there was more space for them to play in. After the February half term, when the weather improved, more of the outdoor activity stations were moved from the covered area to the open playground. Figure 2.1 depicts the structure of the school day.

Figure 2.1: The school day

Time of day	Activity
8.55 a.m.	School starts—on arrival practice writing name
9.10 a.m.	Registration and formal learning session (on the carpet area)
9.30 a.m.	Indoor choose session and guided activities in small groups
10.30 a.m.	Outdoor choose session
11.30 a.m.	Lunchtime—lunch in the dinner hall and outside play
12.40 p.m.	Formal learning session (on the carpet area)
13.00 p.m.	Indoor choose session and guided activities in small groups
14.00 p.m.	Outdoor choose session
14.45 p.m.	Story time and sharing session
15.10 p.m.	School finishes

Doing ethnography

My study at Sunnyside was conducted using an ethnography. The term ethnography literally means 'writing culture' (Seymour-Smith, 1986) and is based on the foundation of studying a culture (or 'group') within its natural environment. There are three key characteristics that make this a distinct approach—focus, process and output (Wolcott, 1995; 1999)—all of which are particularly appropriate to this research project. Ethnography can then be described as 'generat[ing] or build[ing] theories of culture—or explanations of how people think, believe, and behave—that are situated in local time and space' (LeCompte and Schensul, 1999: 8).

Due to the fluid and complex nature of identity, this approach was particularly appropriate in the present study as it facilitated a deep understanding of the inter-play between patterns of interaction, identity, diversity and inequality. To capture this nuanced data this study utilised an applied ethnography built on the foundations of a constructionist ontology and subtle realist epistemology.

Familiarisation

Ethnography should be viewed as a process of becoming familiar with a social puzzle. This process requires continual reflection throughout all stages of the study. To aid this process, as I have argued elsewhere (Barley and Bath, 2014), the inclusion of a familiarisation period can serve as the foundation stone on which this continuous process can be built.

Therefore before commencing fieldwork in September 2010, I undertook a familiarisation period that allowed the study to be setup and me to build relationships with participants. This period was conducted in the school over a period of six weeks during the second half of the summer term in the academic year 2009-2010. The key aims of this period were to learn the routines and rules of the school, locate and build relationships with participants, negotiate a researcher role within the classroom and learn how to effectively collect and record data within the field location. In addition to allowing me to become familiar with the school context and build up relationships, this period also revealed a number of ethical issues relating to negotiating a researcher role within the classroom. This period highlighted that the researcher role needed to be further explored within the full ethnography as an ongoing (re)negotiation process (Barley and Bath, 2014).

My familiarisation period was conducted with the 2009-2010 reception class, who moved up to Year-1 after the summer break. I did not move up with them but stayed in the Reception class, with the support staff with whom I had built up relationships during familiarisation and also within the classroom where I had previously worked. When setting up my familiarisation period, it had been hoped that teaching staff would also remain the same but due to school commitments it was decided by the school (during this period) that the nursery and reception teachers would swap roles after the summer break.

While there was no formal contact with the children who would be taking part in the study, this period gave the then nursery children the chance to see and observe me from a distance (in the outdoor play area) before I had any intentional interaction with them. Near the end of this period, after watching the reception children involve me in their games, the nursery children also began to ask me to take part in their activities. Punch (2002) suggests that his slow process of familiarisation is important for young children as they often need time and space to observe adults in a setting before they are ready to interact and confide in them. Once I started my fieldwork I was already a familiar figure to the children I would be working with and was soon asked to participate in their activities and games. Similarly, children's family members also had a chance to get to know me before formal contact was made with them as they dropped off and collected their children from school. By including a familiarisation period in this study and by taking forward these principles into the fieldwork stage the challenges highlighted above, surrounding informed consent and accessing children's 'voices' were minimised.

Focussing the lens

When employing an ethnography, Hammersley and Atkinson (2007) recommend that two stages of (purposive) sampling are undertaken: selecting cases and selecting within cases. They see this process as important to ensure that the researcher is able to meaningfully focus her observations and to guard against seeking to observe everything and ending up seeing nothing. Hammersley and Atkinson state that using cases in this way gives the ethnographer a number of different lenses in which she can view the field location. While it is acknowledged that the choice of lens clearly determines what is seen by the ethnographer, meaning that aspects of the field location will be missed, this is understood as a necessary practical tool to ensure that in-depth data is gathered effectively.

They describe the first stage, of selecting cases, as the process of breaking down the research population into 'sub-categories' that have different characteristics. They recommend that this is done as part of what they describe as 'casing the joint' (Hammersley and Atkinson, 2007: 41) or in other words conducting a familiarisation period. Within the current study this first stage of sampling was informed by a paired interview with the Early Years Co-ordinator and Multi-lingual Support Worker near the end of my familiarisation period where linguistic background (most notably Arabic and Somali) was highlighted as important for patterns of interaction within the school. Linguistic diversity therefore initially informed the strategy for selecting focus children as 'vehicles of representation' around which to base observations and research activities.

When selecting within cases, Hammersley and Atkinson (2007: 46) contend that three key dimensions should be taken into consideration: time, context and people. They contend that time, understood as 'a dimension of obvious importance in social life ... [as] attitudes and activities often vary over time in ways that are highly significant for social theory', is often neglected in sampling strategies. Time was an important criterion round which to focus observations and activities in the current study as not only was the school day split up into formal and informal learning sessions but throughout the course of the day some children (particularly at the start of their school year) became tired and at times irritable and argumentative with their peers. This was particularly true of children with little or no English who seemed to struggle with spending the whole day in a predominantly English speaking environment. Working within this dimension, I observed activities for the whole school day but only undertook research activities with children during the morning session or initial stages of the afternoon session before fatigue began to set in.

In relation to context, Hammersley and Atkinson (2007) clearly argue that this should not be understood as a synonym for place. Rather, in line with Goffman's theory (1959) of dramaturgical analysis (which will be discussed in more detail in Chapter 3), context refers to a situation that prompts different types of behaviour. In the present study, the contextual dimension refers to the different activity stations within the indoor and outdoor learning areas. Some of these stations were commonly used by children as social areas (e.g. the role play corner and construction) and others as individual areas of learning (e.g. the interactive white board and computer stations). Spending time within the classroom context as part of my familiarisation period helped me to map the dimensions of each context. This mapping exercise was then used as one of the ways to structure future observations.

In response to Hammersley and Atkinson's (2007) third dimension, people, six focus children were identified to centre observations and activities around. Focus children should be understood not as case studies but as 'vehicles of representation' through which the field is viewed. To allow for time to build up relationships with children before starting research activities, all focus children were selected from the group of September starters. Initially during the October half term I listed the children (n=11) who regularly involved me in their classroom activities and initiated interaction with me. I then observed them more closely until the end of this first term when I asked them if they would like to help me with my project. This self-selection was important for two reasons. Firstly, on a practical level I was able to access these children's values and beliefs and secondly, by involving me in their activities the children and I were actively engaged in negotiating ongoing informed consent (Thomas and O'Kane, 1998). It should be noted that, although for practical reasons six children were selected as focus children around which I structured my observations, all children who self-selected to take part in the study were included in research activities so as not to 'favour' certain children over others.

In line with applied ethnography's principle of working closely with gatekeepers and guides in the design and development of a study, classroom staff helped to develop further criteria for selection. Therefore in addition to children's self-selection, the final selection of focus children was based on two further aspects: as mentioned above, staff within the school had highlighted that language plays a role within patterns of interaction in the classroom. Therefore (using this participant identified category) focus children were selected from a range of linguistic backgrounds. Additionally, initial analysis of non-participant observations (in January) revealed that play, particularly within the indoor area, was largely gendered. To ensure that all child-initiated 'groups' (using a very loose interpretation of the term 'group') within the class were included in the study, three male and three female focus children were selected i.e. as an observer-identified category of selection. Also it should be noted that gender and linguistic background are not (purely) viewed as demographic variables, but as social attributes which can and, as will be seen in subsequent chapters, do qualitatively affect children's conceptualisation and operationalisation of identities.

Introducing the focus children

Figure 2.2 presents some basic background information on each focus child. As for the figures in previous sections, information in Figure 2.2 has been taken from school registration data, apart from religion and the predominant nature of patterns of interaction within the school. All focus children regularly identified themselves as being Muslim or Christian. Therefore the information regarding religion in Figure 2.2 is their self-defined religious identity

Figure 2.2: Focus children's background information

Child	Gender	free school meals	Ethnicity	First language	Religion	Student family
Annakiya	Female	No	Other Black African	Other	Christian	Yes
Nasra	Female	No	Other	English	Muslim	No
Deka	Female	No	Somali	Somali	Muslim	No
Amir	Male	Yes	Other	English	Muslim	No
Daud	Male	Yes	Somali	Somali	Muslim	No
Kareem	Male	No	Other Black African	Arabic	Muslim	Yes

It was hoped that it would be possible to identify an Arabic-speaking girl as a focus child. However, the only Arabic-speaking girl, Aafia, who self-selected me went back to North Africa with her family in January. However, as Kareem's patterns of interaction were not as gendered as the other boys' interactions I was also able as the year progressed to gain an insight into the beliefs and values of this 'group' of girls via Kareem's introduction.

While a number of focus children speak a first language other than English, only Kareem and Annakiya were on the EAL register at the start of the school year. Daud and Deka had both been on the EAL register when they were in nursery. Kareem was the only focus child who was identified as in need of additional language support.

It should also be noted that throughout this study the emic term '*the older girls*' refers to Annakiya, Deka, Nasra Aniso, Fariido, Fazia and until she returned to North Africa (in January) Aafia. This group of girls regularly played together and engaged in shared activities throughout the course of the year. The other female September starters, i.e. Dahlia, Cala and Lina (who were all quieter, more reserved girls), were not part of this 'friendship' group.

The older girls also named a group of boys in the class, Amir, Daud and Mubarak, who more often than not played together, *the gang*. Throughout the course of the year Barak and Ferran also become part of this group. This group of boys soon took ownership of the name *the gang* that *the older girls* had ascribed to them.

Annakiya

When she started school in September, shortly after arriving in the UK from West Africa, Mary identified Annakiya as being able to understand an intermediate level of English. On a one to one basis with staff she spoke in words and phrases. However, she was very shy in groups and subsequently very quiet. Throughout the first term she began to speak fluently on a one-to-one basis with staff and peers. By the February half term she had become friendly with *the older girls and had* gained confidence and fluently engaged in group conversations in English.

During the second term Annakiya was put on the Gifted and Talented register for both literacy and numeracy. Annakiya was one of three non-Muslim children in the class. She discussed 'being Christian' and 'being Muslim' with Deka and was interested in why some of the other girls in the class, and some adults, wore hijab. Annakiya's parents had concerns about their children (all girls) attending a school where most of the pupils come from Muslim families and throughout the course of the year talked about moving schools. Annakiya's older sisters did move but Annakiya stayed as her parents believed that at her age the religious identity of her peers was not as important for Annakiya as it was for her older sisters. As Annakiya had taken a relatively long time to settle into school, staff also felt that it was better for Annakiya to stay for at least the whole year rather than having to cope with another upheaval soon after her arrival to the UK.

Nasra

Nasra was born in the North of England to a white English convert (mother) and a Somali father. Nasra and Deka are parallel cousins. Nasra, who has light brown hair, hazel eyes and olive coloured skin, strongly claimed her Somali heritage and Muslim identity. New adults to the school, e.g. supply teachers, more often than not assumed that Nasra was from one of the Arabic-speaking communities in the school. She was always quick to correct them and assert her Somali identity. Nasra regularly wore hijab to, but not necessarily at, school. 'Being Somali' habitually featured in Nasra's conversations. For Nasra this aspect of her identity was closely interwoven with 'being Muslim.' Nasra, Deka and their siblings regularly spend time together outside school, particularly at their paternal grandmother's house. Nasra's and Deka's mothers are close friends and often picked up each other's children from school. During the school year Nasra started to attend Koranic school, at the local mosque, and increasingly talked to me about this as the year progressed. She often played with the other *older girls* in the class but at times also liked to play quietly on her own (or with one or two other children) rather than with the big group of 'noisy girls'. Nasra's mother was also friends with Amir's mother and both children spent time together outside school. However, at school both children regularly engaged in gendered play and did not actively work together. As well as these family connections to children in the class, Nasra also attended Sunnyside's nursery where she got to know a number of other children who moved up to the reception class with her.

Deka

Deka is the eldest child of a Somali family who now live in the North of England. She was born in London and moved north as a toddler to be closer to where her extended family, including Nasra's nuclear family, had lived for a number of years. Deka previously attended Sunnyside's nursery and her younger sister was in the nursery class during the 2010-11 school year. Like Daud, Deka was put on both the EAL and School Action registers by nursery staff. At the start of reception, Deka was fluent in English though continued to be on the School Action register as at times she displayed, what staff described as, 'challenging behaviour'. When the children started school in September, a number of the *older girls* in the class soon started to 'hang out' together. Deka was a key part of this group. Like Nasra, Deka habitually wore hijab to school (though not always at school) and regularly talked about 'being Muslim' to her peers.

Amir

Amir was born in the North of England. His mother is a white English convert to Islam and is the second wife to Amir's father, who is from Morocco. His father's third wife still lives there so Amir's father splits his time between his first two families in the UK and his family in North Africa. Amir has a strong Muslim, and Arabic, identity and regularly incorporates aspects of this in his imaginative play. He also talks about going to the mosque and the activities that he does there at Koranic school. Amir attended Sunnyside's nursery with a number of other children in the class. When he arrived at reception he was already in his own words 'good friends' with two Somali boys, Daud and Mubarak. When allowed, these three boys would do everything together. The *older girls* nick-named these boys *the gang*, a name that the boys themselves soon took ownership of. Amir and Mubarak were the leaders of this group and directed *the gang's* activities between them. Amir is a very bright boy and was put on the Gifted and Talented register for literacy and numeracy at the same time as Annakiya. More often than not he was the first child in the class to master a new aspect of learning and regularly got bored when he understood the new concept but it needed to be reinforced for other children in the class. Because of this, Amir often misbehaved and then got into trouble.

Daud

Daud was the third original member of *the gang* but he took on a more passive role than Amir and Mubarak. Daud could often be observed wandering round the classroom, with his hands in his pockets, contemplating the world. When Amir and Mubarak were organising a joint activity, Daud would invariably join in but, when left to his own devices at times tried to get the attention of an adult in the room or would wander around watching the other children play. As part of a big Somali family, Daud is the second youngest child, with a younger sister and a nephew in Sunnyside's nursery during the 2010-11 school year. When at home, his mother depicted a similar scene where Daud was happiest working alongside his father. When this was not possible, he would watch and listen to his older brother and other adults in the house. Daud attended Sunnyside's nursery before starting school, where he was put on the EAL and School Action (i.e. Special Educational Needs) registers. By the time he started school Daud was fluent in English but still received Special Educational Needs (SEN) support for literacy and numeracy. During imaginative play, Daud incorporated aspects of going to the mosque, particularly when playing with Amir and Mubarak who would normally initiate the game. In conversations attached to research activities, where he and I worked on a one-to-one basis, he would regularly initiate a conversation about going to the mosque with his father and the things that he had learnt there.

Kareem

Kareem had no English when he first arrived at Sunnyside from Libya a few weeks after the start of the new school year. He struggled at first with the language barrier and got frustrated and upset when he couldn't communicate effectively with his peers. As he started school a few weeks after the other children, staff also noticed that he struggled to become friendly with other children in the class (even with the other Arabic speakers) as they had begun to form their own friendship groups before Kareem arrived. By the February half term Kareem's English vocabulary had grown considerably and he was able to communicate effectively with staff and children. At the start of the year, during indoor choose sessions, he invariably chose individual activities, such as the interactive white board and the computer, where he played on his own or with one other child and therefore was not required to speak much English. When these options were not available, he would sit at a nearby activity station playing on his own and watch for a free space at the computer or white board. Outside Kareem regularly played football with some of the other boys in the class. As the boys all knew the rules, and mostly agreed on them, Kareem was able to join in without the need to verbally negotiate the rules of play as most other activity stations required. When football was not an option outside, Kareem regularly chose to go on the bikes i.e. another independent activity. To help Kareem integrate into the classroom, staff encouraged the other Arabic-speaking children to speak to him in Arabic. As a result of this, Kareem began to work more closely with Aafia until she returned to North Africa in January. Aafia not only spoke to Kareem in Arabic but also helped him to communicate with their peers in English. After Aafia left, Mustafe, who Kareem regularly played football with, voluntarily took over this role of peer interpreter.

Fieldwork

The fieldwork aspects of this project took place over the 2010/2011 academic year. To gain access and maintain a sense of naturalness, I entered the setting and worked as a classroom assistant while still retaining an overt research identity. Weekly observation sessions (full day—including arrival, morning activities, lunchtime, afternoon activities and home time) were conducted and research activities with children were carried out throughout the course of the year. In agreement with the school fieldwork started in the third week of the Autumn term after allowing the children a few weeks to settle into their new school environment. A total of thirty-four days were spent in the field over the course of the academic year. Unplanned school closures and personal circumstances meant that three extra planned days of fieldwork were missed.

As has been previously mentioned, at the end of my familiarisation period an unstructured formal paired interview was conducted with the Early Years co-ordinator and multi-lingual worker to explore in more detail themes that had arisen in familiarisation observations and also to gain a fuller picture of the norms, beliefs, rules and rituals of the field location. Children themselves were also instrumental in guiding the focus and direction of my study. By listening to their views and experiences in the early stages of my fieldwork, I discovered the issues that were important to them. In line with an inductive approach, children's voices guided the course of the project.

Throughout my fieldwork, practitioners acted as research guides in not only helping me to build relationships with children and their families but also in making note of their own observations that might be of interest to me (i.e. when I was not at school) and by helping me to make sense of the data that I had collected e.g. mapping out the family connections between children in the class. As the year progressed and I began to build relationships with family members, they also helped me to make sense of my data by clarifying a point that their child had made or confirming their behaviour at home. These informal conversations with practitioners and family members were an invaluable part of data collection and analysis.

As is recommended by Eriksen (2001), formal and informal fieldwork methods were combined. Additionally the challenges in combining and interpreting these different types of data were considered and prompted a collaborative approach to analysis with focus children. Due to the emergent nature of this project, an exact timetable of events was not clear at the start of the study although it was anticipated that non-participant and participant observation sessions would be conducted throughout the year, with research activities with children taking place after the February half term. However, as the project took shape, and relationships with children were formed and developed, the nature and timing of my fieldwork was adapted. Figure 2.3 outlines the broad timeline of fieldwork activities that emerged:

Figure 2.3: Fieldwork timeline

Aspect of fieldwork	2010/11		
	Autumn term	Spring term	Summer term
Non-participant observation			
Participant observation			
Focused research activities with children			
Collaborative analysis with children			

Observation

At the start of each day, I would hover round the entrance to the classroom and greet the children and parents as they arrived at school. Invariably one child or another would then ask me to help them write their name. Once the formal morning session started, just after 9 a.m., I would sit at the back of the carpet area to observe the lesson as a non-participant. As Thorne (1993) highlights, the location that the ethnographer chooses to observe from becomes a lens for the observation and can both enable and constrain the data that is produced. By sitting at the back of the carpet area I was not able to see the facial expressions of the children but was in Mary's eye line. At times Mary would ask me a question to involve me in the session or would communicate with me (non-verbally) over the children's heads. My positioning during these sessions also made it difficult for me to read the children's body language. To try and counter this, I started to sit with the children on the carpet. However, the children found this distracting and tried to talk to me or catch my attention rather than listening to Mary. After a few weeks of trying this strategy I returned to my place at the back of the carpet.

After this formal session, the children were able to choose in the indoor area. As the children were choosing I would sit at a table in the middle of the classroom and observe the children playing from there. As children invited me to take part in their activities I would move with them to the different activity stations and become involved in their games as a participant observer. Aspects of Mandell's (1988) 'least-adult role' and Milstein's (2010) concept of 'horizontal relationships' were also important allowing me to join in children's games and peer conversations when invited; and, as far as is possible, experience classroom life from their perspectives.

Each day at round about 10.30 a.m. we would go to the outdoor area where I would initially sit, if the weather was nice, on the stage or, if it was raining, on the bench in the covered area and observe the children as a non-participant. Like in the indoor area, I would move to other areas as invited by the children and take part in their activities.

The afternoon session was again split up into a short formal session, indoor choose time and outdoor choose time. During these sessions I would take up the same observational places as for the morning sessions.

During observations I always had my fieldnote book to hand to note down what was happening around me as it occurred. When asked to take part in an activity, I would put my fieldnote book to one side until we had finished our game. I then noted down what had occurred as soon as possible after finishing the activity.

Fieldnotes as a research tool

As Breglia (2009) points out, the rules surrounding when and how fieldnotes are recorded need to be carefully negotiated with participants as part of the 'work-break game'. In my study, learning how to play this game was particularly important as the children had not before encountered a researcher. When introducing myself to the children, I explained to them that I was doing a project at university and related this to their own project work at school. I positioned myself, as Mayall (2008) advocates, as an adult who lacked knowledge about children's worlds and needed them to teach me.

My fieldnotes also became a research tool in their own right as children increasingly wanted to directly contribute to my fieldnotes via mark makings, drawings and writing.

Figure 2.4: Extracts from fieldnote book

Above: Amir—I want to go to the mosque

Above: Nasra—Picture of Barbie

The meanings that children subscribed to their fieldnotes will be explored in subsequent chapters.

Additionally at times, when children were too engrossed in their activity to take time out to write for themselves, they would come and tell me what they wanted me to write about them. One example of this can be seen when we were in the outdoor play area. Daud comes over to where I am sitting on the edge of the stage and stands and looks over my shoulder. He scans the page of my fieldnote book and asks 'Why have you not written my name?' I explain that I couldn't as he has been inside working in the classroom and has only just come outside a few minutes ago. He agrees that this is a valid reason for not writing about him and then says 'But now I'm having a sleepover. Write that!' I tell him that I will and he runs off back to the climbing frame where the other boys are playing.

While this interest in my fieldnotes can be seen as a way of ensuring ongoing consent from children, children's interest also enabled the collaborative analysis of data as it was being collected, enabling me to check and where necessary revise my interpretations. Following Pryor and Ampiah's (2004) 'data chain model' I was then subsequently able to devise new research questions and areas to focus on. This child-directed approach to collecting and analysing data (as well as designing research activities) was an important part of my study.

While at times I allowed children to write and contribute to my fieldnote book, I had discovered, during the familiarisation period, that this was not always appropriate for two key reasons: (a) only one child could participate in this way at a time; and (b) at times I was without my fieldnote book for extended periods meaning I was unable to record ongoing activities. To counter these difficulties I gave children who asked individual pieces of paper from my notebook so that we could all take notes at the same time. We were then able to discuss and analyse their data, allowing them to direct the focus of the study, as well as freeing me up to continue observing other ongoing activities. Discussing my fieldnotes with children as, and shortly after, they were written enabled me to ensure that my first level of data analysis was not interpreted through the lens of my own ideological stance but that children's emic interpretations of their social worlds were elicited. To ensure confidentiality I only shared the sections of my fieldnotes with children that related to their own activities and interactions.

Focused research activities

Within ethnography observational data is always integrated with other data sources with visual methods becoming an increasingly prevalent feature of ethnography (Russell, 2007; Spencer, 2011). As Russell (2007) highlights, when using visual methods, a distinction needs to be made between images as a tool to construct or elicit data and images as data in and of themselves. By creating visual data participants are able to influence the course of a study as their position within the research project shifts reducing power differentials between the researcher and participants. Within my study both approaches were adopted and are made explicit below.

A number of visual research 'lenses' were used in the current study to initiate conversations with focus children (as well as the 'extras' who self-selected to be involved in the study) and gain a 'snapshot' of children's views and beliefs. These are described in more detail below. As well as incorporating children's own ideas for research activities, a range of activities were designed to allow children with different learning styles (i.e. auditory, visual and kinaesthetic) to all participate in the study using their preferred learning style on at least one occasion, allowing me to access 'the hundred languages of children' (Malaguzzi, 1993).

These activities were recorded using a *Dictaphone* both to ensure that our conversations were fully captured and as a symbolic marker to remind children of the purpose of my questions in relation to the 'on the record' nature of my study. All children liked to use the *Dictaphone* and we regularly listened to the recording together after completing the activity. Occasionally children asked that the *Dictaphone* was turned off for part of an activity. More commonly, though, if children wanted to tell me something that they didn't want the *Dictaphone* 'to hear' they would whisper it to me so that the *Dictaphone* could not pick up their voice. These parts of our conversations are not included in the study.

At the start of each activity, I told the children what the activity entailed and what its purpose was so that they were aware of the task that they were being asked to participate in. Using the research activity as a starting point, I directed our conversation to an aspect or theme of my study. This process resulted in children actively constructing both verbal and visual data. Each child responded to these activities in a different way. Where the activity caught the child's attention, this prompted an in-depth conversation, allowing the child to express themselves both verbally and via the activity e.g. drawing, building etc. Each activity was particularly well received by some children but not so engaging for others.

The six research activities were:

Children's tours
Children's learning journeys
'My friends are' picture
'Where I am from: Scotland' book
'Where I am from ...' digital books
Model identities

It should be noted here that Children's learning journeys refers to the folders that educational settings are required to keep to evidence how individual children are meeting the Early Years Foundation Stage areas of learning.

Each of the activities are outlined below.

Children's tours

During observational sessions, some children actively took me on a tour of the play area that we were located in, i.e. indoor and outdoor, showing me where they like to play and with whom. This approach was always initiated by children and therefore was not conducted with all focus children. Using children's tours, in combination with observational techniques and other research activities, as advocated by Clark and Moss (2001) is a useful tool to gain young children's perspectives (particularly those under the age of five) and perspectives of older children who do not speak English as a first language or who have other communication difficulties.

Children's Learning Journeys

Throughout the year I looked at children's learning journeys and talked with children about individual pieces of work that they had done. Where a piece of work focused particularly on aspects of their identity and/or patterns of interaction, I asked the child if I could use the piece of work in my project. After copying the piece I asked the child to interpret their picture and/or mark makings, utilising the drawing as a means of exploring further the child's understanding or experience of their social world. As the year progressed, individual children started to show me pieces of work that they had done that week and in particular during the day I was at the school. They at times specifically told me that they wanted me to have it or that they had made it for me.

Figure 2.5: Examples of items from children's learning journeys

Above: Abia's picture of her family in Libya

Above: Nasra's picture of a girl playing football

The meanings that children subscribed to their drawings will be explored in subsequent chapters.

'My friends are' picture

Drawing on the work of Coates (2004), I decided to further use children's drawings and their accompanying narratives to explore their perspectives of their peer interactions at school. As I was reflecting on how best to do this, Daud gave me an idea for how this research activity could be framed and subsequently gives me permission to use this as part of my project, taking pride in his contribution to the design of my study.

> During an observation session in January, Daud comes over to where I am sitting writing my fieldnotes and says to me 'I want to do some writing too.' I tell him to go fetch some paper and a pencil and bring it over. He comes back and tells me that he wants to write his friends' names down and say 'we are going to the park.' He asks me to help him spell his friends' names so I ask him whose name he would like to write first, to which he replies Amir. I start spelling Amir's name for him and as I do Amir comes over and joins us saying he wants to help. Daud then decides he wants to write Mubarak's name and asks Amir if he can help him. The two boys work together writing down their friends' names as well as the sentence 'we went to the park.'
>
> As they are doing this I reflect that this child-inspired activity could be used as a research activity to initiate conversations about children's patterns of

interaction. Based on Daud's activity I subsequently created an activity sheet to use with children to facilitate a conversation about who they like to play with at school. Engaging children in the design of research activities in this way (as co-researchers) can help to reduce the power differentials between researcher and participant. Additionally, using children's ideas for research activities allows them to communicate their ideas and feelings in the medium of their choice and ensures that they are comfortable with and have experience of using the required research tool (Johnson, 2008).

To ensure the anonymity of children, the majority of these pictures are not included in the thesis though an example of an easily anonymised picture is shown below.

Figure 2.6: Deka's 'My friends are' picture

'Where I am from: Scotland' book

During observational sessions, I observed a number of children regularly talk about the different countries that they are from with their peers. To facilitate similar conversations with focus children, I designed a book around my own national and cultural identity called 'Where I am from: Scotland'. After telling the children something about where I am from, I then asked them a similar question about their own background. By telling my own story, and highlighting that I am not from 'here', I was not only able to build up a relationship with children through sharing information about my own background, but more importantly did not fall into the trap of 'othering' children as can often be done when trying to explore these issues (Raj, 2003). The framing of the questions in the book allowed children to say that they were from 'here' just as easily as from another part of the world and also allowed them to express the fluid and complex nature of their identities.

'Where I am from ... ' digital books

After reading the Scotland book with Mustafe and Kareem, Mustafe asks me if I have a Libya book. I tell him that I don't but ask if he would like us to make one together. He replies saying that he does as 'Libya, it's important' and I tell him that we can on another day.

Initially, before this conversation, I had thought of getting the children to write and illustrate a book about their own identity. However, due to time constraints of only being able to spend one day a week in the school, I decided to put this idea on hold. Additionally, a similar activity was being used in literacy lessons and, to help keep the boundaries between research and school work separate, and to reinforce each child's voluntary association with the study including their ability to negotiate ongoing informed consent, I decided that it was not appropriate to adapt a school work activity into a research tool.

However, after Mustafe's interest in creating a book about where he is from, Libya, I revisited this idea. Reviewing the transcripts of conversations with Mustafe and other children when reading the Scotland book as well as my observational notes, I developed an online picture library informed by themes that the children regularly talked about as being important to them. This digital approach differed from the books created in literacy lessons. Copies of these images were printed off so that children could easily access them and decide which pictures they wanted to use when creating their book. When the child wanted to include an image that wasn't in the picture library, I either asked them to draw the picture for me, which I later scanned and included in their book, or together we used functions in word to create the image.

Collaboratively the children and I created a digital book called 'Where I am from ...' The collaborative production of visual data, such as this book, has been highlighted within ethnography as an important way of empowering individuals within the research process through having direct control over the images used to represent themselves and/or aspects of their culture (Banks, 1995; Morphy and Banks, 1997).

Model identities

Inspired by Gauntlett's (2007) approach to exploring identities and relationships with adults through the use of *Lego*, I designed a hands-on activity to explore children's identities via the places that are important to them. Using *Lego* pieces and other materials (e.g. wooden bricks) from the construction activity station, I asked children to firstly make or find a person to represent themselves and secondly build the different places that are important to them. While they were building their models, as well as at the end of the session, we talked about the different places that they were building, why they were important to them, what things they did there and who they went with/liked to play with there.

While cultural minority children are often disadvantaged by the tools that are available to them in school because of their minority cultural capital (Brooker, 2002; Brown, 2007), the use of *Lego* and bricks for this activity did not disadvantage any of the children as all had been observed choosing to use *Lego* and the other construction tools throughout the course of the year. However, to ensure complete familiarity, this activity was employed as the last research activity in late May to allow children who do not have construction toys at home to participate fully in the activity after learning to use the materials for their own purposes over an extended period of time at school. As Gauntlett (2007) highlights in his work, building time into the research strategy like this to ensure that participants are familiar with the research tool is a crucial part of the process.

The kinaesthetic nature of this activity was clearly welcomed by some of the children as they got visibly excited when they realised that they could physically and verbally explain to me the places that were important to them. This was particularly true of Kareem who was able to use his ever increasing English language skills alongside physical actions to communicate with me. When he was unsure of a word he would show me, using his model and/or an action, what he wanted to say. As he had previously stated that he no longer wanted to work with me via bilingual support (i.e. when reading the Scotland book) but that he wanted to talk to me directly, this combination of verbal and physical communication proved to be a useful tool allowing me to access his *hundred languages* (Malaguzzi, 1993).

Considering and operationalising research ethics

Undertaking an ethnography poses some specific ethical challenges, such as entering and withdrawing from the field; maintaining an overt research identity through continually negotiating informed consent; positionality; reflexivity and insider/outsider status. Additionally, conducting research with children requires further ethical considerations, for example gaining and negotiating on-going informed consent; appropriately managing power differentials; ensuring beneficence and non-malfeasance; and employing appropriate dissemination activities (Cocks, 2006). Many of these ethical implications are also related to conducting research with ethnic minority 'groups', though some additional challenges are also posed, such as employing culturally appropriate research methods; being alert and able to respond to possible language and cultural difficulties (Salway et al., 2009b).

These ethical issues were all considered before starting the fieldwork aspects of the project, both initially at the proposal stage when the research design was reviewed for scientific rigour (Spring 2009) and additionally through gaining ethical approval from the Faculty of Development and Society's Research Ethics Committee, at Sheffield Hallam University (Spring, 2010). While there is no one specific code of practice that researchers have to follow in respect to child protection issues (Furey and Kay, 2010), in line with good practice, I adhered to Sunnyside's own child protection policy including gaining an up-to-date Criminal Records Bureau (CRB)[4] check prior to starting my familiarisation period in the school (Kay et al., 2009). The Association of Social Anthropologists of the UK (ASA, 2011) ethical guidelines informed the ethical processes undertaken throughout this study.

As well as gaining scientific and ethical approval and complying with Sunnyside's child protection checks it is also as, if not more, important that ethical issues are considered and acted upon throughout all stages of a research study. Working through the day-to-day practicalities of research ethics is an ongoing process that requires (re)negotiation with research participants (ASA, 2011). In the current study, the familiarisation period revealed a number of ethical issues relating to negotiating a researcher role within the classroom that needed to be considered further within the research setting, most notably these related to protection from harm and negotiating ongoing informed consent, with both adults and children.

As an adult in the classroom who was not a member of staff or a teaching student, there was initial uncertainty concerning my resistance to taking on the role of disciplinarian. To allow me to observe how children negotiated their

4. In 2012 the Criminal Records Bureau (CRB) and Independent Safeguarding Authority (ISA) merged to form the Disclosure and Barring Process (DBS). The DBS is a non-departmental public body of the UK Home Office.

patterns of interaction, I decided that unless there was potential for harm I would not step in. I also remained neutral in arguments and negotiations between peers, where other staff members would repeatedly get involved. Negotiating the boundaries of this role, i.e. when a situation was potentially harmful, was an ongoing aspect of fieldwork. One example of when I did decide to step in to take on a more disciplinary role was when we were returning back to the classroom from an assembly. As we were going back to the classroom, I was one of two adults with the children. When we got to the top of the stairs Amir, Mubarak and Callum decided to crawl down the stairs head first. Concerned that they might slip and bump their heads, I told the boys to stop, stand up and walk down the stairs holding onto the banister.

Through conversations with research guides, during my familiarisation period, it also became evident that the boundary between informal interviews and 'off the record' conversations can become blurred. Setting boundaries and markers to indicate when a conversation was not part of the project was an important part of building up relationships with research guides. As these boundaries were negotiated over a period of time, my familiarisation period allowed time for this to be naturally built into the study design and paved the way for the establishment of ways of working throughout the whole fieldwork period.

Researcher positionality

Recognising your own values and beliefs and how these frame your world view and consequently your research are crucial aspects of ethnography. To successfully achieve this, the ethnographer must engage in an internal dialogue that repeatedly questions 'what the researcher knows and how the researcher came to know [what they know]' (Berg, 2009: 198). Being reflexive consequently requires the ethnographer to have an ongoing conversation with herself concluding in 'not merely report[ing] findings ... but actively construct[ing] interpretations of experiences in the field and ... question[ing] how these interpretations ... arose' (Berg, 2009: 198). Engaging in this reflective process is particularly important when researchers are seeking to access children's voices as a researcher's values and beliefs as an adult need to be additionally taken into account on top of other aspects that influence how the ethnographer frames her worldview.

This study adopted a two-fold approach to understanding and employing reflexivity, i.e. academic reflexivity, or in other words methodological reflections (which include theory, research methods and ethics), and non-academic or personal reflexivity (which incorporates life based experiences or what anthropologists refer to as 'the researcher's cultural prejudice') (Davis, 1998: 321). This reflexive approach is particularly important as this study worked with children from ethnic minority backgrounds where I was an 'outsider' to children's lives on two accounts i.e. firstly as an adult and secondly as an individual with a White Scottish identity.

Analysis

In keeping with ethnographic principles, analysis was conducted as an ongoing process alongside data collection, and in many respects the two cannot be completely separated (Hammersley and Atkinson, 2007). As has been previously mentioned, practitioners and children alike were involved in the ongoing process of analysis and interpretation through helping me to check and, where appropriate, revise initial interpretations. Involving participants in the analysis process helps to reduce potential power differentials between participant and researcher (Flewitt, 2005). Additionally, as Emond (2005) highlights, the researcher working with children needs to be careful to not filter data through an adult lens, which can distort the stories and experiences that children have shared. Consequently, as an ongoing part of the study, I asked children to explain their meanings and interpretations of a specific action or game either during or as soon after the activity as possible through asking questions such as 'why did you choose to play that game' or 'why did you decide to play with ...'?

To complement this collaborative analysis with children and practitioners, I themed (or coded) my fieldnotes using an inductive approach. As this process was started before analysis with participants, this fed into the collaborative analysis which in turn fed back into the final stages of fieldnote analysis. This allowed me to utilize LeCompte and Schensul's (1999) three levels of inductive analysis: the item; the pattern; and the constitutive.

Item level analysis

Item level analysis consists of extracting discrete themes from the data. To do this I used the software programme NVivo 8 in an ongoing process of analysis at five key points in the fieldwork year. In January at the end of Term 1, I conducted the first point of this analysis and coded the data using the following emergent themes (free nodes): methodology, methods, field location, ethics, capital, identity, racism, multiculturalism, good practice, friendships, family, home school relationships, reflection, staff perceptions, views of childhood. This first point of analysis helped to inform the sampling of focus children. After focus children were identified, data was reviewed again and themed by focus child. During the second and third terms, while I was employing research activities with children, a point of analysis was formally employed every half term to identify gaps in the data and help inform the design of subsequent research activities e.g. the aspects covered in the Scotland book. It is interesting to note from this information that, as the year progressed, children became more open about discussing aspects of their identity with me. While some of this can be directly linked to the research activities that were conducted during the second and third terms, it is also important to note that once I had built up a relationship with the children and they had learnt that they could trust me, they started to tell me more about their own values and beliefs.

As the wealth of data that I collected grew, I discussed with the children which themes they thought were the most important. Out of these discussions, I decided to focus our analysis on the free node 'identity.' I converted this free node into a 'tree node' and with the children's help created sub-categories to further theme this umbrella category. Additionally, I converted the free nodes ethics, methodology and reflection into tree nodes to aid further analysis on the process of the study. The data that has been included in this study are based on these four tree nodes. There is consequently a wealth of additional data that needs to be explored outside the confines of this book.

NVivo, like all other software packages used to analyse qualitative data, is often critiqued for taking sections of data and viewing them out of context. To minimise this, both text and reference views of nodes were referred to when interpreting findings. Additionally focus child nodes were compared with thematic nodes during this process to further ensure that data was interpreted within the context in which it was produced in line with LeCompte and Schensul's (1999) pattern level of analysis that seeks to discover the connections between item level codes.

Collaborative analysis with children (pattern level analysis)

As well as conducting ongoing analysis with children throughout the fieldwork stage, I also facilitated a more 'formal' or 'official' period of analysis near the end of the school year. In early May I began to feel that my data had become saturated and that my observations were no longer revealing new insights. Following the advice of seasoned anthropologists who recommend as 'a sound rule of thumb ... that when the ... culture you are studying begins to look normal, it is time to go home' (Barley, 1983: 153), I began to design collaborative analytical tools to use with focus children after the May half term holiday and focused our energies on analysis rather than additional data collection. However, as has been previously discussed, the close nature of data collection and analysis within ethnography (where there is no fixed boundary between what some other research strategies see as bounded stages of research) meant that this change in focus did not exclude new pieces of data from emerging from conversations surrounding analytical activities.

Adapting the increasingly popular Early Years planning tool *Possible Lines of Development* (PLOD) plan (Arnold, 2010), I designed a *Participatory Analysis Tool* (PAT) to use when conducting collaborative analysis with children. PATs are designed to be a child-directed form of analysis where the child and the researcher can both contribute to the analysis through reviewing extracts from the data narratives together. The researcher can then 'check' that the child agrees with her interpretation of previous research activities and observations. PATs can be completed using a range of mediums (e.g. writing, pictures, drawings, mark-making, etc.) of the child's choice and, while some guidance is given to help children understand the nature of the exercise, children are encouraged to direct the activity as they choose. In the current study two key activities were used to create PATs.

The first analytical activity centred on collaboratively mapping children's identities. Children were presented with a piece of A1 paper with two concentric circles on it. The circles were designed to give children a starting point to work with rather than being restrictive.

After writing their name in the inner circle, the child and I collaboratively filled in the second circle (or sometimes the whole sheet) with words, drawings, pictures, mark-makings etc. to describe the child's identity or 'who you are'. In doing this I said to the child 'when watching you play I saw you ...' or 'when we made the digital book you said that ...' and asked the child to say if the theme that I had mentioned or the story that I had recited (from my fieldnotes) was important to them. By doing this I was able to check if the themes that I had pulled out of my initial stages of analysis had been interpreted in a way that was meaningful to the children who were involved in the activity or observational session. Our conversation was recorded during this activity and afterwards I listened back to the recording and further annotated the analysis sheet with the child's explanations of aspects of their identity that they wanted to be included in the sheet. This was done at a later time to ensure that everything the child had asked to be included was and that a particular aspect had not been accidentally missed off during the activity. In a separate session these notes were then 'checked' once again with the child to ensure that they were 'correct'.

Following on from activities outlined in Clark's (2004) *The Mosaic Approach*, the second analysis activity focused on collaboratively analysing data relating to patterns of interaction. Using pictures of the different indoor and outdoor activity stations, I asked children to pick their three favourite activities at school. We ranked these in order of first, second and third. I then asked the children who they liked to play with at each activity. After discussing these choices I showed the child their PAT and after checking that they were happy with the identity data (and where necessary updating this information) we collaboratively filled in the remainder of the page with information about the child's patterns of interaction at school. At the end of this session, most children decided that they had completed their PATs, however Daud and Amir asked if they could do some more work on these in a subsequent week. In these sessions we reviewed all of the material on their PATs before filling in the gaps (using drawings, pictures, mark-making etc.) until they were satisfied that they had completed the activity. When each child had decided that they had finished this activity I took a photo of the child with their PAT to give to them. This symbolised that we had completed our collaborative analysis as well as the child's formal involvement in the study.

Some additional children also asked to do the activity mapping their favourite activity stations. As a number of these children were mentioned by focus children during this exercise, and vice versa, this was a good opportunity to match up children's perceptions on their patterns of interaction from a number of different angles (or children's perspectives).

Constitutive level analysis

The final level of analysis, constitutive analysis, looked for relationships among patterns to build an overall picture of the phenomena under examination (LeCompte and Schensul, 1999). This level of analysis was conducted after the first two levels of analysis, item and pattern, had been finalised. At this stage I compared themes in the data with themes from the literature that I had reviewed as an ongoing process before and during fieldwork. Further literature was reviewed after fieldwork to follow up on themes that arose from the data. This level of analysis laid the foundations for the final written ethnographic output which can be found in subsequent chapters.

Withdrawing from the field

At the end of the second analytical activity, focus children were individually debriefed about what stages of the study I still had to do and how their data would be used i.e. in an anonymised form. On my last day in school I also debriefed the class as a whole and thanked them for their participation. I separately debriefed school staff and arranged to meet with them after the summer holidays to discuss my initial research findings and proposed dissemination activities.

As the end of my fieldwork tied in with the end of the school year, this natural break allowed me to withdraw from the field and working with the children as they were preparing to move to their new class after the summer holidays. This 'natural' end to my fieldwork minimised some of the potential challenges that withdrawing from the field can bring (such as sensitively concluding researcher-participant relationships) as the field, i.e. the class, was also moving on and child-adult relationships in the school were naturally drawing to a close.

Chapter 3

Being me: Theorising children's identity discourses

'Identities are ... not the so-called return to roots but a coming-to-terms with our 'routes' (Hall, 2000: 4).

'I am Muslim. All my family are Muslim ... but not all of my friends': The importance of identity in a 'strong structuration' framework

As Nasra is drawing her 'My friends are ... ' picture in early February, she tells me 'I am Muslim. All my family are Muslim; my mum, my dad, my sisters, my grandma and all my cousins but not all of my friends.' She then goes onto explain this further saying 'They [my friends] don't all wear hijab. Aniso isn't [Muslim] 'cause she doesn't wear hijab.' Deka and Fariido who, like Nasra, regularly wear hijab to school, from time to time join Nasra in questioning Aniso about why she doesn't also wear hijab. This particularly concerns these girls as Aniso, like them, is Somali, which for them all equates with 'being Muslim'. However, 'Being Somali' and 'Being Muslim' are also a strong part of Aniso's self-defined identity and she regularly talks to the other children about going to the mosque and joins in with their theological discussions about Allah and 'hellfire'.[5] When she is challenged by one of the other girls about why she doesn't wear hijab, Aniso doesn't say anything but looks towards the floor or focuses intently on the activity that she is doing, close to tears. In early June Aniso comes to school wearing a brightly coloured hijab. When the other girls comment on how pretty it looks, Aniso smiles proudly and happily compares her hijab with the other girl's headscarves.

Interestingly Aniso is the only other Somali girl in the group of *older girls*. This may explain why her Muslim identity is called into question. In contrast, Fazia and Aafia, who are both from North Africa, are not under the same pressure to defend their religious identity. Annakiya, the other member of this group, is Christian. Hijab can therefore be viewed as primarily symbolic of these girls' national, cultural or ethnic identities, which for them is a potent symbol of their religious identity i.e. as in Nasra's words 'All Somalis are Muslim but not all Muslims are Somali'.

5. 'Hellfire' is the emic term that children used to talk about *Jahannum* i.e. the Islamic concept of hell. While children utilised the Arabic term for heaven, i.e. *Aljana*, in their conversations they did not use the term *Jahannum*.

In contrast to Aniso's compliant reaction when her identity is called into question, Nasra's response to the questioning of her own identity is met with a clear assertion that her self-defined identity is more important to her than the ascribed identity that she is repeatedly given by others. For example, in early April a supply teacher is in charge of the class. As she introduces herself to the class she tells them that she can speak 'schwe, schwe [a little] Arabic' as she lived in Dubai for two years. Some of the Arabic-speaking children laugh at hearing the words 'schwe, schwe' and seem pleased that their supply teacher knows some of their language. Later on in the day, when we are in the outdoor play area, the supply teacher is sitting with Saida. Saida asks the teacher to speak to her in Arabic and the teacher shares the words that she knows with her. Nasra, who is sitting on her own nearby, looks up as they are talking and the teacher asks her what words she knows in Arabic. Nasra confidently tells the teacher that she is Somali and can speak some Somali but not Arabic. The teacher, responding to Nasra's correction, asks her what she can say in Somali and Nasra teaches her some words that she knows. As they are doing this, I think back to the other times when I have seen Nasra's linguistic and national identity questioned by others. Her olive coloured skin and light brown hair often cause those who don't know her to assume that she is from one of the Arab states. Nasra, however, is always quick to correct them and assert her Somali identity.

Identity, as this chapter reveals, is not only important to children at Sunnyside (as the examples above reveal) but is also a central concept in anthropological and sociological understandings of the social world 'because of the way in which it focuses the sociological imagination on the mundane dramas, dreams and perplexities of everyday human life' (Jenkins, 2008: 16). In this way, the notion of identity marries Mills' (1959) key concepts of 'public issues' and 'private troubles', with both concepts, when viewed together, helping to explain the significance of 'the other' (Griffiths, 1995). Identity can therefore be understood as a meta-concept that, for the most part, 'makes as much sense [when viewed] individually as collectively' making it a strategically significant concept in which to understand wider theoretical debates, most notably around the notion of structuration (Jenkins, 2008: 16; Stones, 2005). The central role that identity plays in anthropological and sociological interpretations of the social world stems from the way in which it bridges these 'public issues' and 'private troubles' (Mills, 1959).

Within this discussion it is important to highlight key aspects of the structure-agency debate that has long dominated both classical and contemporary anthropological and sociological understandings of the social world and continues to be one of the most persistent issues in current social science thinking. Classical social theorists such as Durkheim (1893) and Marx and Engels (1948) who subscribed to the notion of holism (i.e. the notion that the whole is greater than the sum of its parts) advocated that social structures are fundamental in determining, or limiting, an individual's actions. In contrast, theorists such as Weber (1930), who subscribe to the notion of atomism (i.e. the idea that individual parts are key rather than the collective manifestation of these said parts) argued that an individual's agency is fundamental to how they (re) construct their social world. Each of these theorists assumed that the concepts of structure and agency are fundamentally different. Unconvinced by these arguments, more recent thinkers such as Giddens (1984) and Bourdieu (1990) have questioned the assumed dichotomy of these two concepts. This questioning in turn has paved the way for the development of Giddens' *structuration theory*. This theory argues for *the duality of structure* where structure and agency are understood as being intertwined; contending that social structures influence an individual's actions in the same way that the individual can change the social structures which influence their lives. Social structure can consequently be understood as both the catalyst for and product of social action. Structure is therefore not permanent but rather is maintained and altered by social action in a form of reflexive feedback. As can be seen from Aniso's and Nasra's stories, structure and agency are interconnected at Sunnyside in the way that Giddens envisioned.

Over the years, Giddens' interpretation of structuration has been critiqued from many sides. Two key critiques include arguments for the dualism (rather than the duality) of structure that attempt to counter the apparent conflation of structure and agency (Archer, 1995, Mouzelis, 2000) and the notion of the concept of structural differentiation, which proposes that while semantic rules are relevant to structure that these rules are differentiated along lines of diversity such as ethnicity, class, gender etc. (Thompson, 1989).

Despite these critiques, Stones (2005) argues that structuration is an important and useful concept that needs to be further developed rather than set aside, as some have argued, due to the flaws in Giddens' interpretation. He states that:

> Structuration theory has reached a decisive point in its trajectory, a point that could see it fade as a distinct approach or, alternatively, establish

itself more strongly than ever as an integrated perspective able to offer invaluable kinds of systematic explanatory power and critical insight to social theory. There has been a certain paradox or irony in the fate of structuration in recent years, at the theoretical level it has been the negative target of sustained and detailed criticisms, whilst at the empirical level its history ... has been one of overwhelming success as scores of researchers have found that its concepts have allowed them to gain critical purchase on empirical phenomena'. (Stones, 2005: 2)

Building on Giddens' work, Stones has developed a revised theory which he has termed 'strong structuration'. This theory addresses and responds to both his own and others' critiques of Giddens' original theoretical framework. Holding onto aspects of Giddens' interpretation, namely the centrality of *the duality of structure* and what Stones (ibid.: 5) terms the 'structural-hermeneutic core', strong structuration also systematically addresses methodological and empirical critiques of Giddens' work. Stones also notes that Giddens himself at times 'underestimated the significance of *the duality of structure*.' By developing a strong structuration theory, Stones places the 'structural-hermeneutic core' at the heart of the discussion and, in doing so, counters Giddens' overestimation of the relevance and application of this theory.

Giddens' work is primarily concerned with structuration at the abstract level, resulting in the birth of an ontological concept that addresses the overarching nature of 'being' rather than specific experiences of 'being' rooted in a particular social context. Stones (ibid.: 7) terms this approach as 'ontology-in-general.' Building on this abstract concept, Stones (ibid.: 10) argues for 'a developed structurationist ontology [that] can shape empirical insights' in specific social contexts, or in other words at the *ontic* level. This he terms 'ontology-*in-situ*.' In grounding strong structuration, Stones unlocks the potential of structuration theory in unearthing empirical insights. In developing an understanding of strong structuration as 'ontology-*in-situ*' Stones contends that a quadripartite cycle of structuration be employed to explain the nature of *the duality of structure*. The quadripartile cycle consists of the following four aspects:

external structures as conditions of action;

internal structures within the agent;

active agency, including a range of aspects involved when agents draw upon internal structures in producing practical action;

outcomes (as external and internal structures and as events)' (ibid.: 9).

In adopting this approach, strong structuration 'provides an array of structural-hermeneutic tools and insights that ... make meaningful and nuanced links between large historical, geographical and social forces, proximate networks of social relations and practices, and the sung and unsung phenomenological experiences ... of diversely situated human beings' (ibid.: 11). Therefore, as the concept of identity bridges the 'public issues' and 'private troubles' of Mills' (1959) *Sociological Imagination*, so does the theory of strong structuration. The ways in which these links are played out at Sunnyside will be explored in the following chapters.

However, Stones (2005) also cautions against over-reliance on structuration theory and calls on theorists and researchers alike to recognise the scope and limitations of this theoretical framework. Consequently Stones argues that strong structuration should always be used in conjunction with other theoretical perspectives that can flesh out structuration's skeleton. In line with this, the current study uses a strong structuration framework as a way to draw together theoretical perspectives of identity.

My study adds to the growing body of literature that continues to uncover 'structuration theory in action' as it provides 'critical purchase on empirical phenomena' (ibid.: 2; 10). In this chapter, three identity theories that continue to be dominant within the social sciences—Goffman's (1959) *dramaturgical analysis*; Hughes' (1945) *master status* [sic]; and Jenkins' (1996, 2008) dialectical work—will be considered within a strong structuration framework. The remaining chapters in this book will build on this chapter showing how a strong structuration framing of identity can, and does, shed light on the salient lived experiences of young children's daily negotiations surrounding identity, diversity and inequality.

Irrespective of where theorists position themselves in relation to the structure/agency debate, the need to belong, or be part of a 'group', has long been acknowledged across a wide range of academic disciplines and has formed the basis for countless theoretical questions and debates since the times of Socrates through to Freud and beyond. While achieving such a sense of belonging, or shared identity, is difficult to delineate, it is widely understood as being foundational to an individual's and a group's wellbeing (Marranci, 2006; Jenkins, 2008; Bath, 2009) and as in the case of Aniso (mentioned above) the need to belong can at times over-ride an individual's customary expression of their identity. Interestingly, while an individual may think that they belong to a particular group, the group itself, and external onlookers, may disagree with this identification and ascribe the individual with an external identity or assume that they belong to another group (Marranci, 2006; Jenkins, 2008), as seen in the case of Nasra above. An individual's response to this questioning may result in them re-asserting their group membership, as Nasra did in the conversation with her supply teacher, or may result in them being denied group membership and either accepting their exclusion, or as Aniso has shown, re-negotiating the way that they express their identity to ensure that group membership is ultimately granted. As can be seen, from both Aniso and Nasra, identity, and the need to belong, directly impact on the day-to-day lived experiences of children at Sunnyside.

Within the class a number of children from North Africa clearly identified as 'being white.' Juxtaposed to this self-definition they at times came up against external discourses that told them that they could not be white, as they were also Muslim, but should refer to themselves as Arab. The way in which different aspects of identity intersect will be explored in more detail in Chapter 4. It is interesting to note here, though, that exclusion of group membership, at times, did not just relate to one aspect of an individual's identity but to the ways in which different aspects of identity interweaved. Before unpacking children's experiences in more detail I will further examine the concept of identity itself.

'They aren't Arab': Similarity and difference

First, to begin exploring this concept it may be helpful to examine the etymological roots of the word 'identity'. Etymologically the term 'identity' is derived from the Latin word 'idem', which can be translated into English as 'the same'—highlighting the central role that concepts of similarity and difference play in developing an understanding of identity. As can be seen below, notions of similarity and difference are often discussed by children at Sunnyside both with myself and with their peers.

When working with Amir in late January using the 'My friends are ...' research activity, Amir decides that he wants to draw a picture of himself playing football with his friends. Before starting to draw, Amir tells me that he likes to play football with Daud, Mubarak, Mustafe, Barak and Seif while at school and that they often pretend that they are England, Spain or Barcelona because these are 'good football teams'. After telling me this, he reaches over to the pen pot and picks up a brown pen which he starts drawing with. 'This is Mubarak' he tells me. He then draws Daud using the same pen telling me that Daud and Mubarak both have the same skin colour. After finishing this part of his picture he looks again in the pen pot and informs me that there isn't a pen for his skin colour.

He shows me his hand and says to me 'Look, there isn't the right colour'. He then picks up a blue pen and says 'let's pretend its white' also commenting that 'blue is a good boy's colour'. He draws a picture of himself (with the ball), and then draws a picture of Barak and Seif using the same blue pen. As he is doing this, he tells me that he is *the same* as these boys and that they are all Arab and Muslim. He then picks up a green pen and draws some grass. With the same pen he draws Mustafe. He tells me that, when they play football, Mustafe is always the goal keeper and that the goal keeper needs to be a different colour from the other players.

After he has finished drawing Amir looks at his completed picture and tells me that Daud and Mubarak are also Muslim like himself and the other boys. However, he explains that 'they aren't Arab', like the other boys, as they are not white but rather that they are Somali. During this activity Amir shows that he understands that there is social meaning behind the differences that he sees between himself and his friends and that their different skin colours can also relate to other aspects of their identity. Amir does not, however, place these differences within a social hierarchy but rather purely comments that these differences exist. In depicting his peers in this way, Amir utilises skin colour as a collective marker of difference and in doing so emphasises the relevance of group identity and notions of sameness.

When drawing Mustafe, Amir uses the colour green to depict Mustafe as a goal keeper rather than representing him via his ethnic identity as he does with the other boys. Throughout the course of the year, when playing football, Mustafe always chooses to be in goal and relishes this role. As the other boys prefer to play in other positions, Mustafe soon becomes known as the class goalkeeper. It is therefore not surprising that in this context Amir chose this as the over-riding aspect of Mustafe's identity to depict. In this respect Amir shows that he is aware of the multiple identities that he and his peers have. The salience of these identities, for Amir, also appear to change depending on the social context, as at other times Amir refers to Mustafe as primarily 'being Muslim', highlighting shared aspects of their religious identities. The importance of context or social environment in the conceptualisation and operationalisation of identity will be discussed in more detail in the next section.

Interestingly, although Seif and Mustafe are not members of *the gang*, Amir has recognised that they too like to play football and has depicted them with *the gang* in his drawing. While Kareem is also regularly found playing football, particularly with Mustafe, he was not mentioned by Amir during this activity.

As Chapter 6 shows Kareem's own patterns of interaction are largely based on language. As Kareem spoke little English and Amir little Arabic, despite classical Arabic forming part of his religious identity, lack of a shared language appears to strongly impact on how both boys view this peer relationship.

While Arabic is often thought of as being one language for collective identity purposes (e.g. socio-political, ethnic), modern Arabic dialects are often 'mutually unintelligible'. Additionally it should be noted that classical Arabic and modern Arabic dialects are also distinct and in linguistic terms can be understood as separate entities (Heath, 1997). The varieties of classical and modern Arabic dialects make communication across different forms of Arabic difficult.

As my conversation with Amir reveals, children at Sunnyside are aware of, and discuss, concepts of similarity and difference in relation to their understanding of their own and others' identities. The seventeenth century philosopher Locke reflected a similar understanding in his quest to discover why human beings feel the same over a long period of time. Locke (1959: 449) came to the conclusion that human consciousness is continuous, stating that it is consciousness that 'makes everyone to be what he [sic] calls self, and thereby distinguishes himself from all other thinking beings, in this alone consists personal identity.' Building on this there are two key concepts that are foundational in understanding the fundamental nature of identity—similarity and difference:

> The notion of identity involves two criteria of comparison between persons or things: similarity and difference ... Identifying ourselves or others is a matter of meaning, and meaning always involves interaction: agreement and disagreement, convention and innovation, communication and negotiation. ... Identity is our understanding of who we are ... it too is negotiable. (Jenkins, 1996: 4-5)

As Jenkins highlights above, understanding similarity and difference, and leading on from this who we are (and similarly who others are), is a negotiated process which involves interaction between individuals so that meaning can be established. Jeffs and Smith (2005: 48) support this claim by stating that 'we are [only] what we are because of our interactions with others.' Notably, as Bath (2009) points out with reference to early years practice, and particularly in relation to child-centred approaches, identity is often viewed as asocial. However, as this study shows, many social theorists, such as Goffman (1959) and Jenkins (1996, 2008), argue that identity is deeply social. Social theorists working within the field of early years education, such as Van Ausdale and Feagin (2001) and Connolly (2003), also argue that identity is social. Indeed, the children at Sunnyside reveal that, for them, identity is intrinsically social. In research conversations, different aspects of identity appear to be more salient for some children than others. For some, their social interaction with their peers comes to the fore while for others their collective family identity appears to be the predominant shaping force. In all cases, though, identity is social. Consequently 'Traditional' Early Years interpretations of concepts such as identity can be developed and enriched by drawing on relevant literature from other academic disciplines, such as social anthropology and sociology, which also highlight the social nature of identity.

Drawing on Giddens' (1991) notion of identity as a reflexive project of the self, identity can therefore be described as 'a work in progress' or 'a negotiated space between ourselves and others; [that is] constantly being re-appraised and [which is] very much linked to the circulation of cultural meanings in a society.' (Taylor and Spencer, 2004: 4). This negotiation, as discussed above, is important for Amir as he depicts the similarities and differences that he sees between himself and his football peers at school.

The ways in which children at Sunnyside understand these two concepts of similarity and difference will be explored further in Chapter 5 in relation to conceptualising and operationalising social abstractions of difference, discourses of discrimination and hierarchies of difference.

'I've been a good school boy': The role of social agency in identity (re)negotiation

Building on the fundamental nature of identity as being concerned with notions of similarity and difference, an individual's social environment is also important within this discussion and can contribute to which particular aspects of their identity a person places most emphasis on in any given situation (Goffman, 1959). Theorists who subscribe to this understanding of identity highlight the importance of social agency in their theoretical constructions.

Children at Sunnyside, most notably members of *the gang*, carefully perform to their immediate audience and in doing so they (as social actors) guide the impression that their parents and other family members (the audience), who bring them to school, have of them as school pupils. Therefore, as Goffman's (1959) work highlights, context is central to how children at Sunnyside fluidly perform different aspects of their multiple identities. Amir, Daud and Mubarak (almost) always seem pleased to see each other when they first arrive at school in a morning and often have a story to recount about what they have done the previous evening or bring something to school to show the other boys. When they arrive at school separately, they often say to me that they are waiting for their friends to come to school or that they need to tell them something.

One morning in late January, Amir and Mubarak arrive before Daud. As the children arrive in the morning they are expected to select whether they are having school dinners that day or a packed lunch by putting their name card in the correct basket. After doing this they are encouraged to practice writing their name on individual wipe-able boards. Having chosen their lunch options, the two boys sit and chat while writing their names. Daud arrives and his mother directs him towards the meal options board where Daud selects his name and puts it in the basket for school dinners. Amir and Mubarak see him and run over to greet him. Daud starts to tell them something but his mother shoos away the other boys and regains Daud's attention. She tells him that he has to be good at school, work hard and not spend all day chatting to his friends. Daud nods as she tells him this and meekly follows her over to the table where his name card is located. He sits down and begins to write his name. His mother watches him write the first few letters and then leaves. As soon as she is out of sight, Daud drops his pen on the table and stands up. Amir and Mubarak come over to him and Daud lifts up his trouser leg and shows them a scab on his knee. He then excitedly tells them how he fell over earlier that morning on the road ('where there could have been a car!') explaining that he had to go back home to get cleaned up, resulting in him arriving at school after the two other boys did. Mary rings the tambourine to tell the children to tidy up and come and sit on the carpet. Daud comes over to me smiling cheekily and exclaims 'I haven't even written my name yet!' All traces of mother's studious son seem to have left as Daud no longer needed to manage his mother's impression of himself as a diligent pupil. At the end of the school day, when his mother arrives to collect him, Daud once again acts the role of the hardworking son and carefully chooses which aspects of his day to tell her about, while also emphasising that he has 'been a good school boy' and has 'not got his name on the board' (i.e. got into trouble). In this account, however, I do not hear Daud mention his friends and the games that they have played during the course of the day.

Goffman's (1959) theory of dramaturgical analysis clearly explains the importance of social environment when developing an understanding of identity and in doing so also highlights the performative nature of identity that Daud has demonstrated above. Employing Shakespeare's imagery from the play 'As You Like it', Goffman (1959) likened social interaction to a theatrical performance. His analogy states that in social interaction, just as in a theatre, there is a front stage where the 'audience' can see the 'actors' performance' and a backstage, which is a private place, where the 'actors' can 'be out of role.' Goffman argues that within any social context an individual will consequently attempt to draw attention to a particular aspect of their identity within a particular social environment or to a particular audience to try and guide the impression that others within the social environment will make of him or herself. Thus individuals are actors creating identities by playing different roles on different stages. Identity can therefore be defined, for Goffman, as the act of presenting oneself to an external audience and by its very nature must be understood as multiple and situated. For Goffman an individual's social agency is key to this presentation.

As this study uncovers, the children at Sunnyside demonstrate a high level of fluidity and performance in their identity (re)negotiations. Through employing their social agency children are able to (re)negotiate their identities against a backdrop of social discourses relating to ethnicity, gender, religion and other social attributes. While emphasising the performative nature of identity my data does not show any evidence to support Goffman's concept of a backstage. The children reveal that to a certain degree their identity performance is strategic, for example Nasra's portrayal of a 'nice, friendly girl' (below). While, as Goffman states, context determines the identity performance, this does not necessitate a backstage where the 'actor' can be 'out of role.' What if there is no backstage? What if identity is purely triggered by context without relating back to a core aspect?

As Daud's behaviour (above) shows this performative nature of identity is enacted by children in the same way as the adults that Goffman used to illustrate his theory. While Goffman himself did not directly relate his findings to the actions and experiences of children, instead viewing them as nonpersons, Brown (2007) points out that in numerous studies children actively engage in complex identity performance. Jeffcoate's (1979: 13) research in Bradford clearly highlights this:

> The head teacher in an all White nursery school in Bradford invited four year-old children to talk about non stereotypical pictures of Black and White people doing a variety of jobs. As they made no reference to skin colour during the ensuing discussion the head teacher's contention that children do not discriminate between skin colour was confirmed.

> However, in the afternoon when the same set of pictures were left on the tables without any input from the head teacher, the children responded differently. Not only did they refer to skin colour but their increasingly negative and derisory comments forced the head teacher to step in and end the session.

As can be seen from Jeffcoate's work, young children do actively respond to their social environment and consequently choose how to present themselves to an external audience, guiding the impression that others make of them in a way that is consistent with perceived social norms. Van Ausdale and Feagin (2001) discovered that the children who they were working with (three to six year-olds) likewise changed their behaviour and more specifically the ways in which they discussed ethnic difference when teachers and other school authority figures were present. Similarly all of the instances that I observed at Sunnyside of children discussing and operationalising the hierarchical nature of difference (Chapter 5) were out of sight and earshot of school staff. By building up trusting relationships with children over the course of the year that minimised power differentials (Chapter 2), I was given access to aspects of children's lives that they kept well hidden from school staff.

In addition to managing their identities with family members, children at Sunnyside, like those in earlier studies (Jeffcoate, 1979; Van Ausdale and Feagin, 2001), actively manage staff and peer impressions of themselves. A conversation that I had with Nasra as she is about to begin the 'My friends are ...' activity reveals this aspect of performance. I give Nasra the 'My friends are ...' sheet and explain to her the activity before asking her who her friends are. She tells me that Deka, Aniso and Fariido are her friends. Then looking around to make sure that no-one can hear us, she quietly tells me that Fariido isn't really her friend. She begins to write down Deka's name on her sheet of paper. As she is doing this she says to me, 'Don't tell Fariido. She thinks that she's my friend but she's not. She bothers me.' She then goes on to explain why, even though she plays with Fariido, she doesn't think of her as her friend. She then tells me that she has to 'pretend' to be friends with Fariido otherwise Fariido will be nasty to her and tell the other girls that they also shouldn't be Nasra's friend. She further explains that she has to pretend to be everyone's friend because that is also what school staff tell her that she has to do. Within this context Nasra has decided that the best way to deal with Fariido is to be nice to her as in doing so she can successfully manage peer and staff impressions of herself as a friendly girl who gets on with everyone. In acting out this performance, Nasra hides her true feelings about Fariido while also creating a 'good' impression of herself. She believes that this will protect her from the backlash of any individual arguments that they may have as her peers and staff consider her to be 'a nice, friendly girl' and will therefore, according to Nasra, not blame her for any arguments that she and Fariido may have in the future. In doing this Nasra tactfully engages in Goffman's (1959) impression management.

As Russell (2011) highlights, structure and agency both have a part to play in how young people interact with their peers conceptualising, as Nasra shows above, that resistance is multifaceted and complex. For Russell, resistance can be placed on a continuum of complete resistance, at one end, and total acceptance, at the other. Russell (2011: 71) argues that 'dimensions of resistance ... fall within and between the following continua: covert or overt, individual or collective, intentional or unintentional, and engaged or detached.' On these continua, Nasra's actions can be described as a covert, individual, intentional form of resistance that is detached from wider social interactions.

Sunnyside has a policy of inclusion and inclusive play as advocated by Paley's (1993) work in American kindergartens. Paley discovered that while practitioners had long ago 'outlawed' hitting and name-calling, children still regularly excluded their peers from their games and in doing so had found new ways of ostracising other children in a way that appeared to be socially acceptable to staff members. Through implementing the rule 'You can't say you can't play' Paley tried to re-address this issue. However, as Nasra reveals, children are able, even within this context, to resist school rules and effectively manage others' impressions of themselves. Observations of Nasra's patterns of interactions show that she only plays with Fariido as part of the group of *older girls*, or via an adult's direction, and does not directly initiate contact with Fariido or invite her to play any of the games that Nasra herself has set up. Devine's (2000) work similarly reveals that children actively create and manage their own strategies for resisting adult rules. Drawing on a Foucauldian interpretation of power, Devine argues that adults can never have complete control over children's actions and social agency.

While Paley's research shows that policies like 'You can't say you can't play' have helped to further the inclusive nature of classrooms, Goffman's (1959) theory of impression management coupled with Russell's (2011) theory of pupil resistance and Devine's (2000) understanding of power suggest further subtleties that need to be unravelled. Complex forces may be at work when children offer reasons for not wanting to play with others. This is beyond the scope of the current study, but is an important area that warrants further exploration. Importantly, though, this section highlights that social agency plays a fundamental role in how children interact with their peers and resist adult rules.

'That's a boy's job!': The role of social structure in identity (re)negotiation

While, as Goffman's (1959) work shows, social agency is an important feature of identity formation, his work fails to account for the part that social structure, and wider social discourses, play in identity formation and maintenance. Structural discourses, as will be seen below and in following chapters, alongside agency, play a part in the identity negotiations of children at Sunnyside. From this perspective it is important to consider Hughes' (1945) notion of *master status theory* [sic], which highlights the role of structure, within this discussion. Before exploring Hughes' work I will, however, return to Sunnyside to see how social structure influences children's identity (re)negotiations.

Peer conversations at Sunnyside often comment on what are considered to be 'appropriate' activities for girls or boys to do. Phrases such as 'boys don't do that!' or 'pink is for girls' can regularly be heard as one child admonishes another for their actions. Almost all children adhere to these discourses and encourage their peers to also do so (Chapter 5). For the most part, boys and girls also voluntarily engage in gender segregated play though outside the classroom sometimes come together in mass chasing games where the boys typically chase the girls. Annakiya is the only girl in the class who does not conform to the traditional female role of being chased. During research activities we discuss this and Annakiya tells me that she likes to chase the other children but believes that she 'really should not do this' but rather 'should like to be chased by the boys.' She then asks me not to talk to the other children about this, saying that she does not like it when they ask her why she does not behave like the other girls. While Annakiya exercises her agency in taking on what the other children consider to be 'a boy's job' in the class' chasing games she is still influenced by wider social discourses relating to gender roles that the majority of her classmates adhere to and promote. Walter (2010) argues that wider social discourses pertaining to 'acceptable' gendered behaviour are widespread and that children from a young age are bombarded with messages telling them how they should behave. It is, therefore, difficult for children, like Annakiya, who do not want to conform to these ascribed roles to find a way to express their gendered identity in a non-stereotypical way. At

Sunnyside very few children are questioning these discourses and those that do are often disparaged by their peers who tell them how they should behave and in doing so often ascribe each other with a gendered master status'.

The term master status refers to the primary aspect of identity [or to use Hughes' (1945) terminology 'social position'] that an individual promotes, achieves or is labelled with by others. Consequently an individual's master status can be either self-defined or ascribed. Hughes suggests that a person's master status overshadows all other identities in the majority of (if not in all) situations, for example, if a working mother feels that her role as a mother is more important than her role as an employee, a daughter, a wife or a sister then she is most likely to label herself first and foremost as a mother in all situations and not just when she is interacting with her child or her child's school and other networks. Hughes' theory goes on to state that in all social settings she is also most likely to identify with other women who also view being a mother as their master status. It should be noted that Hughes' (1945) term master status is problematic due to inherent gender discourses that promote male dominance. However, no replacement term has been found in the literature that conveys the same signified concept that lies behind the term. In re-coining this term I will use a gender neutral replacement—*dominant status*—to convey the same signified concept that Hughes' conceptualised

An individual's *dominant status* affects an individual's behaviour in social situations (Hughes, 1945). Furthermore this identity, and the 'perceived social standing' that is connected to this, can be foundational in shaping an individual's 'entire social status' (Hunt, 2011). While the notion of fixed identities has been widely critiqued due to widespread views of identity's transient nature (Bauman,1996), social discourses of discrimination show that institutional racism (Hall, 2010) and caste systems (Rao, 2010) can over-ride identity's fluid nature, as individuals are often strongly identified by others using their ascribed dominant status. These discourses can have a profound impact on an individual's sense of self (Chapter 5). Social structure is, consequently, an important consideration in identity (re)negotiation.

As Modood (2010: 308) points out, while 'we may have a principled political objection to wide group identities that connect so many aspects of a person's life ... under a single 'master [sic] signifier'', ascribed group identities do have a very real impact on the lived experiences of many minority individuals. While the salience and agency of identity is not under question, structural discourses of discrimination can, and do, impact on how an individual (re)negotiates their identity. Consequently, while abstractions of difference, such as ethnicity, gender etc., are socially constructed and may not be considered to be 'real', related structural discrimination, such as racism, sexism etc., are *very* real and directly impact on real people in real situations (Modood, 2007). A strong structuration framework, that highlights *the duality of structure*, can help us to understand the complexity of the relationship between social abstractions of difference and structural discrimination. This will be explored further in Chapter 5.

It is important to note that, in a similar way to which Goffman's (1959) theory of agentive identity fails to recognise the importance of structure, Hughes' (1945) work does not adequately account for the role of social actors in renegotiating the identity that they are ascribed with. While the level of agency that social actors can employ will depend on the prevalence of the social structures that are dominant in their social environment, all actors to a greater or lesser degree can, as the children at Sunnyside show, reconstruct these discourses. Consequently, while both Goffman and Hughes highlight some important points in their respective identity theories, both fail to access the crux of the problem and therefore both are inadequate to fully explain the complexities of how children at Sunnyside conceptualise and operationalise their identities. As seen above, both *structure* and *agency* impact on how children interact with their peers, for example Annakiya's role in the class' mass chasing games. A theory of identity is therefore needed that incorporates both of these theoretical concepts and highlights *the duality of structure*.

'Somalis can be white': The dialectical nature of identity

As the children's narratives above reveal, structure and agency are both intrinsic to the make-up of identity. These narratives resonate with findings in Van Ausdale and Feagin's (2001), Corsaro's (2003) and Russell's (2011) work that also uncover the role that structuration plays in children's and young people's social interactions. Returning now to concepts highlighted by Stones' (2005) strong structuration theory, described above, I will discuss the *duality of structure by* considering Jenkins' (1996, 2008) work on the dialectical nature of identity and how this played out at Sunnyside.

Some children at Sunnyside are aware of apparent conflicting aspects of their identity. This is particularly true for children from multi-ethnic backgrounds, such as Nasra and Amir, and for children whose families have sought asylum in the UK, such as Daud, Jabir and Aniso. In response to the questioning of her identity, Nasra has developed a discourse that incorporates the dialectical nature of identity. Within this discourse, Nasra equates 'being Somali' with adopting a specific socio-political position rather than a specific ethnic identity. Consequently, in Nasra's terms 'being Somali' means wanting Somalia to be a unified and stable country which exiled Somalis can return to and live in safety. A desire to visit this 'new Somalia' strongly features in Nasra's peer conversations as does her explanation of how she can be Somali, 'because Somalis can be white' since for Nasra 'being Somali' is not equated with ethnic identity but rather within a socio-political discourse.

Nasra holds a nuanced view of what 'being Somali' means for her. Her father is influential in developing Nasra's views of Somalia as he tells her stories of his experiences living there and his hopes for the future of his native land. Nasra also likes to listen to her *Ayeeyo*,[6] and other family members, talk about Somalia. As will be seen, though, in Chapter 6 Nasra's mother tries to discourage Nasra from identifying as 'being Somali' instead encouraging her to identify as 'being Muslim.' While Nasra's views of Somalia seem to be influenced by the Somali members of her family, she is also an *active agent* in constructing her own understanding of what 'being Somali' means and positioning herself within this discourse. Though she states that some people think that 'being Somali' means that 'you have to be dark,' Nasra has developed a socio-political discourse that allows her as a white girl to be Somali. Interestingly though Nasra does not challenge the dominant discourse that equates 'being Somali' with 'being Muslim.' As she clearly positions herself as 'being Muslim' she seemingly does not feel a need to re-construct this discourse.

As well as explaining apparent conflicting aspects of identity that arise from being part of a multi-ethnic family, children at Sunnyside also regularly discuss with their peers other dialectical aspects of identity, formulating a way of reconciling contradicting features as they (re)negotiate their identities amongst themselves. In the remainder of this chapter I will examine identity's anchored and transient; self-defined and ascribed; as well as individual and collective dialectics. Firstly, I will consider the ways in which identity can be both anchored and transient by exploring Daud's 'Muslim Father Christmas.'

The 'Muslim Father Christmas': Identity as anchored and transient

At the end of November the children are all sitting on the carpet near the end of the school day. Mary mentions to the children that there is only one month left until Christmas and asks them if Father Christmas comes to their house.

6. Grandmother

Amir responds saying, 'I'm Muslim', while Deka replies that Father Christmas does not come to her house. When asked to contribute to the group discussion, Daud tells the class that, 'a Muslim Father Christmas comes to my house.' As it is the end of the school day I do not get a chance to immediately follow this up with Daud. However, when I am next at Sunnyside I ask him to tell me more about the Muslim Father Christmas. Daud explains to me that, since he is not a Christian, 'Mary's Father Christmas' can not come to his house so instead a 'Muslim Father Christmas' comes and brings him and his family presents. He then goes on to tell me 'I'm always Muslim' and further explains that while his family did not celebrate Christmas when they lived in Somalia (before he was born) they have started to have a 'Muslim Father Christmas' come to their house since moving to England.

As discussed in previous sections, Goffman's (1959) work reveals the importance of social environment when developing an understanding of identity. Leading on from this within postmodern thinking, identity is primarily viewed not as anchored (or fixed) as it was throughout modernity but as transient (or fluid) (Bauman, 1996). This change in thinking in anthropology from anchored to transient notions of identity came out of another shift in thinking regarding anthropology's key concept of culture. In structuralist and modern thought, culture was viewed as coherent and stable and notably as being meaningful to all actors in the same way, regardless of their social position within the 'group.' However, in post-structuralist and postmodern thinking, the notion of 'plural cultural imaginaries' has arisen which reveals that social divisions, e.g. gender, class, ethnicity etc., directly impact on an individual's lived experience of 'group' membership. This theory argues for example that a Muslim girl may experience group membership of 'being Muslim' differently from a Muslim boy. The concept of 'plural cultural imaginaries' has consequently paved the way for a change in thinking regarding the nature of identity (Mumford, 1990; Holland and Lachicotte, 2007).

However, it should also be noted that, as Marranci (2006, 2008) points out, some aspects of identity can remain anchored even when an individual's expression of this aspect of their identity can be transient. As identity is fundamentally a social construction, an individual's experiences (or in other words their social environment), that can challenge their notion of identity and at times conflict with previous and/or concurrent experiences, play a key role in how they (re)negotiate their identities. Coining a new term, it may therefore be helpful to understand anchored aspects of identity as *relative fixity* within the wider context of plural and fluid identities.

Influenced by Goffman's (1959) work, Barth (1969) views identity[7] as fluid, situational and in a state of perpetual (re)negotiation. Hall (2000: 4) supports this notion, stating that identities should be viewed as if in a continual state of becoming, claiming that identities should not be viewed as 'the so-called return to roots' but instead as 'a coming-to-terms with our 'routes'' or in other words making sense of the experiences (social environment) that challenge and call into question our notion of who we are. Connolly's (2003) work with young children also starts from the premise that identity is primarily fluid and situational. Borrowing a term from Gilroy (1993: 122), identity can therefore be viewed as the 'changing same', where aspects of identity are in a continual state of becoming (i.e. are transient), while at the same time relating back to the same anchored core, such as Daud's identity of 'being Muslim.' Leading on from this, identity can be conceptualised as 'a process through which multiple and changing subject positions are given some sense of coherence' (Gunaratnam, 2003: 111).

As can be seen from Daud's explanation, being Muslim is an anchored part of his identity which requires him, and his family, to adapt apparently conflicting practices, such as celebrating Christmas, to ensure that his anchored identity is not compromised. Additionally, it is interesting to note that Daud recognises that moving to the UK has changed aspects of his family's identity as they have begun to adopt cultural traditions that are practiced by the dominant culture in the UK. Here, Daud shows that he is aware that elements of his family's collective identity, which, from previous conversations with both his peers and myself, he clearly subscribes to, are also fluid and situational. Children at Sunnyside, as Daud has revealed, consciously (re)negotiate their identities with their peers, actively engaging in a process of becoming, as their identities are called into question. This is particularly salient for children from minority families.

Aniso's understanding of her national identity is also at once anchored and transient. During a conversation in July, Aniso tells me 'I'm Somali.' She then goes onto explain to me that she was born in the Netherlands and can speak some Dutch, commenting that she used to also be 'a little bit Dutch.' 'Now', she continues, 'I live in England and am a little bit English.' As can be seen from this conversation Aniso clearly self-defines herself as being Somali. This for her is anchored and does not change, over successive migrations, as she and her family

7. While Barth's (1969) work primarily focused on ethnic identities, he also discussed social identities more generally within his argument.

repeatedly move. However, she also recognises that living in different countries is important for her sense of self and consequently subscribes to a transient national identity based on where her home currently is.

As can be seen at the start of this chapter, Aniso is also aware of identity's *internal-external* dialectical nature in relation to Nasra, Deka and Fariido's communal assertion that Somali girls should wear hijab. It is interesting to note here that in recent years the Netherlands (where Aniso was born) has shifted from promoting liberal multicultural policies and practices to assimilationist models of working (Entzinger, 2005). As a result of this, hijab is currently forbidden in certain arenas in the Netherlands, such as the police force and court systems (Hadj-Abdou et al., 2011). Additionally schools also have the authority to require their pupils to wear a uniform that does not include a head covering (McGoldrick, 2010). A separate conversation that I had with a Somali community member reveals that a number of Somali refugees in the Netherlands (and in Denmark) strive to move to the UK as they believe that there is greater religious freedom here. Families in the local community who previously lived in the Netherlands or Denmark reportedly feel more able to express their religious identity in the UK, most notably in relation to wearing headscarves. While it is unclear if living in a country, such as the Netherlands, where an assimilationist model has been adopted, has directly impacted on Aniso and her family's dress code, it is interesting to note that, as the only child in the study who was born in a country that adopts this approach, Aniso is also the only Somali girl in her class who did not wear hijab at the start of the school year. The other Somali girls in the class were all born and brought up in England where wearing hijab is the cultural norm for Somali girls and women. While the impact of repeated migration is beyond the scope of the current study, it is an area that warrants further exploration, particularly in relation to its impact on young children's conceptualisation and operationalisation of identity. One thing that is clear, though, is that aspects of Aniso's self-defined identity are anchored, irrespective of where she and her family currently reside, while other aspects are transient, changing in relation to her social environment.

While postmodern interpretations of concepts such as culture and identity have moved anthropological thinking forward, as seen in this section, postmodernity's pre-occupation with change and fluidity cannot, on its own, adequately explain how children at Sunnyside conceptualise and operationalise their identities. The dialectical nature of identity, which reveals how apparent opposing aspects of identity, such as anchored and transient features, are interconnected is therefore important in this discussion. A strong structuration framework that emphasises *the duality of structure* at the *ontic* level grounds this discussion and allows us to unearth the ways in which identity's dialectical nature is played out in every day lived experiences.

'No I'm not!': Identity as self-defined and ascribed

As well as highlighting the dialectical nature of anchored and transient identities Jenkins' (1996, 2008) work also discusses the importance of the *internal-external dialectic. This* duality is important for some of the *older girls at S*unnyside, such as Nasra and Aniso, where *external and internal structures, active agency and outcomes, as* conceptualised by Stones (2005), come into play as the girls (re) negotiate their identities amongst their peers.

A conversation between Amir and Mustafe in February highlights that Amir, like the girls mentioned above, also makes a conscious effort to manage the impressions that others have of him in relation to the *internal-external dialectic*. Amir arrives at school and sits down next to Mustafe and begins to practise writing his name. As they write, the two boys chat about playing football. Mustafe says to Amir, 'My name is Mustafe football.' Amir laughs at this and agrees that Mustafe does like to play football a lot. He then whispers something into Mustafe's ear to which Mustafe replies out loud, 'No you're Amir Morocco.' 'No, I'm not!' Amir retorts, drawing on his *active agency*. 'Yes', chips in Annakiya who has been listening to the boys' conversation, 'cause you want to go to Morocco.' Amir smiles and nods at this confirming that he does want to visit Morocco and his extended family who live there, but still insists that he is not called 'Amir Morocco' rather asserting that he is 'Amir Arabic'. Up until this conversation, Amir has regularly talked in class about visiting Morocco with his father. After this point in the year though, Amir stops discussing this with his peers on a regular basis and only occasionally can be heard telling his closest friends, Daud and Mubarak, about why he wants to visit Morocco. Visiting Morocco also stops featuring in the boys' games, whereas previously they had gone on trips to Morocco as part of their exploring games in the outdoor play area. Interestingly, even when Amir's family begin to plan a holiday to Morocco, during the summer holidays, Amir rarely discusses this with his peers though he does mention this to Mary and myself when working on a one-to-one basis. A week before this conversation the other gang members try to ascribe Amir with an English identity. Again Amir, drawing on his *active agency*, ardently refutes this ascribed identity and, in a similar way to the young people in Russell's (2011) study, resists his peers' labelling. On both of these occasions, Amir refuses to accept the national identities that his peers try to give him, instead choosing to unmistakably express his identity as Arabic, which he equates with 'being Muslim' (Chapter 4).

In day-to-day situations, an individual's identity, as Amir's interactions with his peers reveal, can be questioned in routine social interactions. As Jenkins (1996: 8) suggests: 'one of the first things that we do on meeting a stranger is attempt to locate them on our social maps'. An individual's own identity is then either re-established or not, depending on the nature of the social encounters that they engage in (Jenkins, 1996, 2008; Marranci, 2006). 'Whether or not another's 'identification [of you] is correct ...—in your eyes—may make no difference' to the outcome of the encounter, with identity often described as being in 'the eye of the beholder' (Jenkins, 1996: 2). Therefore others' perceptions of who we are can have a profound impact on our everyday lives as individuals, as well as collective groups (Jenkins, 1996, 2008). Aniso's pride in wearing hijab and her peers' subsequent acceptance of her identity of 'being Somali' illustrates this. However, as in the cases of Amir's and Nasra's assertions of their identities, an individual's self-defined identity is also important, revealing that the dialectical nature of identity is key to understanding this concept.

By exploring further Jenkins' (2008: 42) theory of the *internal-external dialectic*, it can be seen that the identities that others ascribe to us (or with which we are labelled) are as important to our (re)negotiation of identity as our own self-defined understanding of who we are. It is therefore 'not enough to [purely] assert an identity [as] that identity must also be validated, or not, by those with whom we have dealings. Identity is never unilateral'. Identity must therefore be understood as an ongoing interactional process. Since we cannot control the way that others will interpret the act that we display to them, Goffman's (1959) understanding of 'impression management strategies' are important to consider. According to Goffman, all individuals, either consciously or unconsciously, engage in this process of impression management by controlling the information that they give to others in all social situations. Nasra's presentation of herself as 'a nice, friendly girl' who gets on with everyone is a clear example of one individual's conscious effort to manage the impressions that others have of her.

Hall (2000: 4), however, points out that an individual is not always able to manage the impressions that others make of them, and suggests that our identity can be formed by 'the misrecognition of others', such as in the case of Amir's ascribed national identity above. Hall goes on to argue that 'misrecognition can inflict harm and can be a form of oppression imprisoning someone in a false, distorted and reduced mode of being.' Because of this it can be seen why Goffman's (1959) concept of impression management is important as it (at the very least) attempts to regulate the impression that others have of ourselves. However, while recognising the importance of this concept, Hall's (2000) critique of it must also be acknowledged highlighting the role that ascribed identities also play in identity performance and (re)negotiation.

Like Hall, Frith (2000: 125) contends that 'identity is thus ... a matter of ritual' that describes an individual's 'place in a dramatised pattern of relationships.' Consequently a person cannot express themselves autonomously but rather their self definition of their identity always 'depend[s] on audience participation, on shared performing and narrative rules.' Barth (1969) states that it is not enough to just present an act that portrays our (public face of) identity to others, but that this message has to be accepted by the external audience before the individual is able to 'take on' this identity. Butler's (1990) work also proposes that the audience has a larger role to play within identity performance than Goffman's theory suggests. These theorists all challenge the level of agentive action that Goffman's actors appear to possess, and propose that individuals to a greater or lesser degree are scripted by dominant social discourses.

Marranci (2008) disagrees with this emphasis on wider structural factors, stating that an individual's self definition of their identity (i.e. their social agency) is more important than the identity that others ascribe to them. While, as Marranci highlights, an individual's own interpretation of their identity may be the most important aspect to them, this is an aspect that it is not always actualised. We only have to think of Nazi Germany to see that powerful ascriptions of identity can, in certain circumstances, over-ride all other considerations.

Additionally, as seen above, the other girls' denial of Aniso's Somali (and Muslim) identity based on her practice of not wearing hijab reveals that others need to accept our self-definitions. This is in line with work by Barth (1969), Butler (1990), Hall (2000) and Frith (2000). Further Nasra's strong assertion of her national and ethnic identity, despite questioning by others, reveals that Marranci's (2008) emphasis on self-definition is also important. Consequently, a theory of identity needs to take into account these two aspects which Jenkins (2008) terms as the *internal-external dialectic*. Unlike the previous identity theories discussed that adhere to one side of the traditional structure-agency debate, a dialectical interpretation of identity allows for *the duality of structure* to come to the fore where both structure and agency are considered to be not only important but also interlinked.

For Cohen (1985) this negotiated process of (re)constructing identity requires an understanding of boundaries (i.e. definitions of terms such as black, white, etc) to be permeable. Identity, according to Cohen, is then constructed in 'transactions that occur at and across the boundary' to form what Jenkins (1996: 24) subsequently calls the *internal-external dialectic*.

In the run up to Christmas, Jabir revealed that the maintenance of boundaries between self and others are important for some families at Sunnyside.

> In late November I am sitting at the indoor creative area with Fariido, Cala and Gamal. Gamal is cutting sellotape to help Fariido make her model, while Cala is quietly working on her own. After a few minutes, Jabir comes over and shows me the Father Christmas ring that he has on his finger, telling me 'My Dad gave me this Merry Christmas.' I tell him that it looks nice and he explains that he went with his father to a bakery where his father bought them both a fairy cake. The cakes had rings on them (for decoration) which Jabir explains they had to take off before eating. He goes to get some materials to start making a model from the resource trays and comes back to the table and stands next to where I am sitting. He starts to put the separate pieces of his model together and asks me to help him 'with sticking.' I cut some sellotape for him as he tells me that he is making spears—one for Amir and one for himself. 'It's not Merry Christmas today' he informs the group 'my dad says'. The other children don't respond but I agree with him saying that there are still a few weeks left before it is Christmas. Jabir then volunteers 'My Dad isn't allowed to do Merry Christmas.' 'Why?' I ask him. 'My sister says', he replies. He goes on to tell me that his (adult) sister says that his family cannot celebrate Christmas because they are Muslim, and should only celebrate Muslim festivals like Eid. Jabir then tells me that his sister often makes the rules, but he and his father sometimes secretly break them, as they did when they got the 'Merry Christmas cakes.'

In doing this, Jabir and his father actively resist their family's rules in a similar way to how the young people in Russell's (2011) study exercise their social agency in resisting school rules.

The example shows that Jabir's sister contends that one of the ways to maintain her family's collective religious identity is to only celebrate Muslim festivals. In maintaining this boundary, she forbids her family members from crossing this symbolic frontier. A number of Jabir's classmates, such as Amir and Deka, also support this assertion that Muslims should not celebrate Christmas. For Jabir's father though, this is not important as he views buying Christmas themed items as harmless fun. Jabir also reveals that breaking his sister's rules takes on a deviant meaning where he and his father can jointly rebel from her authority and secretly revel in their shared mischief. While being part of a Muslim family is important for Jabir, his own and his father's deviant identities are also significant. The dialectical nature of (multiple) collective and individual identities will be explored in more detail in the following section.

'We are all kind of the same': Identity as individual and collective

Daud's conceptualisation of a 'Muslim Father Christmas', described above, also reveals that he understands that his own identity is connected with his family's collective identity. While Daud clearly asserts that he himself is always Muslim, he additionally reveals that his family's collective identity as UK residents is also important to him through the way in which he describes their ways of adopting cultural practices associated with the dominant group. Interestingly, while on other occasions Daud describes his family as all being Muslim, he doesn't do this when discussing the 'Muslim Father Christmas', but rather asserts his own personal religious identity. It is unclear from our conversation why Daud chooses to assert his personal, rather than his family's collective, religious identity, though conversations with his peers sheds further light on this emphasis. In the lead up to Christmas, Daud, on more than one occasion, explains to Amir—who ardently questions how Daud can celebrate Christmas in addition to the Muslim festival of Eid—how it is possible to have a 'Muslim Father Christmas'. In this context Daud's perceived need to justify this to his peers may explain his clear assertion of his own personal identity when discussing his family's collective practices. In doing so, Daud effectively manages the conflicting structures that his family and his peers adhere to.

Most anthropological literature on identity emphasises identity's collective nature. As Sökefeld (1999) highlights, this often minimises the role of the individual and social agency in the process of identity (re)negotiation. He argues that, since individuals constitute a culture or society, and consequently shared identity, questions of individual identity cannot be ignored. Leading on from this, Marranci (2008) views individual aspects of identity as being more important than collective aspects, since without individuals cultures and societies can't exist. He argues, similarly, that individual identity forms the foundation for collective identities. Cohen (1994), Sökefeld (1999) and Marranci (2006) all argue that, in uncritically adopting Durkheim's concept of the collective consciousness, anthropologists have unwittingly over-emphasised the importance of society and neglected individual and interactive perspectives. Marranci tries to re-address this imbalance by centering his identity theory on the individual and their self-defined identity. However, I argue here that in doing so he has committed a similar offence to that which he accuses anthropologists, who built their theories on Durkheim's work, of doing i.e. sacrificing one element of identity for the sake of another. In Marranci's case, though, he has sacrificed the collective at the expense of the individual. I therefore argue that aspects of the individual and the collective need to be carefully balanced when (re)constructing a definition of identity. To do this it is important to unpick further anthropological and sociological assumptions around these two terms. As Jenkins points out there are two key assumptions that are important within this discussion:

> 'The first is the assumption that individual and collective identity are qualitatively ... different. This is rooted in the foundational axiom that there are concrete things called individuals, over and against which stands society. ... Having distinguished the individual-personal from the social-cultural, one is assumed to be more important—if not actually more 'real'—than the other'. (Jenkins, 1996: 14-15)

As can be seen from the quote above, Jenkins (1996) identifies the distinction between individual and collective identity as being foundational in forming the idea that one aspect of identity is viewed as being more important than the other. Hence, we fall into the trap of scholars, such as Marranci and those from a Durkheimian school of thought, who sacrifice one element to promote the other.

Building on Giddens' (1984) structuration theory, which holds that structure and agency are interconnected, Jenkins' (1996, 2008) takes this argument one step further. In doing so Jenkins argues that concepts of the individual (the social agent) and the collective (structure), which are manifest in his theory of identity, are fundamentally the same. In this he departs from Giddens' (1991) interpretation which holds that while the individual and the collective are inter-connected there are still distinguishing features that separate them. For Jenkins these differences, which he also acknowledges, are not fundamental but rather 'a matter of ... emphasis' (Jenkins, 2008: 38).

Rather than being viewed as fundamentally different, individual identities (individuals) can therefore be viewed as the foundation stones of collective identities (groups or societies) and consequently as fundamentally the same—as one consists of, or makes up, the other. As Griffiths (1995) highlights, individual and collective identities can be understood as continually reconstructing each other.

Using Mill's concept of *The Sociological Imagination*, Jenkins (1996: 17) shows that 'the social is the field upon which the individual and collective meet and meld.' Jenkins (2008: 37-8) goes onto argue that 'the individually unique and the collectively shared can be understood as similar in important respects ... [They] are routinely entangled with each other ... [and] only come into being within interaction.' While individual identities may place more emphasis on difference, and collective identities on similarity, Jenkins, as mentioned above, views this as 'a matter of ... emphasis', rather than as a fundamental difference between the two. Using Jenkins' model to understand concepts of the individual and the collective in this way we are able to grasp more of the complex nature of identity.

While Daud and Jabir express how their own individual identities are interwoven with their family's collective identities, some children at Sunnyside also articulate the ways in which they share a collective identity with their peers.

> In October I am sitting at the Maths area writing in my fieldnote book. Fazia and Aafia are also in the area doing jigsaws. As I look up from my notebook, Fazia tells me 'Aafia and me can speak Arabic.' 'Do you speak Arabic or English when you play together?' I ask in response. 'Both' she replies. Pointing to Gamal she then says 'And he speaks Arabic too.' 'Are you all from the same place?' I ask. 'No,' she replies, 'They are from Libya and I'm from Egypt.' She then explains to me that although they are from different countries that they 'are all kind of the same' as they can all speak Arabic.

As Fazia reveals, identity is a complex concept that incorporates a number of different aspects—but fundamentally relates back to two key concepts of similarity and difference. In this chapter children at Sunnyside demonstrate in their narratives the roles that structure and agency both play within identity (re)negotiation. A number of children have also highlighted the intersecting nature of their identities.

'I am and I can': Summarising the complex nature of identity

> In late March, the teacher from nursery comes into the Reception classroom while all of the children are sitting on the carpet and asks if the bilingual support

> worker can go to nursery that morning as there is a new Somali boy in nursery who can't speak English. As she is explaining this to Mary, Aniso, who is sitting near to the nursery teacher, turns and says to her 'I am Somali but I can't speak Somali.' The teacher laughs at this and repeats the sentence back to her saying 'So you are Somali but can't speak Somali?' She looks at Mary as if to question Aniso's claim of her national identity. Nasra then pipes up saying 'I am [Somali] and I can [speak Somali].' The teacher looks at her and nervously laughs. Her body language suggests that she is also questioning Nasra's claim of being Somali, though this time I assume that this is based on Nasra's skin colour. However, she doesn't comment, but makes a hasty retreat with the bilingual support worker. As she leaves, Mustafe, who is sitting next to Aniso, asks her why she can't speak Somali. Aniso explains to him that she was born in the Netherlands and then moved with her family to England so can speak Dutch and English. This answer satisfies Mustafe's curiosity.

While the incident above again reveals the dialectical nature of identity, and the ways that children at Sunnyside negotiate their identities, it also reveals that some staff members at Sunnyside are not always aware of the complex nature of identity or the ways in which young children conceptualise who they are. Van Ausdale and Feagin (2001) similarly found that staff members were not always aware of these complexities. Despite this, the children themselves have clearly shown in this chapter that they do understand the *performative, situated and dialectical nature of identity* and how these aspects relate to their lived experiences.

Therefore the nature of identity can be seen as a complex whole made up of distinctive individual parts. It is at once layered and situated, self-defined and ascribed, anchored and transient, individual and collective. It is only when all of these aspects are drawn together into a complex whole, within a model that recognises *the duality of structure*, that the nature of identity can be fully understood.

Chapter 4

Being all of me: Uncovering children's intersecting, symbolic and dynamic experiences of identity

> *'We always have to reckon with, and to deal with history, and the particular ways in which constructions of difference are produced and have effects at any historical moment. Yet these meanings are also dynamic and contingent, and can be negotiated, resisted and reworked by individuals'*
>
> *(Gunaratnam, 2003: vii-viii).*

The intersecting nature of identity

Amir's religious identity overshadows other aspects of his identity and in doing so forms his dominant status in almost all of his social interactions at Sunnyside. He regularly talks with his peers about going to the mosque, praying, and what 'being Muslim' means to him. He also consistently incorporates aspects of his religious identity into his school activities where he encourages the other members of *the gang to* pretend that they are at Koranic school and 'do Arabic writing', build mosques in the construction area, or incorporate praying into their imaginative play. While this aspect of Amir's identity is extremely important to him, he does not see this as being segregated from other aspects of his identity and clearly verbalises the interconnected nature of identity and how all aspects of his identity intersect with each other.

Before uncovering in more detail how Amir interweaves different aspects of his identity, I will discuss the concept of intersectionality which can be used to interpret Amir's lived experience. The messy and complex relationship between different aspects of an individual's identity, which Amir hints at below, are now widely acknowledged as not only important in theoretical, but also in methodological discussions about how the intersecting nature of identity can be explored (Gunaratnam, 2003). Before exploring these implications in more detail, however, it is helpful to return to the roots of the concept of intersectionality itself.

The concept of intersectionality, coined by Kimberlé Crenshaw, has its origins in the late 1980s in re-visionist feminist critiques of dominant approaches to understanding and responding to discrimination. Dominant approaches viewed gender and ethnic discrimination as two separate entities (Crenshaw, 1989). In contrast, the concept of intersectionality suggests that discrimination should be viewed as multidimensional (McCall, 2008). Black feminists in the 1980s recognised that the discrimination that white middle-class American women were facing differed greatly from the experiences of black, working-class or disabled women. The ways in which different aspects of identity combined, consequently, determined an individual's social positioning. Developing Crenshaw's term, Collins (2000) further developed the concept in the 1990s as part of her discussion on Black Feminism.

Appropriate methodological and theoretical frameworks need to be adopted in order to respond to 'the relationships among multiple dimensions' of identity in all of their complexities (McCall, 2008: 49). Starting from the premise that socially constructed categories (such as gender, ethnicity etc) do not act independently of each other but rather interact on multiple levels, intersectionality holds to the argument that forms of inequality (such as sexism, racism etc) should also not be viewed as separate entities but rather as part of a 'system of oppression' (Harro, 2000: 19). This understanding builds on the concept of holism, that social theorists such as Durkheim (1883) and Marx and Engels (1948) had previously adhered to, that state that the whole is more than just the sum of its parts. This non-reductionist understanding of forms of inequality as a 'system of oppression' requires a sophisticated epistemological base that allows the complexities of the social world to be explored alongside an individual's own interpretation of how these socially constructed concepts impact on their day-to-day lived experiences. Subtle realist approaches, such as the approach that forms the philosophical framework for this study, allow for this. Intersectionality can therefore be understood as an everyday heuristic device that can produce 'particular identity positions' (Phoenix, 2011b: 147) and in doing so can make evident the impact that different socially constructed concepts (such as gender, ethnicity etc) have on an individual's life.

McCall (2008) has highlighted the methodological challenges of exploring issues of intersectionality, and in particular the need for methodological approaches that are able to address the complex nature of this concept. Ethnography, as highlighted in Chapter 2, is one approach that is well equipped to explore such complexity since its in-depth approach is able to facilitate a deep understanding of the nature of such multifaceted concepts. McCall has identified three key approaches to exploring intersectionality which she calls anticategorical complexity, intercategorical complexity and intracategorical complexity. Anticategorical complexity views social life as being too complex to be reduced purely to fixed, bounded categories and consequently deconstructs previously recognised categories of analysis as it understands such categories as trying to over-simplify micro-concepts related to this discussion. At the other end of the spectrum McCall's second approach intercategorical complexity works to use existing categories to explore the relationships between them. Lastly intracategorical complexity, which can be understood as the traditional approach to exploring intersectionality, places its key focus on social groups whose identities cross boundaries of traditionally thought of bounded groups. As McCall rightly points out though, not all research on intersectionality falls neatly into one of the above approaches, with some studies borrowing from more than one of the above ways of studying this concept.

Phoenix (2011a) agrees that these three approaches to studying intersectionality should not be viewed as bounded separate entities but, like the concept of intersectionality itself, should be viewed as intersecting with and complimenting each other. However, one important aspect that Phoenix argues is missing from McCall's theory is the role of social agency and the need to incorporate an individual's self-defined identity into this analysis. Phoenix' interpretation consequently recognises *the duality of structure*.

The current study adopts Phoenix' approach to researching intersectionality. While it relies heavily on principles contained within intracategorical complexity, it does so with a strong leaning towards anticategorical's understanding of the social world as being too complex to be purely reduced to categorical analysis. Through exploring meaning with children about how they conceptualise and operationalise the terms that they use to describe their identity, this study uncovers how children (re)negotiate their identities within a complex social framework.

Children at Sunnyside, as Amir shows, operationalise a complex understanding of their own and others' identities in their conversations and peer interactions revealing that they are acutely aware of the intersecting natures of their identities as well as the associated multidimensional character of discrimination. The way in which Amir understands the complex nature of identity is further evidenced by two conversations he has with me and his peers over a period of a few weeks.

The first conversation arises while Amir is drawing a picture of his friends playing football as part of the 'My friends are ...' activity in late January. As has been discussed in Chapter 3, when drawing his friends Amir comments on their skin colour, and carefully chooses different pens to depict children from different ethnic backgrounds. He uses a brown pen to draw fellow gang members Daud and Mubarak and uses a blue pen to draw himself, Barak and Seif. Pointing to the boys in blue he then goes onto tell me that he is also Arab like these boys and that they are also all Muslim. Looking back at his picture he looks over at the figures of Daud and Mubarak and tells me that they are Muslim too but not Arab and explains to me that while all Arabs are Muslim not all Muslims are Arab. Daud and Mubarak, he continues, cannot be Arab as they are not white.

Our second conversation on this topic occurs during an indoor free choice session in early February.

> Daud comes over to where I am sitting at the writing table and asks if he can write in my fieldnote book. As I pass my notebook over to him, Mubarak and Callum join us and start to draw independently on the pieces of paper that have been set up at the activity station. After a few minutes Callum looks up from his picture and asks Daud, 'Can you learn me Arabic tomorrow?' 'Yes' Daud replies. Interested in their conversation and unaware that Daud speaks Arabic, I ask him about this. He replies, telling me that he can speak some Arabic as he is learning the Arabic alphabet at the moment. Mubarak then tells me that he can speak some Arabic too. 'Where do you learn it?' I ask them both. Mubarak replies, 'At the mosque.' Daud looks up from his writing, so I ask him 'do you learn at the mosque too Daud?' 'Yes', he replies. During this conversation Amir has wandered over to the writing table and is standing next to the resources tray, fiddling with the pot of pens, listening to our conversation. He looks up at me and smiles. 'Amir speaks Arabic too, don't you?' I ask. 'Yes', he replies looking pleased that I have included him in our conversation. Daud then looks at me and says, 'But he's English.' Amir turns to face him and hotly replies almost shouting, 'No, I'm not!' as if he has been accused of doing something wrong. Sensing his unease I ask him to tell us what he is. 'I'm Arabic' he replies actively asserting his agency and resisting the label his peers try to give him. 'No, you are English.' retorts Mubarak. 'No, I'm not' Amir insists ,'I'm Arabic. English are Christians. I'm not!' The other boys don't respond to this, so I ask him, 'What are Arabic people?' 'We are Muslim' Amir replies. As the other boys turn back to their drawings, I ask him if English people can be Muslim too and he tells me that they cannot, as they have to be Christian. He then goes onto explain to me that he doesn't feel like he is from any country, since although he was born in England he can't be English and tells me that being Arab doesn't mean that you are from any one particular country but it means that 'you are not English.' He then informs me that 'all Arab people speak Arabic, and are Muslim' and tells me that these are the things that they have in common with each other.

As can be seen from the two conversations above, Amir views the concept of 'being Arabic' as connected with an individual's skin colour and linguistic identity. For Amir this identity also clearly intersects with religious identity, whilst not being synonymous with it, as he explicitly states that it is possible to be Muslim and not be an Arab. In contrast 'being English' for Amir is synonymous with 'being Christian', an identity which he ardently resists. Amir's interpretation corresponds with Nasra's understanding of her Somali and Muslim identities. As well as articulating the relationship between 'being Somali' and 'being Muslim', Nasra is also able to clearly express how 'being white' intersects with these aspects of her identity.

In conversations with her peers and with me, Nasra can regularly be heard asserting her identity of 'being Somali'. However, when exploring this aspect of identity in more detail (via the Scotland book in late March), the complexities of Nasra's identity are uncovered as she explains to me that her own identity is formed as a combination of her father's identity as Somali and her mother's identity as English. Nasra reconciles these two aspects of her mixed heritage by saying 'I'm Somali and a little bit English.' I prompt her by asking 'So you're a little bit English?' 'I'm half an' half in that I am full Somali but half English' she replies and again explains that as her mother is English she is also 'a little bit English.'

The complex and fluid nature of Nasra's identity means that different aspects of her national identity come to the fore in different social situations, in line with Goffman's (1959) imagery of the actress who promotes certain aspects of her identity dependent on her social environment. While Nasra's conceptualisation and operationalisation of her national identity is complex and context specific, her identity of 'being Somali' forms the overriding discourse relating to how Nasra understands her dominant status. This is consistent with Van Ausdale and Feagin's (2001) research which suggests that young children of mixed heritages construct a narrative to conceptualise and operationalise dual (or in some cases multiple) aspects of their ethnic and national identities. This is particularly important in Nasra's case where her self-defined identity was regularly challenged by others based on her skin colour. Likewise in Van Ausdale and Feagin's (2001) work a number of mixed heritage children responded in a similar way to Nasra, by primarily subscribing to their self-defined national identity as their dominant status. In this way persistent questioning of an individual's self-defined identity can cause the individual to actively assert their social agency and reject an ascribed identity. The *outcome* of this is dependent on the level of pervasiveness of dominant social structures.

Van Ausdale and Feagin (2001) additionally point out that children's statements about identity, which at first may appear to be contradictory—such as Nasra's statement, which asserts that 'I'm half an' half in that I am full Somali but half English'—are in actual fact highlighting the complex and fluid nature of identity. In this statement Nasra is asserting that, while she considers herself to be first and foremost Somali, she also understands that aspects of her mother's identity as English intersect with her father's identity as Somali to create her own identity. In describing the complexities of her identity with me Nasra often uses the phrase 'being all of me' to describe how the different aspects of her identity intersect before describing in more detail one specific aspect of her identity.

While Nasra employs discourses around 'being Somali' in every day conversations, she also informs me at a later date (whilst inserting a picture of the Muslim doll Amina in her digital book) that her mother encourages her to emphasise her religious identity (which she has in common with her doll Amina), rather than her national identity, saying, 'But my mum said only when I am grown up she said I am Somali. When I am a little girl I am a Muslim.' Despite, or potentially because of, this encouragement, Nasra firmly identifies with 'being Somali.' However, since, for Nasra, 'being Somali' is interwoven with 'being Muslim', her religious identity is also an important part of her identity discourse.

When discussing the multilevel nature of her national identity, Nasra also explains how her ethnic identity intersects with this. In doing this Nasra explains to me that she can be white and Somali, 'because Somalis can be white', due to her mixed heritage. Being Somali, for Nasra, is therefore not intrinsic to having a black ethnic identity, but is rather associated with her socio-political positioning in line with how she describes 'being Somali' as important for her family's collective identity. Interestingly while her mother's side of the family is white and Christian—and at times Nasra celebrates Christian festivals with her Grandma—this side of her family's religious identity does not form part of Nasra's own identity as she actively subscribes to 'being Muslim' while clearly stating that she is not Christian.

While Nasra subscribes to her father's identity of 'being Somali', she also subscribes to her mother's identity of 'being white' and positions herself, based on her skin colour, in relation to the other girls in the class. In this respect Nasra actively aligns herself with a relatively high social status within *the older girls'* discourses of 'whiteness.' However, she does not do the same with her national identity but rather subscribes to 'being Somali' despite the often negative discourses around immigration and refugee status that are on the rise in the UK. One interpretation of this could be that, while racially motivated discourses are prevalent at Sunnyside and used by children as a form of stratification, discourses relating to immigration and refugee status have not pervaded Nasra's social world. Additionally, the way in which Nasra marries these aspects reveals that the dialectical nature of identity is key to understanding how an individual can reconcile apparent conflicting aspects of their identity whilst maintaining a holistic view of themselves.

Nasra's gendered identity is also important to her. At school, during free choice activities, she predominantly takes part in stereotypical female activities, such as playing with dolls, playing families and drawing pictures of Barbie and fairies. She also repeatedly tells me that when she is at home she also likes to play with dolls with her middle sister and 'do girls things' like dressing up and putting on make-up. 'Being a Muslim girl' is also important to her and when creating her PAT, Nasra explains to me how her gendered and religious identities intersect. 'At the mosque the boys don't wear hijab' Nasra tells me as she points to the picture of a boy wearing a Kufi hat, 'They wear these. They are like mini hats.' Nasra goes on to tell me girls are not allowed to wear these, just like boys are not allowed to wear hijab. I prompt her and ask why girls wear hijab and boys don't. She tells me that she doesn't know why, but again asserts that she only wears hijab because she wants to since when she does people know that she is 'a Muslim girl.' 'Being Muslim' for Nasra is consequently a gendered experience. While Nasra doesn't know why Muslim boys and girls typically dress differently, she clearly articulates that this is the case and positively asserts that she is 'a Muslim girl' recognising that these two parts of her identity intersect.

The symbolic nature of identity

As seen in the previous chapter, children at Sunnyside actively promote certain aspects of their identity in different social situations, such as Daud's identity as the 'studious son' and Nasra's identity as the 'nice, friendly girl'. Building on his understanding of this performative nature of identity, Goffman (1959) came to view symbols as a tool that allow an individual to adapt the aspect of their identity that they wish to perform for others within the context of their social environment. As well as using symbols to highlight a particular aspect of their identity, children at Sunnyside also used symbols to emphasise the intersecting nature of their identities.

Symbols, and the meanings ascribed to them, play an important part in Sunnyside's day-to-day life and particularly in peer relationships within the class. Hijab is a key symbol that all children in the class, irrespective of religious affiliation, connote with 'being Muslim.' Most children understood the symbolic nature of hijab at the start of the school year with many telling me that their family members, or Koranic teacher, had told them that hijab is an important part of 'being a Muslim girl.' Others, however, most notably children from non-Muslim families, began to attach such meaning to hijab throughout the course of the school year as they explored its meaning with other children in the class. Interestingly, all but one female family member from the Muslim families who bring and collect their child from school wears hijab, with a number also wearing niqab (face veils) and jilbab (long loose fitted gowns). Female school staff who identify themselves as Muslim also all wear hijab, with all but one wearing jilbab. Varying forms of traditional female Muslim dress codes are therefore a visible and symbolic presence in children's lives.

As seen in the last chapter, three girls in the class (Nasra, Deka and Fariido) regularly wear hijab *to* school (though not necessarily *at* school), and frequently discuss wearing hijab amongst themselves. Comparing headscarves, discussions about how their hijabs complement their clothes, and conversations about where and when they have bought new headscarves often form their initial interactions at the start of a school day. For all of them hijab is a sign of 'being Muslim', one that seems to be more important than going to the mosque or praying. For Nasra 'being Muslim' and 'being Somali' are intertwined as she explains by saying 'All Somalis are Muslim.' Consequently hijab is also an important symbol for Nasra of her national identity, 'Somalis we wear hijab. Like this ... I like wearing it' she tells me. Throughout the year, wearing hijab at school becomes a collective act for these three girls. On most occasions half way through the morning (or sometimes earlier) one of the girls will take off her hijab or discuss taking off her hijab with the others. Once one has removed her headscarf, the others do the same with one or all of them vocally justifying their actions to those around them by saying something like 'I'm too hot under hijab' or 'It's too itchy.' The removal of hijab appears to be a symbolic act as the girls re-position themselves with a peer identity (at school) in contrast to their public identity in the outside world. Alongside this practice, all three girls regularly comment that they like to wear hijab in town in order that other people know that they are 'Muslim girls.' It therefore appears that the girls do not feel that they have to wear hijab at school, as they do in public, because their peers already know that they are Muslim and they are therefore able to waive the hijab as an identity marker within this social context. However, it is important to note that the girls always articulate a reason to their peers for removing their hijabs, providing a justification for why, as a group, they have decided to take off their headscarves.

As Cooley (1902) and Mead (1934) highlight, a collective expression of identity, such as the girls' actions above, can develop into an important part of social interaction. At Sunnyside, male members of *the gang* are often amused by the girls' behaviour, confiding in me that the girls always copy each other in wearing (or not wearing) their headscarves. This practice, then, becomes an instrumental way in which the girls' classmates view and interact with this aspect of their identity. As Spencer (2006) stresses, social interaction, such as this, is an important part of the ongoing (re)negotiation of identity.

When individually asked, all three girls tell me that it is their own choice to wear hijab. Deka's mother also confirms to me that Deka actively chooses to wear a headscarf and isn't coerced to do so by her family, stating 'She (Deka) tells me in the mornings that she wants to wear it and if I don't give it to her she asks me why I don't want her to have it.' Her mother then goes on to tell me that she doesn't understand why Deka repeatedly tells her that she wants to wear hijab *to* school since she almost always takes it off when she is *at* school. Nasra likewise tells me that her family does not make her wear hijab, but does also mention that 'We're not allowed to go *to* the mosque without a hijab'. At the same time though, she points out that 'if you don't wanna wear your hijab you can just take it off *at* the mosque.' While all three girls clearly articulate that wearing hijab is their own choice, they all (albeit to varying degrees) also believe that in certain situations, most notably when going to the mosque or praying, that Muslim girls should cover their heads. Here the girls allude to how structural factors influence culturally accepted dress codes, while at the same time revealing that their social agency facilitates an element of choice for their own practice. Implicit in this is a shared understanding that hijab is an important part of 'being a Muslim girl' that is also a fundamental means of conveying their religious identity to others. This shared understanding and associated cultural meaning is significant for understanding the nature of symbols (Spencer, 2006).

During the winter months, particularly when it is snowy or frosty, the girls often put their hijab on when we go to the outdoor play area.

> One day, as we are getting ready to go outside, I am helping Deka put her hijab back on after she has taken it off during the morning indoor session. As I am

> helping her she tells me that, as well as showing other people that she is Muslim, wearing hijab 'will keep us warm' and suggests that I buy myself one to also wear when it is cold and snowy.

There is therefore a practical as well as a symbolic aspect attached to this practice. Interestingly Deka was not concerned that people would think that I was a Muslim if I was to wear hijab, as she explains that 'being Muslim is a good thing'. She also did not seem to think that there was anything hypocritical associated with a non-Muslim wearing hijab for practical reasons. A few weeks after this conversation, I was on a political march in London when the weather turned cold and started to rain. While I had forgotten to take an umbrella to the event I did have a large cotton scarf with me. As I wrapped it over my head and round my shoulders to keep myself warm and dry I smiled to myself, remembering my conversation with Deka. As I did so, I also wondered whether the people around me interpreted my actions as a religious symbol or a practical solution in the inclement weather.

On another occasion during a free choice activity whilst I was working next to Deka, she directly asks me if I have ever worn hijab. When I tell her that on occasions I have worn hijab when I have visited a mosque or have visited a country where lots of girls and women do cover their heads, such as Morocco, she seems pleased and tells me 'that is the right thing to do'. The importance of adhering to social norms in this way appears to be implicitly understood by Deka.

As discussed in Chapter 3, wearing hijab is not just part of an individual's self-defined identity at Sunnyside, but is also important to how children ascribe identities to each other, such as the way in which Nasra, Deka and Fariido declare that Aniso's practice of not wearing hijab is symbolic of her 'not being Muslim.' The use of hijab is consequently important to how children at Sunnyside view and interact with others based on another's use of (or in this instance failure to use) a commonly understood symbol to express their identity.

Over the course of the year Annakiya (the only non-Muslim in *the older girls'* key circle of 'friends') also becomes interested in discussions around wearing hijab and 'being Muslim'. She, like the other girls, understands hijab as being symbolic of Muslim faith and positively asserts that she doesn't wear hijab as she is Christian. She is, however, interested in why her Muslim friends cover their heads and is careful to show her friends wearing hijab in her drawings, as can be seen from her 'My friends are ...' picture, which she drew in late January.

Figure 4.1: Annakiya's friends wearing hijab

In this picture Annakiya has drawn Fariido wearing a pink hijab and the lunch time supervisor in her 'long, black Muslim dress' (jilbab) and black and gold hijab. The other girls in the picture, Aniso and Aafia, at this point in time, did not wear hijab to school. While drawing this picture Annakiya describes to me in detail the clothes that her friends wear 'to show that they are Muslim'. Annakiya actively interprets the actions of her classmates who wear hijab as being symbolic of their religious identity. Blumer (1962), as we will see below, contends that this is an important part of identity (re)negotiation.

Interestingly, Annakiya does not depict Deka in this picture although they often play together at school. After drawing this picture Annakiya asks me if she can show it to her friends. As she is showing it to Aniso, Deka comes over and also looks at the picture. As she does so Annakiya says to her 'I'm sorry I didn't draw you.' Deka doesn't reply to this but saunters back to the creative table where she had previously been working. I ask Annakiya if she wants to add to her picture but she tells me that she does not. Notably after the February half term Annakiya and Deka begin to play together more often.

In conversations with the other girls about hijab, Annakiya at times also talks about 'Christian necklaces' and in doing so shares a symbol that is meaningful to her, and one that represents her own religious identity. While she herself does not wear a cross, she still mentions this symbol to the other girls in the class as her version of their hijabs. The other girls come to understand this as a Christian symbol, with Nasra explaining to me while creating her PAT 'Necklaces with these on [a cross] I'm not allowed them. They are for Christians.' Nasra, as well as actively constructing and conveying her own identity through symbols, also understands the meaning that others give to their symbols. This acceptance of another's interpretation of their own symbol, as Spencer (2006) points out, is crucial to allow meaning to be transmitted.

Goffman's (1959) view of symbols as a tool to promote a certain aspect of an individual's identity has been further developed by Blumer (1962), who coined the phrase *symbolic interactionism*. For Blumer, symbolic interactionism builds on Mead's understanding that social interaction occurs when individuals 'interpret or define each other's actions instead of merely reacting' to them. Their reaction should not be understood, however, as being made directly towards the initial action but 'instead is based on the meaning which they attach to such actions' (Rice, 2011 [online]). According to Blumer (1962), social interaction is therefore mediated by the significance attached to symbols or an individual's interpretation of the meaning of another's actions. Individuals can therefore be described as 'construct[ing] and transmit[ting] culture through symbols' (Spencer, 2006: 96) as seen in both Nasra's and Annakiya's use of symbols above. This interpretation allows individuals to 'move' from one representation of themselves to another and through 'the act of sharing symbols' individuals can 'experience themselves in the roles of others' (Marranci, 2006: 35).

For interactionists, identity is an ongoing (re)negotiated process and social contexts 'are always encounters that have shifting and unstable outcomes' (Spencer, 2006: 96). Out of this theory 'an understanding emerges of the 'self' as an ongoing and, in practice simultaneous, synthesis of (internal) self-definition and the (external) definitions of oneself offered by others' (Jenkins, 1996: 20).

All individuals are engaged in this *internal-external dialectic* process—either consciously or sub-consciously—and all are attempting to highlight particular aspects of their identity and keep hidden other aspects by modifying their behaviour to influence the impressions that others make of them. Identity can therefore be described as *performative, situational and dialectical* resonating with the view that identity always involves a degree of comparison and the notions of similarity and difference.

While Goffman's (1959) work has been foundational in developing our understanding of identity there is one key question that remains unexplained by his theory of dramaturgical analysis, and that is the question of 'how individuals may pass from one identity to another (or to use Goffman's terminology from one character to another) and remain at the same time part of the audience'

(Marranci, 2006: 37). McCall and Simmons (1978: 65) tried to address this question in their 'role-identity theory' by stating that identity can be defined as 'the character and role that an individual devises for himself as an occupant of a particular position.' Within this definition an individual can take on more than one character and therefore occupy a number of social positions and have several identities, such as the working mother who is a mother, a daughter, an employee and possibly a wife and a sister all at the same time. However, according to McCall and Simmons, an individual does not have complete control over which aspect of their identity will come to the fore in any given context as structural forces are also at play. Therefore, as we have seen above in relation to Nasra's negotiation of her identity, while an individual's dominant status may always be key for their self-defined identity, this may not always be the aspect that others ascribe as being important in a given situation. For McCall and Simmons this process is a constant fight against structural discourses to promote the aspect of identity that the individual perceives as needing to take centre stage. Marranci (2006), however, considers an individual's social agency as the most dominant force in this process. He views an individual's social agency as a self-correcting mechanism by which an individual can make sense of their dominant status. Within Marranci's work this is viewed as a negotiation rather than a conflict as McCall and Simmons (1978) previously described it.

The question of how we navigate between identities is thus important to consider. Is identity performance triggered almost automatically by our social environment as McCall and Simmons (1978) advocate? Or do we actively decide, and have the freedom, to promote one aspect of our identity more than another as Marranci (2006) proposes? The children at Sunnyside, similarly to the young people in Russell's (2011) study, are influenced by an interplay between both structure and agency (Chapter 3). While McCall and Simmons (1978) and Marranci (2006) fail to fully explain how structure and agency intertwine in a process of identity (re)negotiation, Stones' (2005) revised notion of 'strong structuration' incorporates both of these aspects without giving primacy to one over the other. This equally weighted interpretation reflects the negotiation process that the children at Sunnyside engage in as they conceptualise and operationalise their identities amongst their peers.

As discussed above, Nasra, Deka and Fariido all equate wearing hijab as a symbolic act that reveals to others their religious identity of 'being Muslim.' This aspect of their identity is, however, also strongly connected with their gendered identity as Nasra explains that by wearing hijab others will know that they 'are Muslim girls'. Consequently, symbols can be used not only to promote one reflection of an individual but also to show the ways in which different reflections intersect.

The dynamic nature of identity

At Sunnyside flags are another symbol that a number of children at times use to express an aspect of their identity and communicate this to their peers. Interestingly none of the children use the Union Jack in this way, although a number did refer to this as 'being England' when they saw a picture of it. This shows, as in the example above of Nasra's interpretation of the Christian cross, that they understand the meaning that others give to certain symbols. All of the children with an English identity who identify with a flag use the St George's Cross to symbolise this. The St George's Cross is in the same way used by children who subscribe to 'being English' and who also subscribe to being from the city where they now live (i.e. they have a localised English identity) such as Daud, who tells me when sticking the St George's cross on his PAT in June 'It's not for England. This is the [name of the city where he currently lives] flag and the [name of the city where his cousins live] flag.'

As in Connolly's (2003) work in Ireland, some children at Sunnyside are also aware of the political and cultural symbolism that flags can embody, most notably in times of political upheaval. This is particularly true of Mustafe who is from Libya where seven flags have been adopted in the last 100 years with a new one being taken on for each new political era that the country has entered. During the course of my fieldwork, the Arab Spring erupted. Some children in the class were directly exposed to these events, such as Alim whose family left Libya after the unrest had begun, while other children, such as Mustafe, soaked up the news via the media. These unfolding global events became the focus of a number of our research activities as children linked macro events to their own micro contexts.

As I collated images for the picture library to use when creating the digital books in January, 2011, I inserted a picture of the solid green flag that was adopted as the Libyan national flag in 1977 by the Gaddafi regime. However, by the time we started to make the digital books, the flag of the Kingdom of Libya (initially used between 1951-1969) had begun to be re-used by the anti-Gaddafi protesters and soon became a symbol of the Libyan revolution and new ruling authority.

Figure 4.2: Recent Libyan flags

Above: Flag adopted by the Gaddafi regime (1977-2011) Above: Flag adopted by the National Transitional Council (February, 2011)

In February, 2011, as we are making the digital books, this flag was formally adopted by the National Transitional Council, which was established to co-ordinate and represent the anti-Gaddafi protesters and freedom fighters. As events unfolded the National Transitional Council began to take control of Libya's key cities and these two flags were often portrayed as symbols of the two different sides in the struggle. News programmes regularly pinned the two flags onto a map to show how the fighting was progressing. Media images of freedom fighters burning Gaddafi's green symbol of power were also prominent. Adults and children were repeatedly shown holding up the flag of the revolution with one hand, while making the peace sign with the other. Although I had included a picture of the solid green flag in the picture library for the digital books, Libya's official flag at the time, my failure to update this and to include the new flag of the National Transitional Council prompted an interesting discussion with Mustafe about his national identity.

> While making his digital book, Mustafe looks at the pictures of flags in the online picture library. As he looks at the flags we chat about the different countries that they represent. As he gets to the green flag of the Gaddafi regime, he points to it and says 'That's Libya's.' I ask him if he wants to put it in his digital book to which he replies 'No, no I ... well ... there's ... there's lots of Libya's flags.' I reply saying 'Yes, there is isn't there? Lots of them.' Mustafe replies saying, 'Yeah', as he looks again at the pictures of all of the flags trying to find the one that he wants to put in his digital book. When he can't find it he says to me, 'It's black. Not all black ... It's dark red and it's black and it's dark green ... and in the middle black we put a shape which is like a banana. Like this.' He picks up my pen and draws a crescent in my fieldnote book. I suggest that he draws the flag saying that we can take a photo of it and then put it in his book. He begins to draw the flag and, after drawing the outline of the flag with the crescent in it, goes on to tell me, 'and we put a star next to it', which he does.

Mustafe colours in his flag and starts to describe to me what is happening in Libya saying, 'But there's fighting now in Libya so can you write that?' As I type what he tells me to in his digital book he continues, 'There is fighting and fires in Libya. So we can't go to Libya. We have to wait. ... We have to wait for a long time.'

After colouring in the black central strip of the flag Mustafe discovers that he cannot colour in a white star and crescent on top of the black pen. Therefore he decides to write the words 'moon' and 'star' underneath the flag to make sure that people looking at the flag know that they should be there.

Figure 4.3: Mustafe's drawing of the Libyan flag that he subscribes to

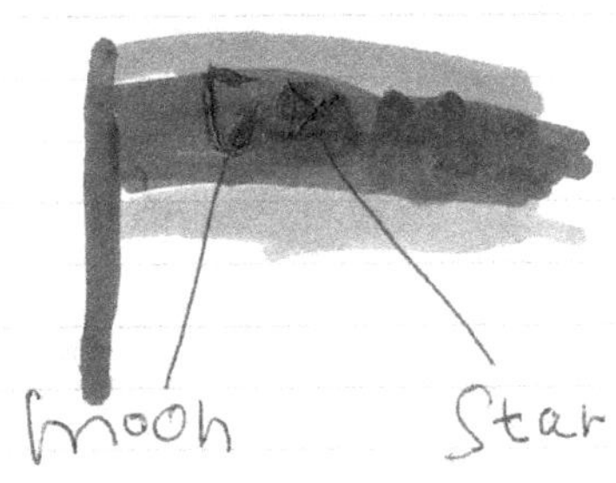

He stops colouring and looks through the picture library and then says to me, 'I can't find fire.' We look through the picture library together, and I point to a picture of a bonfire and ask him if this is the kind of picture that he is looking for. 'Is that Libya?' he asks. I tell him that I'm not sure but that it can be Libya if he wants it to be. He tells me that he doesn't think that it looks like Libya. He continues looking at the different pictures. After looking through all of the pictures he stops at the picture of a policeman and thinks for a minute before continuing, 'There's lots of people fighting. And there's lots of police killing.' 'Police killing?' I ask 'Who are they killing?' 'Yeah,' Mustafe replies, 'With their guns.' 'Are the police good or bad?' I ask. 'They're good,' Mustafe tells me, 'But they're good at killing those who are very naughty. There's someone who is very naughty.'

With further prompting, Mustafe tells me that the police who he is referring to are the revolutionaries who are fighting against Gaddafi (i.e. the naughty person) rather than the official Libyan police force. Mustafe continues to colour in his flag and says to me 'I can't say it in English but I can say it in Arabic.' 'Say what?' I ask him. He then goes onto tell me that he has heard the protesters saying something

> when he watches the TV with his parents. I ask him if he can tell me it in Arabic to which he replies saying 'Libya harra mahama yatla barra' (Free Libya). He then tells me that as the protesters are saying this they hold up two fingers in the peace sign. He repeats the phrase as I write it down but is concerned that he can't explain to me what it means in English. I tell him I will ask someone who I work with to translate it for me. He agrees to this, happy that I will be able to understand him. As he finishes his flag he tells me that this is the flag he wants in his Libya (digital) book as it is the flag that he also wants for Libya.

Throughout the escalating Libyan uprising, Mustafe begins to increasingly discuss the Libyan flag(s) and his views on the ensuing conflict with peers at school. This flag becomes a key symbol of Mustafe's identity which he uses as a way to talk to his peers about the current situation in Libya and his national and socio-political identity in relation to 'the naughty person'. As well as using the National Transitional flag, Mustafe also increasingly uses pictures of fire to express this aspect of his identity and communicate this to his peers. When showing his digital book to Fazia he tells her, 'Its Libya but there isn't any fire', before explaining the meanings behind the pictures and text in his book and why there should also be a picture of fire in it. The symbol of fire with its connotations of danger and destruction become important to Mustafe and also increasingly begin to worry him about the current situation in his home country and members of his extended family who still live there.

On a previous occasion after reading the Scotland book with both Mustafe and Kareem, Mustafe first discusses his use of fire as a symbol for Libya with me. After finishing the activity the boys return to the classroom and re-join the free choice activity session there. I work with another child making their digital book. When I return to the classroom Mustafe comes up to me and shows me the picture that he has drawn, telling me, 'Look it says, I live in Libya. In Libya there was fire and fighting.' He then tells me that the boy in the picture is himself and that he is standing in the middle of the fires in Libya that he has seen on the news. He goes on to explain to me that the fires now need to be in all pictures of Libya as there are lots of them in the country at the moment coupled with the fighting.

Figure 4.4: Mustafe's picture of Libya

Mustafe also shows the other children in the class his picture, explaining to them the symbolism of fire. The children who Mustafe shows his picture to do not seem to be aware of the Libyan uprising, but are interested to hear about the fighting and fires.

As the other children that Mustafe regularly interacts with don't understand the significance of these symbols to Mustafe's identity, or share the meanings that Mustafe gives to them, while important to Mustafe himself, they do not appear to impact on how Mustafe's peers interact with him at school. This is in contrast to the meanings attached to hijab by children at Sunnyside and the way in which this symbol is intrinsic to both self-defined and ascribed identities as well as the ongoing negotiated process of social interaction. In contrast, Mustafe's flag can be viewed as a symbolic marker of identity that is not particularly salient in the context of Sunnyside. It is an important contrast to the hijab, which is well embedded in the daily lives of almost all of Sunnyside's Muslim families. As Mustafe performs this aspect of his identity to a largely unappreciative audience he emphasises the meaning that he attaches to this symbol and, in doing so, attempts to transmit its meaning to his peers. However, as was discussed earlier in this chapter, Spencer (2006) states that a shared understanding of a symbol is needed to allow its meaning to be transmitted from one individual to another. When this meaning is commonly understood culture can be produced and shared via the symbol as we saw in *the older girls* use of hijab. For Mustafe though this meaning cannot be transmitted to the school peers who he interacts with as they do not share his interpretation of the symbolic meaning behind Libya's flags.

The fluid and uncertain nature of the uprising in Libya brought this aspect of Mustafe's identity to the fore in both his conversations with myself and his peers, illustrating how children can and do link global (macro) and local (micro) contexts. Before the uprising Mustafe at times talked about 'being Libyan' with his peers but more frequently emphasised his identity 'as a boy' who likes to do boy's things, such as play football, and still be friends with girls, most notably Aafia who Mustafe met at a local nursery. As this conceptualisation of 'being a boy' who can be friends with girls is not shared by many of Mustafe's peers he worked hard, during the first term at Sunnyside, to (re)negotiate this aspect of his identity. As the uprising commences though, Mustafe's identity performance changes as he responds to the dynamic situation in his home country. The aspect of his identity that he chooses to perform, during the second term, mirrors this fluidity. Consequently 'being all of me' for Mustafe changes in response to an emerging social environment. Gilroy's (1993: 122) understanding of identity as the 'changing same' frames Mustafe's fluid identity as in a continual state of becoming. While 'being Libyan' was always an aspect of Mustafe's identity, the dynamic situation in Libya in early 2011 propelled this aspect to the front of Goffman's (1959) stage where Mustafe emphasised the importance of his dynamic Libyan identity. Throughout the course of the uprising, the meaning of 'being Libyan' changed for Mustafe, from initially being a reference to his birthplace and home to determining his socio-political position in relation to 'the naughty person.' Mustafe's self-defined dominant status of 'being Libyan' is an identity that his peers acknowledge without fully understanding the meaning that Mustafe subscribes to it.

It is also interesting to note that some other children in the class do share Mustafe's dominant status, at this time, of 'being Libyan' (also sharing his socio-political views about Gaddafi) and at times depict scenes from Libya in their pictures and discuss this with their friends. Abia's picture of her family in Libya, which she decides to draw during a free choice activity session, that depicts Gaddafi looking angry while her family are smiling, is a clear example of this.

Figure 4.5: Abia's picture of her family in Libya

The other children who strongly subscribe to and operationalise this aspect of their identity were all female January starters. Mustafe, like most of the male September starters, chooses not to interact with the younger girls such as Abia. Consequently, their common national and socio-political identities are not as important to Mustafe's patterns of interaction as other aspects of his identity, such as age.

After the end of the Libyan conflict I revisited Sunnyside (in the summer term 2012) to explore how the Libyan children conceptualised and operationalised their identities six months after the Libyan Uprising ended. 'Being Libyan' is still a strong feature of Mustafe's identity, however, he does not talk about this as often with his peers as he did during the conflict. 'Being a Muslim boy' is now also a strong feature of Mustafe's identity discourse though 'being Libyan' continues to be his dominant status. Similarly, Kareem's discourses around 'being Libyan' (Chapter 5) are now not as prominent as they were during the conflict. Abia, Gamal (below) and their families had returned to Libya before I revisited Sunnyside so I was not able to explore this with them.

Summarising the signified meanings behind children's identity discourses

Interestingly, while Gamal's family arrived in the UK from Libya, and were in a similar situation to Mustafe's family—on temporary student visas before the revolution began, and then forced by ensuing circumstances to stay in the UK rather than returning home for the summer—Gamal's dominant status of 'being Libyan' relates to his socio-economic rather than his socio-political identity.

Gamal regularly talks to staff and peers at Sunnyside about what life in Libya was like and longs to return to his home country. He describes living in 'two big houses in Libya' with 'lots of toys and clothes', and compares this to the one small house that he currently lives in with his family in the UK. He struggles to cope with this change in his family's socio-economic situation and often states that he wants to go back to his old house where he has lots more things to play with and his family has lots more money with which they can do different things. While Mustafe, Abia and Gamal all self-defined 'being Libyan' as their dominant status this identity has different signified meanings for them relating to their national, socio-political and socio-economic identities. Building on this, the next chapter will explore how some children at Sunnyside are ascribed a dominant status by their peers and how this is often related to wider social structures and discourses of discrimination.

As seen in this chapter, conceptualising and operationalising identity as intersecting, symbolic and dynamic is important for children at Sunnyside. In the next chapter I will further explore how young children conceptualise and operationalise their identities amongst each other whilst at school. To begin with I will look in more detail at how children at Sunnyside perceive identity's fundamental concepts of similarity and difference and how these influence their peer interactions.

Chapter 5

Being different: Exploring children's discourses of difference

> *Children are aware ... that colour, language, gender and physical ability are connected with privilege. Racism, sexism and other forms of institutional discrimination have a profound influence on their developing sense of self and others ... All children are harmed. On the one hand, struggling against bias that declares a person inferior ... sucks energy from and undercuts a child's full development. On the other hand, learning to believe that they are superior ... de-humanises and distorts reality for growing children, even while they may be receiving the benefits of institutional privilege. (Derman-Sparks, 1989: ix)*

Social abstractions of difference relating to ethnic diversity

A conversation between Daud and Mubarak at the start of the school day in late March reveals that they too (like Amir, Nasra, Deka and Annakiya in Chapter 3) understand concepts of similarity and difference and, in the case of Mubarak, that some children are also aware (even if not always fully able to explain the significance) of wider socio-political meanings that are commonly attached to specific terms depicting ethnic diversity. On this particular morning the two boys come into the classroom, together with their mothers.

> After putting their dinner cards into the appropriate baskets, they find their name cards, subtly move them so that they are able to sit next to each other, and begin to write their names. As they are doing this, their mothers chat to each other a few feet away from them, on the carpet area. Nasra comes into the classroom with her mother and, after also putting her dinner card into one of the baskets, comes over to the table that the boys are sitting at and begins to write her name. Her mother stands nearby watching her. Daud looks up from his writing and says to Nasra 'Your mum's white.' Nasra doesn't respond to this but looks up and smiles at her mother who also doesn't comment about Daud's statement. Daud then looks over to the carpet where his mother is still talking to Mubarak's mother and tells the group, 'My mum's brown.' 'No, she's not. She's black' chips in Mubarak, 'My mum's black too.' 'Black?' asks Daud looking confused. He then puts down his pen and begins to inspect his hand and arm before putting his arm in front of Mubarak's face and informs him, 'It's brown. My mum's brown. I'm brown. So

> are you.' Mubarak contradicts this saying, 'No. I'm black. You are black too.' Daud still looks confused so Mubarak explains that people with brown skin are called black. 'Why black?' asks Daud. Mubarak thinks about this for a minute or so before saying that he's not very sure why but that 'being black is a good thing' which isn't just about the colour of your skin.

While Mubarak comprehends that 'being black' represents a socio-political position, his understanding of this aspect of ethnic diversity is not widely shared by his peers. As Van Ausdale and Feagin (2001) reveal, young children can develop sophisticated understandings of abstract social concepts when they have been exposed to such discourses. Mubarak regularly talks to his peers about his older brother who he likes to spend a lot of time with. Unknowingly I meet his brother in late June (when he is doing a placement at the school) as I am trying to photocopy some resources in the school staff room. When I can't get the photocopier to work, Mubarak's brother helps me to fix the problem and we start to chat. A week later I am sitting next to Mubarak as he is doing 'some sticking.' I ask Mubarak who he lives with and, when he mentions his brother, he tells me that he sometimes works at the school and describes what he looks like to me. As he is doing so, I remember the photocopying incident and tell him that I think that I met him the previous week and that he helped me to fix the photocopier. Mubarak tells me that it was probably his brother as he is always 'helpful like that.' He then explains to me that he often talks about 'being black' and 'being Muslim' with his brother and that these are things that they are both proud of. He also tells me that his brother helps him to be a good Muslim by teaching him Arabic and showing him how to pray and continues by saying that his brother also teaches him that 'being black is a good thing.'

Throughout the course of the year *the older girls* in the class also began to take an interest in the differences between their skin colours, and after the Easter break they carefully use a range of skin-coloured tone pencils when drawing pictures of each other. They also began to talk about the colour of their skin with each other, with some of the darker-skinned girls expressing a wish to be white. This is in stark contrast to Mubarak's expressed pride in being black.

Like Van Ausdale and Feagin (2001), I suggest that young children do not just repeat what they have been exposed to but are also able to apply meaning to these social discourses. In this way children do not 'passively reproduce' these wider discourses but 'actively appropriate, adapt ... and reproduce' them (Connolly, 1998: 104). In the conversation with Daud above, Mubarak appropriates the socio-political dimensions of ethnic diversity that he and his brother have discussed, adapts this understanding to relate to the present context, and actively reproduces these discourses in response to Daud's questions. As can be seen below, Mubarak can also clearly articulate the ways in which religion and ethnicity intersect.

Holmes (1995) and Marranci (2006) both point out that individuals with a minority status, and particularly those who have experienced discrimination, often treasure and promote their identities more than those with a majority status. Both also reveal that this can impact on how family members operationalise both individual and collective identities, resulting in them often stressing the importance of this aspect of identity to their children. In a conversation that I had with a Somali community member, the predominant way that the local Somali community views their collective identity was highlighted as being different from the way that collective identities were conceptualised and operationalised in Somalia before the start of the civil war. Previously in Somalia, identities were primarily viewed along tribal lines. In contrast the Somali Diaspora, who fled the civil war, predominantly identify themselves as Somali or with a composite European-Somali identity (such as British-Somali or Dutch-Somali) rather than with a tribal identity. Within this discourse, families encourage their children to celebrate the similarities they share rather than the differences between them that have fuelled the civil war. Out of this, a number of families, such as Mubarak's, actively embrace a collective identity of 'being black' , 'being Muslim' , or both, as a way of countering the tribal factions that are currently rife in Somalia. None of the Somali children in the class identified with one of Somalia's tribal identities. Valentine and Sporton's (2009) research with Somali teenagers living in the UK reveals that they also strongly identified with umbrella identities such as 'being Somali' or 'being Muslim' rather than with tribal affiliations. Their respondents' experiences of racism, however, caused them to distance themselves from emphasising a black identity and in doing so solidified their religious identity. This was also an important part of some of *the older girl's* identity discourses at Sunnyside.

When working with Mubarak, a few weeks later, making his digital book, he further explains to me how he understands difference when choosing which pictures he wants to use.

> Looking through the picture library, Mubarak stops at the picture of the woman wearing niqab and tells me, 'I want to do the picture with the niqab.' 'Does your mum wear niqab?' I ask him as he begins to cut it out. 'No, only Arabic women' he

replies. 'Like Amir's mum? I ask. 'Yea, with the glasses,' he confirms before telling me, 'My mum wears hijab and jilbab.' He then explains that Somali women all wear hijab and jilbab. After sticking down this picture Mubarak decides to cut out the picture of the five women and girls wearing hijab. As he is doing this, Mubarak tells me, 'One is Pakistani and the others are Somali.' 'How do you know?' I ask. 'Because the white one looks like Pakistani and Somali's are black' Mubarak replies. 'Are you black?' I ask him. 'Yes,' he tells me, 'and I'm Somali. Daud is. Deka is. Fariido is.' 'Is Annakiya Somali?' I ask him. 'No' he replies 'She's Christian. Somalis are all Muslim.' As he tells me this, he picks up the picture of the girl wearing the blue and white hijab and tells me, 'She's Muslim. Arab people are Muslim. Maybe she looks Pakistani though. Pakistani people are Muslim too.'

As can be seen from this conversation, Mubarak not only recognises what Connolly (2003: 167) terms as 'physical markers of difference' but also recognises 'cultural markers of difference' in relation to religious identity and additionally understands the ways in which different aspects of an individual's identity intersect with each other. For Mubarak, being black and Muslim are both needed in order to be Somali. As seen in Chapter 4, the lived experiences of intersectionality are also important for other children at Sunnyside. Interestingly, while Mubarak and Nasra both regularly discuss the intersecting nature of their ethnic and national identities with their peers of the same gender and myself, I did not observe them discussing these issues together. Therefore it is not possible to conclude how they might reconcile the contrasting discourses that they both employ in relation to whether or not Somalis have to be black or can also, as Nasra contends, be white (Chapter 4). The predominantly gendered nature of peer interaction at Sunnyside means that some conflicting discourses may not come into contact with each other. Notably, in our conversation above Mubarak does not mention Nasra when listing other Somali children in the class. It should be noted though that Nasra is not the only child who subscribes to a Somali identity who Mubarak does not mention in this conversation.

Studies conducted with young children, such as those by Van Ausdale and Feagin (1996, 2001), Connolly (1994, 2003) and Brooker (2006) in USA, Ireland and England respectively, also reveal that young children can both conceptualise and operationalise notions of similarity and difference in relation to socially constructed concepts such as ethnicity, gender and socio-economic status. Brooker (2006: 118) further argues that young children on starting school 'are able to identify the *socially acceptable behaviour* and *expectations* for males and females and for different ethnic groups in their own society, as presented through the media as well as through their own daily experiences of roles and relationships (emphasis mine).' As this chapter reveals, children at Sunnyside can not only identify but also prescribe the socially accepted behaviours that are dominant in both majority and minority communities in the UK, and for some recent migrants the social structures that are dominant in their countries of origin.

In line with my findings above Van Ausdale and Feagin (1996; 2001) also found that as well as using ethnic markers, such as skin colour and language, to actively construct and define themselves, young children use these markers to define 'the other.' Additionally, children at Sunnyside also revealed that their sometimes fluid notions of self and others are related to how they understand these two key concepts of similarity and difference.

Before moving on to discuss how children at Sunnyside understand notions of similarity and difference, I first address Connolly's (2003) critique of the current body of literature within the field. As Connolly points out, the majority of studies that explore how young children conceptualise and operationalise difference, and by extension identity, do so through focussing on what he terms as physical markers, such as skin colour, with only a handful of studies focusing on cultural markers, such as religion and nationality. Bourdieu's (1977) notion of bodily positions as the production and reproduction of culture informs Connolly's understanding of how these markers are used to operationalise identity. With the rise of more subtle forms of discrimination, as portrayed in Barker's (1981) concept of 'new racism', and the increasingly prevalent notion of Islamophobia, particularly since 9/11 and the ensuing 'war on terror' (The Runnymede Trust, 1997), the need for research to address this gap in the literature is becoming more and more important. Connolly's (2003; 2008) own work in Ireland amongst white children from Catholic and Protestant communities, aged between three and eleven years old, begins to fill a noticeable gap in this literature.

While Connolly rightly critiques past research on the grounds that it only focuses on skin colour and fails to address the complexities of cultural diversity, arguing that cultural aspects need to also be considered, the terminology that he employs to argue this case is problematic. By distinguishing these two aspects using the terms physical and cultural a false distinction has been made. While, in the context of Ireland, the cultural markers of difference that Connolly's work uncovers, such as the symbolic use of flags or participation in religious and/or political rites, are not necessarily employed on a daily basis as a physical symbolic marker, in other contexts cultural markers may also be described as physical markers of difference. For example, the use of hijab is a very physical (i.e. visual) symbolic marker that Muslim women and girls regularly employ. Additionally in some instances, such as Nasra's use of this symbol, hijab can reflect an individual's ethnic identity while in other instances it may reflect an individual's religious or cultural identity. Consequently, there is not always an absolute difference, as Connolly suggests, between physical or ethnic and cultural markers. While the terminology 'physical markers of difference' as juxtaposed against the term 'cultural markers of difference' is too simplistic, the signified concepts behind the terms, i.e. the role that bodily and material difference plays in young children's conceptualisation and operationalisation of identity, are important.

In line with this critique, I propose that the term *bodily markers of difference* be utilised in relation to embodied attributes such as skin colour, hair type etc. (replacing Connolly's term *physical markers of difference*) to refer to aspects of a person's bodily appearance that they have a limited ability to change. While an individual may be able to adapt their bodily appearance, for example through the use of skin lightening creams or by straightening their hair, this adaptation is restricted.

Distinct from this I propose that the term *material markers of difference* be employed to refer to aspects of cultural identity, such as dress code, choice of language, use of a flag or religious symbol, that an individual can actively adopt and adapt as a marker of their identity. Consequently, within this definition, material markers of difference can be both physical and non-physical. It should also be noted that, some material markers of difference, such as accent and body language, though adaptable may be subconsciously employed.

As in Connolly's (2003; 2008) work, material markers of difference are key to how children at Sunnyside understand notions of self and others and, for some children, are more important than bodily markers of difference. Notably, whilst children's conversations around bodily markers of difference did not become common place until after the Christmas break, children could be regularly heard discussing material markers of difference, in relation to religious and national identity, at the start of the school year.

Social abstractions of difference relating to religious diversity

Annakiya, as the only non-Muslim in the group of older girls in the class, is acutely aware of material markers of difference. Throughout the course of the year, Annakiya comes to recognise the religious symbols that some of the other girls adopt and also regularly discusses with Deka differences between their two religions. Annakiya clearly understands that the other girls have a common identity that she cannot (because of her own self-defined religious identity) be part of. While creating her PAT with me, she asks me if she can draw a picture. When I tell her that she can draw or write anything she wants to, she starts to draw a picture of a Christian girl crying at school.

> As she is drawing Annakiya looks up and says to me 'She's sad'. 'Why is she sad? I ask. 'Because no-one is playing with her' comes her reply. 'Oh dear, why is nobody playing with her?' I prompt. 'Because they are all Muslim and she is Christian and that's me. And I am crying' she tells me. I then ask Annakiya if she often cries at school and she tells me that she doesn't as she has lots of friends here but she also knows that they are different from her as sometimes they talk and argue about 'being Christian' and 'being Muslim'. She then tells me that, while they don't argue about this very often, it upsets her when they do—commenting that they therefore cannot be her 'real friends'. After telling me this, she looks back at her picture and says 'I don't like this picture because it's not beautiful. She's crying' and then crosses the picture out saying, 'it isn't nice.'

While taken at an individual level, Annakiya's discussion with the other girls about their different religious identities are often framed within a friendly discussion about difference, the culmination of these conversations and occasional arguments appear to have a long term effect on Annakiya's sense of self and of being different from the other girls in her class, which at times makes her question whether she fully belongs to this group of friends.

After crossing out this picture, Annakiya starts to draw a picture of herself as a princess kissing a prince. As will be seen later on in this chapter, this picture also highlights Annakiya's understanding of ethnic difference as being part of a hierarchy that directly relates to discourses of discrimination. The ways in which children's understandings of difference relate to their patterns of interaction at school will be explored in more detail in Chapter 6.

Social abstractions of difference relating to gender diversity

As well as being aware of ethnic and cultural diversity children at Sunnyside, in line with Brooker's (2006) findings, were also acutely aware of gendered differences and the socially constructed gender roles that young girls and young boys are expected to adhere to. For example, while drawing her 'My friends are …' picture in early February, Deka draws herself into her picture, telling me that she is a princess. She then begins to draw her cousin Nasra and then Fazia who are also depicted as princesses in her picture.

Figure 5.1: Deka's picture 'My friends are ...' princesses

'Do you have princesses at home?' I ask her as she is drawing. 'Yes', she tells me, 'But I don't bring them to school, because boys will touch them.' 'Why don't you want boys to touch them?' I ask. 'I don't want them to', she repeats, 'My mum says that boys can't touch them.' She then tells me that boys can't touch girls' things like princesses and dolls as they will break them because they are too rough. 'Boys', she tells me, 'play running games and are rough. They aren't like girls.' Deka's discourse here highlights that she, similarly to the children in Thorne's (1993) and Brooker's (2006) studies, is aware of the roles that wider discourses expect girls and boys to play.

On another occasion, in early May, Jabir comes up to me in the outdoor play area and tells me that he wants to play with my school ID badge. I tell him that he can not have it because all of the adults in the school need to wear a badge when they are at school so that everyone knows who they are. He, however, appears to be perplexed by this and says that if I give him my badge he will go and get me a pink one instead of the green badge that I'm wearing (incidentally all of the badges at the school are green). Nonetheless, rather than following up this point with Jabir, I instead ask him, 'Why do I want a pink one?' to which he replies, 'Pink is for girls.' I then tell him, 'I like green', because green is my favourite colour. He, however, tells me that green can't be my favourite colour as 'green is for boys and pink is for girls'. I then ask him, 'Who says that?' 'My sister', he replies, before running off to play with some of the other boys in the den. As I watch him play with the other boys I reflect on the other conversations that I have had with children at Sunnyside about perceived gender roles and the symbolic nature of colours that children commonly associate with gender positions. All of the children in the class have not only picked up on but, for the most part, also adopt the gender roles that they are given by the wider social world. Davies' (2003) work with young children (aged between three and six) also highlights that social discourses surrounding gender influence how children conceptualise their own and others' identities, and furthermore how they interact with each other. Interestingly, however, boys in the class (most notably Kareem, Ferran and Umar), while all ascribing to traditional gender roles and vocalising the importance of them, at times throughout the year resisted these ascribed roles and engaged in activities that were generally thought of, by the other children in the class, as girls' activities, such as playing with dolls, cooking and cleaning. In doing so, though, they were always heavily criticised by the other children for not conforming to 'traditional' gender roles, through the use of phrases such as 'boys don't do that' or 'dancing is for girls and for ladies.' Russell's (2011) work also reveals that the young people in her study likewise promoted, and at times contested, wider social structures relating to gender discrimination.

As can be seen from the above examples, young children at Sunnyside are able to understand abstract concepts and apply 'conventional' meaning to situations relating to social abstractions of difference such as ethnicity, religion and gender. Previous studies in UK, Ireland, America and Australia all support these findings revealing that young children are able to apply social meaning to abstract concepts relating respectively to bodily and material markers of difference (for example Thorne, 1993; MacNaughton, 2001; Van Ausdale and Feagin, 2001; Davies, 2003; Connolly, 2003). Building on these findings Brooker's (2006) work in England and South Korea suggests that the family, early years education settings and the media all play a key role, albeit sometimes unwittingly, in promoting stereotypical discourses relating to both gender and ethnicity, which children then embody.

As seen above, Annakiya's understanding of religious diversity cannot be viewed as purely modelling adult behaviour as, in her interactions with Deka, both girls discuss aspects of their religious identity that they have been taught in relation to their patterns of interaction at school. As a result of these discourses, Annakiya concludes, despite her parents' and staff members' encouragement to interact with and 'be friends with' the other girls, that she doesn't fully belong to this group. Deka's mother is also instrumental in encouraging Deka to be friends with Annakiya at school and not promote the differences between themselves, most notably in relation to their religious identities. It should be noted though that in other instances family members may (subconsciously) convey a message of difference as they promote and enact aspects of their identity.

Similarly Jabir's conversation with me about my favourite colour reveals that he has *internalised discourses* around gender which he has heard from his sister, as he is genuinely puzzled that my favourite colour is green. After this conversation Jabir regularly tells me that 'girls like pink' and 'boys like green' and challenges me on why I don't conform to this understanding of gender norms.

Discourses of discrimination

Following on from the events above, in which children at Sunnyside reveal that they are able to apply meaning to social abstractions of difference, I observed that some children are acutely aware of wider social structures and discourses of discrimination and how these impact on their own identities.

In November I am in the outdoor play area during the morning session.

> Annakiya picks up a ball and asks me to play with her. We throw the ball back and forth to each other. After a few minutes Kareem comes up to us—also with a ball in his hands—and asks me to throw his ball to him. I throw Annakiya's ball back to her and then Kareem's ball to him and so on alternating between the two children. Fariido comes, looks at Kareem, and asks if he will throw his ball to her so that she can also join in. He says 'No' and throws the ball directly back to me. As I throw it back to him, Fariido asks him again if he will throw the ball to her, and again Kareem replies, 'No', but this time also shakes his head resolutely to emphasise his meaning. He then turns to me and says 'She black', offering an explanation for why he won't throw his ball to her. I tell him that isn't nice and that everyone can play.[8] Kareem, however, keeps a tight hold on his ball and starts

8. While I normally did not get directly involved in social encounters and disagreements between children so that I could observe how they resolved them on their own, in this case I felt that there was potential for harm if I did not step in and tell Kareem that his behaviour was unacceptable and to reassure Fariido (and also Annakiya) that this type of behaviour was not allowed at school. Brown's (2007) work supports this approach by saying that quick responses that promote equality and inclusion

to back away from us. Annakiya turns to Fariido, who is upset by the encounter, and says to her 'Play with me.' The two girls then start to throw Annakiya's ball to each other.

As Hall (2000: 4) points out, identities can be understood as being 'constructed within, not outside [of], discourse'. Further observations reveal that cultural discourses surrounding ethnic hierarchies play a part in how Kareem views his classmates. During a free choice session, a few weeks after this incident, I am chatting to Gamal who is showing me a picture that he has drawn of his house in Libya. He tells me that he had 'a big house' in Libya and that there were people there who 'helped him.' As I explore this further with him, I determine that he is referring to domestic workers who were employed by his family. Kareem comes over to us as we are chatting and listens to our conversation. As Gamal finishes discussing his picture, Kareem says 'Me too. Black helpers in Libya' before telling me about the type of jobs that these 'helpers' did. After Gamal and Kareem tell me about their domestic workers back home, I investigate further the social context of Libya and discover that in February 2010 the UNHRC (2010: 2) issued a written statement calling for Libya 'to end its practices of racial discrimination against black Africans.' It appears that these migrant workers are often employed as unskilled and domestic workers. The UNHRC has been alerted to the way in which ethnic minority workers are commonly mistreated within Libya, as well as the commonly practiced ethnic segregation of the population as a whole. The above statement was issued after several concerns had been raised by the United Nations Committee on the Elimination of Racial Discrimination over a period of twelve years. Kareem's and Gamal's recollections about their experiences of life in Libya confirm that ethnic segregation is still common practice. When analysed alongside daily life at Sunnyside, practices and discourses such as these that originate in families' socio-cultural and geographic contexts appear to influence how children conceptualise and operationalise their identities in a new social environment. This reveals the interrelationship of macro and micro contexts and the ways in which they can impact on young children's peer interactions.

are needed in situations like this to send clear messages to children. Sending this message was more important to me throughout the course of my fieldwork than collecting data. After this incident, I also immediately discussed what had happened with school staff asking them if they had observed similar incidents and also helping them to plan a longer term strategy to deal with this issue.

Further observations with Kareem show that in his first term at Sunnyside he consistently segregates multi-ethnic classroom resources based on ethnicity. In the maths area during the first term the focus was on sorting. One of the tools that children could use during free choice activities was a set of miniature people. The individual pieces in this set are made up of both boys and girls as well as black and white figures. Kareem frequently goes to the maths area when his first choices of playing on the computer or the white board are occupied by other children. In the maths area, he often chooses to work with the people figures where he sorts the figures by ethnicity and counts them. Interestingly, while the other children often sort the figures by gender, as well as by ethnicity, Kareem does not, but always focuses on skin colour. If these observations were viewed in isolation, it would not be possible to infer how Kareem was sorting the figures. However, when this activity is analysed alongside Kareem's peer interactions, our research activities and his other solo activities, ethnic segregation appears to be a common theme. Ethnography lends itself to such analysis as its methodological framework requires a wide range of data collection and comparative analysis. Van Ausdale and Feagin (2001) contend that it is important to adopt such an approach when working with young children to ensure that their voices are *actually* heard.

Brown (2007) highlights that young children absorb social discourses of discrimination and hierarchies of inequality that are prominent, both overtly and covertly in wider society and incorporate these into their own identities and social interactions in a similar way to Kareem's refusal to play with Fariido because of their differing ethnic identities. In doing this, children consciously reproduce dominant discourses of inequality that associate ethnicity, gender, socio-economic status and other social attributes with power and privilege in their everyday social encounters. The commonly practiced ethnic segregation within Libya appears to strongly impact on Kareem's patterns of interaction at Sunnyside, particularly at the start of the school year, with Kareem's behaviour affecting patterns of interaction within the classroom. Children's peer cultures can consequently be viewed as perpetuating, and being perpetuated by, social structure(s) (Corsaro et al., 2003; Russell, 2011).

Conversations with staff at Sunnyside further revealed that some children, who come from countries where racial discrimination is perceived as the norm (such as Libya), distance themselves from the black children in their class when they initially start school and, when asked, comment that, where they come from, they do not play with black children. As the school acts to counter this discrimination, by rebuking racist behaviour and celebrating diversity, they have discovered that children's attitudes slowly (appear to) change. As Burr (1995) contends, promoting new discourses that compete with established discourses can bring about change and accordingly be a catalyst for how an individual's identity can be (re)negotiated. Kareem appears to be influenced by the school's anti-discriminatory discourse as throughout the year he increasingly begins to play with multi-ethnic tools, such as the black doll in the home corner, as well as with his black classmates adapting his own language and behaviour to the new social norms that he is exposed to. Language also heavily impacts on Kareem's patterns of interaction and, since no black members of the class are fluent Arabic speakers, it is unclear if Kareem's interactions are more strongly influenced by language or ethnicity. The importance of language within the context of peer interactions will be explored in more detail in Chapter 6.

Connolly's (1994) work highlights that dominant discourses around gender and ethnicity are often closely connected. His research shows that young boys are taught from an early age to be competitive and, that when they feel that they have lost face in a competitive and public situation, they can resort to employing racist slurs in an attempt to reassert their perceived dominant social position.

Discourses of discrimination at Sunnyside were, at times, played out in similar ways to those described by Connolly (1994). During a session in late March, Susan, the classroom assistant, tells me of an incident that she observed earlier that week when Amir and Fariido were having an argument in the outdoor play area. The argument starts when Fariido goes up to Susan and tells her that Amir has lied to the other children. Amir denies this and becomes frustrated when Fariido keeps insisting that he has lied and begins to tease him saying that he will get into trouble. The two begin to argue, resulting in Amir retorting that 'Somalis are stupid.' Susan tells me that she feels that Amir responded in this way as Fariido was 'winding him up' and 'he felt like he was being shown up by a girl' in front of his classmates. This interpretation corresponds with numerous previous (and subsequent) incidents that I had observed where Fariido regularly argues with and teases the other children, causing them to get upset and/or angry with her. Additionally, as Amir's two closest friends at school, Daud and Mubarak, are Somali, his derogatory comments about Somalis are likely to stem from frustration, with the aim of insulting Fariido. When creating his PAT (after this event) it becomes evident that Amir does not view his friends, or Somalis in general, as stupid. Despite this, Amir's choice of a racial slur as an insult, rather than any other form of retort to Fariido's teasing, shows that he is aware of the hurtful nature of such a comment.

Hierarchies of difference

Research also shows that discourses of discrimination mean that some young children try to deny aspects of their own identity because of their wish to have an externally validated majority status, for instance in wanting to be considered by others as 'white' (Holmes, 1995; Nayak, 2009). This desire to be light or white also surfaced at Sunnyside. While in some contexts a distinction is made between wanting to be light and wanting to be white (Tate, 2009) the girls at Sunnyside used these two terms interchangeably and did not appear to distinguish between them.

One example of this was prompted through the photograph of the *playdough* table that I took for use in analysis activities relating to patterns of interaction. As can be seen from the photograph, two children were playing at the table while I took this picture and their hands are showing in the resultant photograph. While it is not possible to identify the children from the photograph (Figure 5.2), one of the children is black and the other white. Other photos taken at the same time, however, reveal that the two children were Fariido and Fazia.

Figure 5.2: Photograph of the *playdough* table

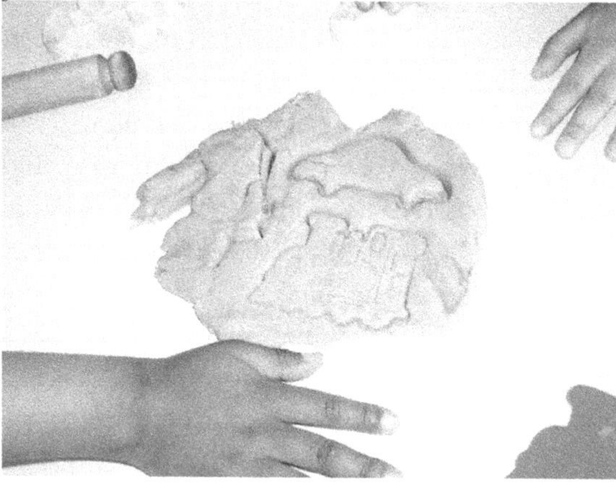

Coincidently, in June, Fariido and Fazia jointly complete their 'patterns of interaction' activity with me. As they are looking through the different photographs they discover this picture and begin to spontaneously discuss who the children in it could be. Neither of them remember that they were at the playdough table as I took the photograph. However, as I had taken the photograph over a month before we completed this activity, this is not surprising.

> After I tell the girls that I remembered them both being at the playdough table as I took the photograph, Fariido points to the hand at the top of the picture and says, 'This is me.' Fazia however points to the hand at the bottom of the picture saying, 'Look that's your hand and that's my hand', as she points to the hand at the top continuing, 'Look its whiter. Look!' Fariido replies, 'Let me see', and turns the picture round. As she does, Fazia points to the hand at the top and says again, 'That's mine.' 'No, that's mine', insists Fariido. 'No', continues Fazia, 'that's mine cause I'm the whiter one. Mine is lighter.' Fariido doesn't respond to this but instead focuses on the picture. I then ask her why she thinks that it is her hand at the top of the picture. 'Cause I want to be white and she the darker one', she tells us laughing. Fazia doesn't laugh with her at this but again insists, 'I'm the lighter one. Look!' as she shows Fariido, and then me, her hand. 'No, I'm the lighter one', replies Fariido. 'Why do you want to be the lighter one?' I ask. 'I like to be white because ... ' Fariido replies before pausing 'because ... because I want to be white, like Fazia. She has a white face.' 'I think you have lovely skin colour', I tell her. 'No I want that', she tells me again pointing to the hand at the top of the picture. 'Why do you want that?' I ask. 'I wish I could take this skin off and put on some like that', she replies pointing back to the photograph.

These views reveal the influence of underlying structural inequalities in society that commonly view 'white as better' and majority forms of capital as more valid than minority capital. Such inequalities can relate both to externalised and internalised forms of racism. When taken to an extreme, these views can lead to ethnic segregation but more commonly impact on a daily basis on an individual's social interactions, such as their friendship groups and social networks. This can then impact directly (in the form of social capital) on an individual's access to resources and services, such as education and healthcare. Holmes (1995), Vandenbroeck (1999), Van Ausdale and Feagin (2001) and Brown (2007) all reveal that young ethnic minority children's desire to be white is a worldwide phenomenon.

As seen in Chapter 1 while working on Annakiya's PAT with her she reveals that, like Fariido, she wants to be light. Annakiya begins to draw a princess who she tells me is a picture of herself as a grown up. As she begins to colour in the princess, she recites to me the different colours that she is using to draw her rainbow dress, her pink shoes, her brown hair and her golden tiara.

> After she finishes colouring in the princess, she pauses and looks at the picture before telling me, 'I'm not gunna colour my face because this is when I'm grown up. My hair is curly, I'm a princess and I am light, like you.' I ask her why she wants to be light when she is older. 'Now I'm dark and you are light,' she continues, 'when I'm grown up I'm gunna be light, like you, and like my mum. My mum's light too.' As I reflect on this last statement, I remember that Annakiya's mother's skin colour is much lighter than her father's and at the same time tell Annakiya that I like the colour of her skin as it is now, saying that it makes her very pretty. She ponders this for a while before saying, 'It's OK to be different, like *Elmer*, but really I wanna be like you.'

Interestingly, the other picture that Annakiya draws on her PAT of herself—again as a princess, though this time kissing a prince—also has light skin though this time the picture is coloured in using skin tone pencils.

Annakiya's comment, 'It's OK to be different, like *Elmer*, but really I wanna be like you', shows that, while school initiatives that promote equality and anti-discriminatory practice, such as the project work about *Elmer* (McKee, 1989), are important in offsetting wider social discourses of discrimination, as Brown (2007) and Bath (2009) both advocate, the deep rooted nature of such discourses make countering them a challenging and long term operation.

Operationalising ethnic and religious identities at Sunnyside

As previously seen, children at Sunnyside regularly engage in peer conversations about their identity. Building on this, I will now explore in more detail how children at Sunnyside operationalise their identities with peers through conversations and imaginative play. As Van Ausdale and Feagin (2001) point out, play can be understood as the means through which a child is connected to his/her social world, enabling them to construct meaning from, and within, his/her social environment. Within an anthropological framework, any universal definition, such as of the concept of play, is problematic as it fails to take into account the variety of cultural interpretations of a concept around the world. As James (1998) argues, play must therefore be understood from an emic perspective to ensure that cultural interpretations are taken into account. Notably this means that children's own meanings about play must be sought. By involving children in collaborative analysis (Chapter 2), I was able to access their interpretations of specific instances of imaginative play with their peers.

At times children's conversations and games at Sunnyside were prompted by my research activities. For the most part the conversations and games in the remainder of this chapter were initiated by the children themselves as part of free choice activities. Additionally, at times I was included as an active participant by the children, although on other occasions children engaged in the encounter purely with their peers.

In early October, a group of children Aafia, Fazia, Mustafe, Amir and Mubarak are all drawing pictures at the writing table during a free choice session. As they are drawing, the children are chatting about their different pictures.

> Aafia puts down her pencil and looks round the table at the other children before asking them 'Do you do this?' She then puts her hands over her face and bends down to the table and up again—going through the motions of Salah (prayer). The three boys watch her and then all join in. As they are doing this, Aafia and Mustafe begin to recite phrases in Arabic. Amir stops and listens to them while Mubarak continues to move up and down, covering his face with his hands. Fazia sits and watches all of this without comment. Suddenly, the children stop and return to their drawings, discussing the different places that they pray and comparing their experiences. Amir is particularly interested in the Arabic phrases that Aafia and Mustafe recited and proudly tells the other children that he has started to learn Arabic at the mosque and will soon also know how to pray using them.

In this encounter children employ *identity's performative, situated and dialectical nature.*

As well as discussing prayer, children could regularly be heard discussing concepts of 'hellfire' and *Aljana* (heaven), both in general terms and also in connection with how their identity positioned themselves in relation to these religious concepts.

> In February, Daud and Mubarak both come to work with me, creating their 'My friends are ...' pictures. After writing down the names of his friends Mubarak rubs his chin as if he is stroking an imaginary beard, saying 'I have a moustache and a beard.' Daud looks up and tells him, 'You are Muslim.' Turning to me, Mubarak explains, 'Muslims have beards.' 'All of them?' I ask. 'Yes', he replies. 'Muslims go to the mosque', Daud chips in, 'My dad has a beard and goes to the mosque.' 'Do you go to the mosque?' I ask them both. Daud indicates that he does. 'I see his brother there', Daud further volunteers indicating towards Mubarak, 'He doesn't go though.' To which Mubarak replies, 'I watch TV at home.' Daud continues saying,

> 'I pray. Muslims pray.' 'Do you pray?' he then asks me. I tell him that I do, but not at the mosque. Mubarak joins in saying, 'I pray at home', and explains that, while he sometimes watches TV at home, he also prays there with his brothers. Daud then tells me that 'Muslims have to pray' and the boys start to talk about 'hellfire' and tell me that, if Muslims don't pray, they 'go to hellfire.' Mubarak also informs me that 'bad people go to hellfire', with Daud mentioning that 'Allah says Christians go to hellfire too.' Mubarak agrees with him about this as Daud explains what being in 'hellfire' entails, saying 'Allah grounds you in hellfire.' When I enquire further about this, Daud explains that you are only grounded in 'hellfire' if you are bad. The boys then tell me that they can't lie, steal or be nasty to other people as they don't want to go to 'hellfire'.

A few weeks after this conversation, Daud and Mubarak return to the topic of 'hellfire'.

> As they are practising writing their names on arriving at school, Mubarak looks up to me and tells me that he stole the pen that he is writing with from a shop in town. He laughs at this. Daud, however, informs me that 'He's lying' and goes on to tell me 'He's going to hellfire', as everyone who lies goes to 'hellfire'. The two boys laugh at this and Mubarak starts to rub two pens together, saying, 'I'm making the fire.' Amir, who has been listening to our conversation from the next table, looks over and tells the other boys that they shouldn't laugh about 'hellfire' as it is a real place.

As can be seen in these encounters identity, for these boys, is operationalised as *performative, situated and dialectical.*

As well as discussing 'hellfire', *Aljana* also featured in children's peer conversations.

> One day, as we were getting ready to go home, Amir, Mubarak and Fariido are sitting on the carpet waiting for their parents to collect them as they start to discuss *Aljana*. Amir tells the others, 'When you die you go [there]. Where the big mosque is.' He then explains that it doesn't happen immediately after you die but it takes a few days to get there. All three children chat about what *Aljana* will be like, imagining what the mosque will look like. While they disagree over some of the details, they all agree that it will be good and that they will like it there. Amir then tells the others that only Muslims can go there and looking over at me tells me that I won't go there as I'm not Muslim. The others agree with him and all tell me that *Aljana* is only for Muslims.

While Sunnyside's children often had theoretical discussions about being Muslim, they also understood that being Muslim had practical implications for their collective identities. This is illustrated by the way in which Amir and Mubarak tell me, 'we are brothers 'cause we are both Muslims'. While both boys understand that there are differences between them, relating to their ethnic and national identities, 'being Muslim' is understood as being important in bringing them together under the banner of a fictive kinship. In this way, the boys' common religious identity becomes the over-riding identity marker by which they identify their special relationship. Interestingly all of the boys in *the gang* are also Muslim and, when Daud becomes friendly with Callum after the Christmas break, Amir repeatedly tells him that it is *haram* (forbidden) to be friends with non-Muslims and actively bars Callum from gang membership. Daud, however, as we will see in Chapter 6, pays no heed to Amir's warnings and increasingly plays on his own with Callum. On more than one occasion, Amir also tells me that as a non-muslim I'll go to 'hellfire'. Interestingly though, as he does this, he always checks that he has not upset me.

'Being Muslim' can, therefore, be interpreted as a 'superordinate identity' for *the gang*, which is defined by Gaertiner et al. (1999) as a salient identity that comes to the fore in diverse social situations as a way of promoting a sense of togetherness. For these boys, the uniting identity of 'being Muslim' is considered to be more important than the divisive ethnic hierarchies that *the older girls* adhere to. Lareau's (2003) work in America similarly found that ethnic difference had a stronger impact on girls' patterns of interaction than boys. The boys in Lareau's study interacted with each other across ethnic 'groups' while the girls segregated themselves based on ethnic difference. At Sunnyside, while most of *the older girls* also self-define as 'being Muslim' they, unlike *the gang*, do not subscribe to Islam's assertion that all individuals are equally valued in the wider Muslim family irrespective of their ethnic background. As seen above, skin colour, for these girls, relates to a hierarchy of difference which incorporates *external* structural discourses of discrimination. While this group of girls do not physically segregate themselves based on ethnicity, as Lareau's girls do, ethnic diversity determines *how* they interact. For other children at Sunnyside, such as Kareem, *external structures* relating to country of origin and segregated macro structures also impact on how they view ethnic difference. The way in which children conceptualise and operationalise difference is consequently related to a complex meshing of religious, gender and ethnic identities, macro and micro social contexts and *the duality of structure*.

As well as discussing the different ways that they express their Muslim identity amongst themselves, children also discuss this aspect of their identity with non-Muslims in the class. During a free choice session in early February, I am sitting with Annakiya and Deka at the writing table.

> The two girls are drawing pictures while I am observing other children in the classroom. Annakiya picks up a new colouring pencil and turns to Deka and asks her, 'Are you Muslim?' Deka, who was concentrating on her picture, apparently deep in her own thoughts, looks up and politely says, 'Pardon?' Annakiya then asks, 'Are you Somali? Are you Muslim?' to which Deka replies, 'Yes', before turning back to her picture. Annakiya watches her draw for a moment and then says, 'My sister says that Muslims don't like god.' Deka doesn't respond to this statement but, intrigued by the conversation, I start to give the two girls my full attention. I ask Deka if what Annakiya says is right. Deka replies first to me that, 'Muslims do like god', and then turning to Annakiya, 'Your sister is lying.' Annakiya responds to this by saying, 'She's only joking', and laughs at her previous statement. Deka turns back to her drawing. I then ask Annakiya if she goes to church. She replies saying, 'Yes but Muslims don't.' 'No', I agree with her, 'they go to the mosque.' 'To pray?' she asks. Deka then re-joins the conversation, volunteering, 'I pray.' 'Do you go to the mosque to pray?' I ask her. 'No', she replies. 'At home?' I ask. 'I don't pray when I'm at my home. I pray at my *Ayeeyo*'s house', she clarifies. Annakiya then tells us that she prays too, but in church. The two girls begin to discuss the different ways that they pray and Deka is fascinated by Annakiya's simple explanation of how Christians pray, finding it hard to believe that they don't pray in a step by step way as she has learnt to.

Annakiya and Deka often discussed different aspects of their religious identity and the ways in which their religious beliefs are similar and different from each other. As mentioned in Chapter 4, throughout the course of the year, Annakiya began to recognise how Deka, and other girls in the class, used hijab as a symbol of their religious identity. While, for the most part, these discussions were part of a friendly and curious interest in each other's backgrounds, at times their discussions spilt over into arguments, revealing their awareness of wider social tensions relating to religious diversity. One such occasion, when Deka and Annakiya's discussions turned into an argument, occurred the day before my weekly visit to the school and resulted in Deka being excluded from school for the remainder of the day.

When I arrive at Sunnyside, Deka does not appear with the other children. As the teacher, Mary, finishes the first carpet session of the day (around 9.45 a.m.), Deka arrives with the deputy head. She goes to sit on the carpet next to her cousin Nasra who gives her a big hug. Annakiya creeps forward from where she has been sitting to join them. As the children are released in small groups to choose an activity, Deka does some guided work with Susan (the classroom assistant). As they are doing this, Mary comes up to me and tells me that yesterday at lunch time Deka and Annakiya had been discussing different aspects of their religion. Their discussion had got heated and Deka had told Annakiya that Christians are bad people. Mary was not sure of any details of the incident but later on that day one of the bilingual workers, Aziza, explained to me further what had happened. As the two girls were discussing the afterlife, Deka reportedly told Annakiya that Christians go to 'hellfire', to which Annakiya replied that it was Muslims and not Christians who go to hell. It was at this point that, in Aziza's words, 'their theological debate got out of hand' and descended into name calling on Deka's part, with a heated argument ensuing. Aziza attributes Deka's reaction to low self confidence which caused her to lash out when she felt threatened. This event, and Aziza's explanation has parallels with the behaviour of the young boys in Connolly's (1994) study who reacted aggressively when they felt that they were losing face in front of their peers. Aziza told me how, at this point, the deputy head teacher was called and Deka was taken to the office. She kicked out at school staff and was subsequently sent home for the remainder of the day. As Annakiya's first reaction on seeing Deka the next day was to go and chat to her, resuming their friendly interactions, she did not appear to be still upset by the previous day's incident.

Interestingly, even after this event, the two girls continued to initiate friendly theological debates, like their conversation above at the writing table, about the nature of god, the after-life and what it means to be Christian and Muslim. As they do this, they explore the differences between their two religions and, at times, touch upon wider social tensions. The extent of these discussions about difference did appear, however, to take its long term toll on Annakiya. As seen above, near the end of the year, while creating her PAT, she drew a picture of a Christian girl crying at school that she identified as herself. While doing this, she explained to me that she doesn't have any 'real friends' at school as they are all different from her. In saying this, Annakiya reveals an understanding of how notions of similarity and difference are important for social relationships. Despite this, she is able to play with, and even at times describes herself as 'being friends' with, the other girls. While creating her PAT, Annakiya acknowledges the ambiguities of her experiences of discussing diversity with her peers, where at times they explore difference in a harmonious way and at other times there is conflict. Following on from this, identity for Annakiya can be understood as *performative, situated and dialectical*. In acknowledging these ambiguities Annakiya is situating her experiences within a multifaceted social environment as she explores the complexities of identity (re)negotiation.

Children at Sunnyside were clearly influenced by wider social discourses of discrimination around hierarchies of religious identity. While in the case of Deka and Annakiya above, this spilt over into an argument, children's conversations about a particular religious group being good or bad were also at times a non-judgemental way to explore and question these wider discourses.

> As Annakiya and Mustafe are tidying up the writing table at the end of an indoor choose session in early June, I go over and help them. As I do, Annakiya asks me, 'Are you Muslim?' I tell her that I'm not and she then asks, 'Are you Christian?' to which I nod in response. 'I'm Christian too', she tells me. Mustafe, who has been listening to this, says, 'I'm Muslim' and then asks us, 'Are Christians bad?' Annakiya replies that they aren't bad, and Mustafe then asks 'Are Muslims bad?' 'No', replies Annakiya again and then tells us, 'My dad says Muslims are not bad either.' I tell them that I agree with her dad. After a minute or so, in which Mustafe appears to contemplate this, he sums up his thoughts by saying 'So no-one is bad then.'

While it is unclear from this exchange the extent to which Mustafe is challenging social discourses regarding inter-faith tensions, it is important to note that he is beginning to question these as he meets non-Muslim individuals. In their diverse school environment, children test and challenge discourses that are influential outside Sunnyside, as they negotiate their interactions with their peers.

It is also important to note that some parents, such as Annakiya's, are encouraging their children to not view difference as hierarchical and are, therefore, playing a role in countering discourses of discrimination. Over the course of the year, my conversations with other parents, however, reveal that some *do* view religious difference as hierarchical and feel that it is important to impart this understanding to their children. Parents' roles in perpetuating and countering discrimination, although outside the scope of the present study, is an area that warrants further exploration.

Children also regularly operationalised aspects of their religious identity in their imaginative play, such as acting out going to the mosque, the girl's Eid parties or the boys' resistance fighters' expeditions in the Arab World. Play, as Corsaro et al. (2003) and Engel (2005) highlights, is not only an important part of children's formal learning but also enables them to operationalise their identities amongst their peers. Leading on from Daud's and Mubarak's conversation about 'hellfire', which was prompted by Mubarak stroking his imaginary Muslim beard, these two boys often pretended to have Muslim beards in their role play games, where they would be 'Muslim scientist boys' or 'Muslim taxi drivers.' During these games, Daud would regularly come up to me and say something like, 'Can you see my little beard?' or 'I've a Muslim beard' and often instruct me to 'write that down' in my notebook.

In late March, as we go outside to the outdoor play area the nursery children are also out.

> The majority of the reception children run over to the bikes, but Mary tells them that, as nursery are also out this afternoon, they will have to take it in turns to have a go on a bike and play with the other activities when they aren't able to have a bike or scooter. Daud and Mubarak both start off on a bike. There isn't one for Amir though, so he sits on his own at the *Lego* tray and makes a car and trailer which he proceeds to blow up telling me that 'it has a car bomb.' Daud and Mubarak race around with Barak and Umar but after a minute or so Daud (who isn't feeling very well today) says to the others, 'Let's not play this game' and shouts over to me, 'It's boring.' He then cycles off on his own. Lina comes to stand next to me by the building blocks in the construction area. She asks me to help her. I pass her the first bricks (which are high up) then sit on the bench behind the pile of bricks and watch as she continues to make what she tells me is a shop, just under the covered area.
>
> At this point, Mary tells the children on bikes to swap over with those who don't have them. Amir and Kareem both run to get one while Mubarak plays football with Mustafe. Daud stands and watches. Lina has now finished building her shop and has collected toy cakes, buns and other food items from the home corner and puts them on display. I move from the bench behind Lina's shop and sit on the climbing frame steps so that I can get a better view of the children on the bikes. Amir cycles past me calling, 'I'm trying to get the bun,' and cycles past Lina's shop, reaching out for a bun that is on the counter without stopping his bike. He doesn't get it the first time but races round again, circling the climbing

frame, and tries to grab it next time round. However, like last time he again doesn't manage to pick anything up. After another circuit he succeeds and smiles at me as he circles again, holding the bun up for me to see. Daud, who has been watching, calls over to him, 'Get one for my dinner' and runs after Amir as he circuits again. Mubarak leaves the football game and races across to the shop to also join in. Amir calls out to him, 'I want the chicken.' Mubarak picks it off the counter and holds it out for him to collect as he passes but pulls it away at the last minute so Amir can't reach it. Mubarak then runs off with the chicken, pretending to share it with Daud. Both boys laugh. Amir goes round on another lap, reaching out for more items of food. Lina silently watches as the boys swoop round taking her food and continues to tidy around them.

Mary calls for the children on the bikes to swap again. Amir gets off the double bike, giving it to Daud and goes over to Lina's shop and helps her to sort the food, putting back the items that he has taken. 'Lina, I'm the shop keeper', he tells her. Lina lets him carry on and doesn't object to him taking over responsibility for the shop.

Daud cycles around on the double bike and then stops in front of me saying, 'I'm a taxi driver, a Muslim taxi driver', as he strokes an imaginary beard on his chin. 'Who's your customer?' I ask. 'I don't have one', he replies before cycling off on another lap. Jabir gets on Daud's taxi and they race around in front of me before circling behind the climbing frame. When Daud returns he is on his own and as he comes to a stop in front of me he sighs and ruefully shakes his head telling me, 'I've still no customers.' 'What about Jabir?' I ask. 'No', he says shaking his head. 'He wasn't a customer. I've had no customers for ten days.' He cycles off again, sighing enthusiastically. After another lap, he comes back with Barak sitting in the back seat. They cycle round again and, as they pass Lina's shop, Barak shouts, 'Let's all pray!' Daud stops the bike and watches while Barak runs over to the side of Lina's shop (i.e. the storeroom) where Amir and Mubarak are standing side by side. Barak stands next to them and all three boys put their hands up to their shoulders, cover their faces, kneel down then bow to the floor and prostrate themselves before sitting up again silently going through the ritual of Salah (prayer). Daud still on the bike watches them as does Lina, who continues to stand behind the shop counter. *The older girls* stop their chasing game and also watch. When the boys stand up again they all unceremoniously go back about their daily business.

As can be seen from the above example, praying becomes a normal part of the boys' game, mirroring the way in which prayer is naturally incorporated into daily Muslim life. The boys do not go to a mosque to do this but instead remove themselves from their female company and pray in the all male environment of the shop's storeroom. While Daud does not join in this part of the game, his Muslim identity also features in his role of a taxi driver. This is just one example of where Daud talks about Muslim taxi drivers, equating the occupational role of his father with his own, and his father's, Muslim identity. In doing this, Daud and the other boys, as Corsaro et al. (2003) and Engel (2005) describe, operationalise aspects of their identities in their game.

Food also featured in children's games within the context of halal (permissible) and *haram* (forbidden) food choices. As James (1997) points out, within anthropology, food has long been thought of as a cultural marker of identity both between and within localised, nationalised and globalised identities. Within this framework, food is often thought of as 'provid[ing] a fluid symbolic medium for making statements about identity' (ibid.: 74). Children at Sunnyside at times utilised food in this way in their imaginative play.

> In early January I am sitting in the corner of the indoor role play area with Kareem, Daud, and Jabir. It has been set up as a café with pretend food such as rolls, cakes, vegetables and sausages. 'We are making a picnic', Jabir tells me. He brings me some food to try and invites me to join the boys at their table. As I sit down, Daud eats some pretend sausages. 'You can't do that!' Jabir tells him, without elaborating on why he shouldn't eat the sausages. Daud looks at him, smiles cheekily, but continues to eat. As he does I wonder if this is a reference to halal and *haram* food choices—but don't ask why the sausages aren't allowed, instead deciding to wait and see what happens next. Barak wanders into the café. He stands and watches the others for a while and then sits down next to Daud and also begins to eat. Daud, Kareem and Barak all pretend to eat the sausages. All this while Jabir has been making tea in the corner, with his back to our table. He brings me a cup, which I drink. He then looks at the other boys eating sausages and says to them 'That's *haram*! You can't eat them!'

While children's religious identities were often woven into their games, children at times also used play as a way to challenge an ascribed socially accepted way of expressing their identity, such as the boys' consumption of sausages. In doing this, children would often explain that they had been told not to do the said activity by their parents and/or teacher at the mosque, while smiling cheekily and instructing me not to tell. Children overtly and intentionally resist, as a collective 'group', rules surrounding food choices, as conceptualised by

Russell's (2011) theory of resistance. Marranci (2008) highlights this process of challenging socially accepted behaviours as an important part of identity maintenance. *The duality of structure* is therefore at play here.

Another example of resisting religious rules was related to music.

> During a free choice session in January, Amir comes over to where I'm sitting and says to me 'You say you're going where I am going. Come on!' referring to our conversation that morning where I asked him if he would like to help me (as a focus child) with my study. He leads me over to the maths table. We sit down and begin to do a number jigsaw together. As we take out the pieces, I notice that the pictures are of children playing different musical instruments. While sorting the pieces, I ask Amir if he plays an instrument. He replies, saying, 'I don't do music because I'm Muslim', and goes on to tell me that his parents have told him that music is *haram*. On other occasions during research activities, Amir also brings up this subject and tells me that he doesn't listen to music as it is *haram*.

However, at the end of March, as the school were auditioning for their 'Sunnyside's Got Talent' contest, Amir shows an interest in music, and in particular, the boy band JLS.

> After a few performances from other children, Amir whispers to me that he wants to dance to JLS. Mustafe, Daud and some other boys are planning on doing a breakdancing act (to a JLS song) and Amir asks if he can join in. He stands up and begins to dance with the other boys. As they are doing this, Aziza, the bilingual assistant, says to me that it is strange to see Amir dancing like this 'as his family are very strict. No TV, no music [at home] but he can still do it.' After this audition session, the children get to choose an activity before home time. Amir comes up to me and says 'I like JLS. I have two favourite songs.' He then tells me what they are but, as I'm not familiar with the band, the names of the songs don't mean anything to me. 'Do you listen to them at home?' I ask him. He replies saying that he doesn't, and I reflect on Aziza's earlier comments. As we are chatting, Daud and Mubarak come up to us and all three boys go to the role play area together. After a short while they come out again, pick up some beads from the maths area, thread them onto a shoelace and ask me to tie them into 'necklaces' for them, telling me that JLS wear them. As I'm helping them make their chains, Mubarak says to me 'We are going to practice in there' and points to the role play corner. 'JLS?' I ask. 'Yes', confirms Amir. All three boys go to the role play area and start to practice their breakdancing. After a few more minutes they all come out again with Daud

> saying, 'Let's not practice now.' As they pass me Mubarak tells me, 'We'll practice at home.' As Amir walks past he doesn't say anything but looks disappointed at Mubarak's suggestion.

Despite telling me on more than one occasion that music is *haram*, Amir seems to also be in conflict over this assessment. While he isn't allowed to listen to music at home, he re-enacts musical songs at school as he negotiates his peer interactions. Interestingly, when creating his PAT, Amir's favourite activity station was the listening area where he told me that he liked to listen on his own, or with one friend, to lots of different songs. Amir's tendency to incorporate music into his life at school does not (from other observations and research conversations) appear to stem from a desire to rebel against his parents and their religious values, but rather from a desire to try and fit in with his peers. His actions could also stem from a genuine love of music. Irrespective of the reasoning behind his actions, Amir appears to be in conflict about the rules relating to music that he feels he should adhere to. However, as Russell (2011) advocates, resistance is multifaceted and dynamic allowing individuals, such as Amir, to manipulate social structures to achieve their own aims. What is unclear, though, from these examples is whether Amir's resistance, borrowing Russell's terminology, is intentional or unintentional.

Operationalising gendered identities at Sunnyside

As well as discussing ethnic and religious identities amongst themselves, children also regularly discussed their gendered identities and reinforced wider gender stereotypes, saying things like, 'Boys don't do that' or 'That's a girls' colour.' During these conversations, some children heed the statement reminding them of the dominant discourses around gender, similar to Davies' (2003) and Brooker's (2006) findings. While others reject the stereotype and show the other children that boys or girls can in reality 'do that'. In doing so, they challenge and re-work the notion of gender roles resisting social structures as the young people in Russell's study do.

> During a free choice session in early February, I am sitting with Deka and Annakiya at the writing table. They are both drawing a picture of a flower. Umar comes over and sits down with us. He reaches for a piece of paper and looks over at Deka's drawing. 'I'm making a flower', he tells us to which Deka replies, 'But you're a boy.' Umar doesn't respond to this but begins to draw his flower, appearing to be unperturbed by Deka's comment and the underlying social discourse that says

> that boys can't like flowers. After a few minutes, Amir comes over and asks if he can join us. I tell him that he can, and pass him a piece of paper. As he sits down Annakiya tells him, 'You have to draw a flower'. He turns his nose up at this, and tells me that 'boys can't draw flowers'. I tell him that he can stay and draw whatever he likes. He, however, decides to go and play elsewhere. As he leaves, Umar looks up from his drawing and says, 'But boys can draw flowers. Look!' as he shows us all his drawing.

At other times, children also used peer conversations to negotiate their gendered identities and justify to others in the class why they could do an activity that was stereotypically thought of as inappropriate for their gender.

> In late November, I am sitting at the creative table with Aniso and Jabir. Jabir asks me to help him 'do sticking', i.e. cut pieces of sellotape for him. Aafia comes over and shows me the picture of Sunnyside on the logo on her jersey. I look at the picture and read out the school motto under the picture before asking her, 'Do you like school?' 'Yes' she replies 'and club', referring to the after school club that she regularly attends. 'What do you do at club?' I ask her. 'Snack' she replies 'and wash our hands.' 'What do you do after snack?' I prompt. 'Play football and basketball', she tells me. 'Do you like football?' I respond. She nods enthusiastically in reply. Aniso then asks Aafia, 'Is it girls' football?' 'Yes, not boys', replies Aafia, 'with a pink ball.' 'Is it girls' basketball?' further enquires Aniso. 'Yes', Aafia replies, and tells her that only girls are allowed to play.

Davies' work also shows that, for some children, rejecting socially accepted gender roles by actively creating a new discourse around a specific activity, such as Aafia's notion of girls' football, is an important aspect of some children's peer interactions.

As the year progressed and the all-female classroom staff began to organise and play games of football during Golden Time,[9] some of the other girls in the class (Aafia had returned to North Africa at this point) also began to play and enjoy this activity, talking more about 'girl's football' (despite this being a mixed activity) as the year progressed. They could also be heard reasoning with their friends about why girls could like to play the game and began to represent girls

9. Golden Time was introduced about half way through the year on Friday afternoons. During this slot children were able to choose a special activity, that was not normally on offer, as a reward for 'being good'. While footballs were regularly available during free choice activities children had to play with them in a smaller area than the area that was made available during Golden Time.

playing football in their pictures and mark makings. Before this, the girls' pictures and mark makings were dominated by fairies and princesses.

Figure 5.3: Nasra's picture of a girl playing football

Nasra became particularly interested in doing this and regularly chose to play football during a Friday afternoon. As the boys were not keen to let the girls play football at other times during the week and monopolised the footballs during free choice activities, it is not clear if the girls would have also chosen to play football outside of Golden Time. As Brooker (2006) found in her work, the choice element and democratic nature of continuous provision (i.e. free choice activities) can consequently stifle as well as facilitate children's operationalisation of their identities and can unwittingly perpetuate discourses of discrimination.

Gendered identities were also acted out when children engaged in imaginative play. Many forms of imaginative play at Sunnyside were segregated activities, such as the girls' dens where they 'play Eid parties' and 'no boys are allowed' or 'the boys' sleepovers' under the climbing frame, where no girls are allowed. Interestingly, Annakiya as a non-Muslim is allowed to the girls' Eid parties, as a special guest, while the Muslim boys aren't. At times I also, as a non-Muslim honoured guest, am invited to these parties 'to learn about Eid.' When outside, the children's play becomes more gender segregated than when they are in the classroom. Although at times boys and girls do play together outside, they more often than not take on stereotypical roles within these games. As Thorne (1993) highlights, this type of play should not be viewed as mixed gender play but as a way of perpetuating gendered stereotypes as children take on socially accepted gender roles.

Outside, Deka likes to be in charge of the girls' games and can often be heard instructing the other girls on how to build their den, or undertaking the role of 'being the mum' in the home corner where she likes to boss the other children around. On one occasion as I am watching her play with Kalila she tells me, 'mums always tell children what to do.' During the first term, play in the home corner is a largely female affair but when the January starters arrive, Deka starts to also play with Callum. The two children can at times be seen on their own while the other *older girls* continue to play together. However, Deka soon begins to incorporate Callum in the larger role play games that she organises, with Callum being instructed to take on the role of dad. While Deka's games often start in the home corner or the den, they are not restricted to these areas, as Deka regularly takes 'her children' out to the shopping centre, McDonalds, and also occasionally to the local secondary school or 'Somali mosque'. As they are going to visit these places, Deka walks round the playground with the other children in tow, loudly telling them off if they generally 'misbehave'. *The older girls* happily take on the roles of naughty children and, while stifling their giggles, play up to Deka's definition of misbehaving where they are then threatened with being sent home. After making their way round the playground, this troop of children normally end up at the climbing frame, where Deka declares to the other children who are there that she is 'the mum'—implying that they can join the game in line with her rules or leave, which most do. Deka and her 'family' then sit on top of the climbing frame which represents the shopping centre or McDonalds until Deka decides it is time to move on. Throughout, Callum effectively plays the role of a downtrodden husband, responding when called upon to do so, but for the most part, taking a back seat, not helping out with household chores, unless he is coerced into doing them, preferring instead to spend the game laughing at Deka's antics.

Davies' (2003) and MacNaughton and Smith's (2008) findings similarly reveal that when boys play families they, like Callum, for the most part play traditional male roles of the father. The boys in their studies also disclosed that they consider the girls to be in charge of these games.

The other outside activities that regularly involved both girls and boys were chasing games. These games were framed in different ways, i.e. of police chasing robbers, monsters chasing children or baddies chasing goodies, but always involve some boys—most frequently Amir and Mubarak—chasing *the older girls*. As seen in Chapter 3, Annakiya more often than not helps the boys chase the girls rather than being one of the children being chased. While making her

PAT, Annakiya explains this role by saying to me that she likes chasing but also asks me not to talk about this with the other children, as she knows that girls normally don not chase but should really like to be chased by boys. Kareem also likes to be involved in these games, but like Annakiya, chooses not to take on a typical gender role and instead likes to run around with the girls being chased. As Thorne (1993) and Corsaro et al. (2003) previously discovered, chasing games, where boys predominantly take on the role of chaser, reinforce gender segregated boundaries that perpetuate stereotypical gendered roles and dominant social structures. Thorne (1993) terms this type of play, where boys and girls play in oppositional ways, as 'borderwork' as the games allow children to explore stereotypical gender roles within a structured framework. As MacNaughton and Smith (ibid.: 168) highlight, children's actions consequently 'shape a gender politics in which 'being normal' and 'doing gender right' [i]s relational ... because being a girl is related to and defined by girls' relationships with boys; and vice versa.' In this way identity can be conceptualised as *performative, situated and dialectical*. The majority of children at Sunnyside spent a lot of time and energy in maintaining these relational gender 'borders' by taking on traditional roles in the class' games and admonishing other children who did not conform to these rules. However, some children, such as Annakiya and Kareem, habitually reject the traditional gender roles that their peers try to ascribe to them when taking part in these chasing games. Additionally, both are conscious of this rejection and articulate to me why they don't want to play in what the other children term as 'the proper way.' Both, however, where possible, actively avoid explaining to their peers why they do not follow the class' rules in these games.

In other aspects of his imaginative play, Kareem also rejects stereotypical gender roles and is the only boy in the class who regularly plays with dolls and cooks and cleans in the home corner. When *the older girls* are not dominating the home corner in the outside play area and no bikes or footballs are free—these are Kareem's preferred outdoor activities—Kareem is often found in the home corner with some of the quieter Arabic-speaking girls. In these games, Kareem takes on the role of husband and father, but unlike Callum's laid back (or in Deka's words 'lazy') downtrodden husband act, Kareem is actively involved in caring for the babies—putting them to sleep and feeding them—as well as cooking and cleaning. While going about these activities, the children mostly speak to each other in Arabic, with the odd English phrase thrown in. Language forms an important part of Kareem's patterns of interaction (Chapter 6). It is also interesting to note though that when one of the more bossy Arabic-speaking girls, such as Saida or Abia, tries to join in these games, Kareem more often than not leaves the game to go and play elsewhere. Kareem's quiet and reserved identity performance at school appears to be an important factor in his peer relationships.

Overall, the home corner in the outdoor play area tends to be used by girls and, where boys are involved, they more often than not take on the role of husband and/or father. At times, though, some of the boys also pretend to be girls. Barak, Ferran and Umar, occasionally act in this way and can be found walking around with 'a ladies handbag', laughingly telling the other children 'I'm a lady', or dressing up in girl's clothing from the home corner 'pretending to be girls.' Even when the other children—both girls and boys—question this behaviour, the boys continue with their games, with Ferran explaining to me 'But we like to pretend to be girls.' Interestingly these same boys can also at times be heard commenting on their peers' non-traditional gendered practices, reinforcing dominant stereotypes saying things like 'dancing is for girls and for ladies' and 'boys don't do that.' In a similar way to how Goffman (1959) conceptualises the performative nature of identity, these boys appear to actively choose which social arenas to challenge dominant discourses of gender in. The extent to which these choices are scripted by wider social structures is not, however, clear.

Contrastingly, Kareem does not reinforce these gendered stereotypes either in relation to his own or to his peers' play. Alternatively, while engaging in a traditional female activity he verbally asserts his own gendered identity, i.e. as a boy, while also commenting that it is OK for a boy to engage in the activity under question. In these encounters these boys enact *identity's performative, situated and dialectical nature* in their peer interactions.

While four boys Kareem, Barak, Ferran and Umar can at times be seen crossing traditional gendered boundaries in their imaginative play, Annakiya is the only girl in the class to do this. This echoes a theme found in both Brown's (2003) and Davies' (2003) studies that showed more boys than girls crossing these boundaries.

As has been discussed earlier in this Chapter, Brooker (2006) contends that current early childhood pedagogies in the UK and elsewhere, which emphasise the importance of continuous provision, or free choice activities, can (unwittingly) perpetuate wider social stereotypes. As Brooker highlights, the pedagogies themselves are not to blame, but rather practitioners for the most part have not created opportunities for children to explore their preferences for certain activities or the underlying social discourses that can influence these choices. While the role play corner in the outdoor play area at Sunnyside was a home corner for the duration of the year, the role play area inside the classroom was transformed each half term into a new imagined place, including a café, garden centre, forest and Space Station. This, unlike its counterpart in the outdoor play area, was regularly used by both boys and girls. By giving children the opportunity to explore role play in a number of different contexts and by encouraging children to choose to explore these areas in counter stereotypical ways (e.g. Kareem's tendency to play with dolls), staff at Sunnyside began to give children opportunities to explore traditional and non-traditional gender roles as well as related underlying social discourses. Davies, like Brooker, also highlights the importance of early years education settings creating space for children to explore play in non-stereotypical ways. Davies argues that children need to be given the opportunity to explore alternative discourses that allow them to position themselves in multiple ways in respect to their gendered identities. The ways in which children at Sunnyside challenge dominant discourses will be explored further in the next Chapter alongside the ways in which staff at Sunnyside encourage children to unlearn discrimination while at the same time holding onto paradoxical views of children's competence and development.

Summarising children's conceptions of being different

While creating her PAT (in June) Nasra further reveals how *the older girls* in the class discuss wider social discourses amongst themselves and reinforce these structural inequalities in their peer interactions.

> Looking at the playdough picture (that Fariido and Fazia discussed above, p. 110), she asks me who the children in the picture are. I tell her that I think that Fariido and Fazia were there when I took the picture. She tells me though that she thinks that it is Deka and Fazia, before explaining that she and the other *older girls* often compare their skin colours and the colour and texture of their hair, confiding in me that the girls all think that 'it is better to be the lightest'. She then goes on to explain that they all also rank themselves based on who has the darkest and lightest skin tones, with the girl with the lightest skin tones being afforded the highest social status and the girl with the darkest skin the lowest status. Nasra identifies Fazia as having the lightest skin colour and Deka as having the darkest by saying 'Outside in the water [area], we said, who's the lightest? Who's the darkest? And we said Deka's the darkest ... then Fariido's a browny and then ... Fariido and Aniso and Annakiya and Deka are the same skin. And we said me and Fazia are together.'

> 'So you have a different skin colour?' I ask. 'Yeah' Nasra replies 'My skin's lighter like Fazia's ... [but] do you know, we're all friends.'

It is interesting to note here that while Nasra clearly subscribes to her father's national identity of 'being Somali' (Chapter 4) that she also clearly subscribes to her mother's ethnic identity of 'being white' and positions herself, based on her ethnicity, in a place of high social status in relation to the other girls in the class.

This conversation effectively underlines a recurrent theme in this chapter—that children are aware of social abstractions of difference, discourses of discrimination and hierarchies of difference and regularly discuss these aspects amongst themselves. In addition, children actively use these structures to reinforce, challenge and contest their own identities within their peer conversations and games.

Within the context of *the older girls'* patterns of interactions, discourses such as these can be often heard when the girls are out of earshot of school staff. These peer conversations, more often than not, follow a similar pattern to my conversation with Nasra above, where the girls compare their skin colours and re-affirm their social status within the hierarchy before reassuring each other that they are all still friends. As there were no white British girls in the class it is not clear how they would fit into *the older girls'* hierarchy.

In the next chapter, I will explore how some girls respond to their ascribed status within this hierarchy and the way that this influences their patterns of interaction. I will also explore in more detail how each of my focus children negotiate their peer interactions both at and outside school.

Chapter 6

Being friends: Uncovering children's patterns of interaction at and outside school

'Identity is at the centre of any form of social interaction, and social interactions help us to make sense of how people may behave and relate to each other within communities' (Marranci, 2008: 94).

Language, identity and patterns of interaction

Language and identity are closely intertwined in children's patterns of interaction at Sunnyside. For some children language has a purely functional value while for others it is a symbolic marker of identity. Similarly, for some children their minority language holds valuable linguistic capital while for others their maternal tongue is viewed as being something to shun.

As discussed in Chapter 5, Aafia, Fazia, Mustafe, Amir and Mubarak, were all drawing pictures at the writing table during a free choice session when Aafia asks the other children if they pray. As this conversation comes to a close, the children all return to their drawings. Mustafe starts to talk to Aafia about his picture but interestingly, while they continue their conversation (mostly) in English, they also intermingle this with some Arabic words and phrases. Fariido—a bilingual Somali English speaker—who is playing at the sand pit, shouts across to them 'Don't say that!' Fazia, an Arabic speaker who is sitting next to Aafia, responds to Fariido 'It's Arabic. It's OK.' Mubarak—who is a Somali English speaker like Fariido—also looks over to her and reassures her that it is OK for the others to speak in Arabic. Fariido looks unconvinced but turns back to the sandpit. As we will see in more detail below for Fariido language holds symbolic value as a marker of identity.

A conversation over lunch with Aziza, one of the multilingual support workers, sheds some light on this encounter.

> We are sitting in the staff room with Mary and the nursery teacher. The nursery teacher and Aziza start to talk about multilingual signs in the classroom before the conversation moves on to discussing linguistic capital. Aziza highlights that in her experience Somali families at Sunnyside do not value their linguistic capital as much as their Arabic counterparts. Therefore, while the majority of Arabic-speaking families encourage their children to use Arabic outside school and take

> pride in their language and cultural heritage, many Somali families encourage their children to speak only English and adopt British cultural practices at the expense, in her opinion, of their Somali cultural background. Aziza primarily attributes this to the residency status that families have in the UK. Many Somali families arrive in the UK as refugees fleeing a civil war and are seeking to settle permanently in Europe putting the horrors of cultural conflict behind them.

Cummins (2001) similarly discovered that families seeking to permanently settle in a new country often sacrifice their own linguistic capital as they seek to encourage their children to integrate into their new environment. By introducing a Somali language programme at Sunnyside the school hopes to support Somali families in recognising and celebrating their linguistic capital. Following on from my conversation with a Somali community member, who highlighted the Somali Diaspora's distancing of themselves from tribal factions, it is also interesting to note that all of the children with Somali heritage who speak a non-European language speak Somali, i.e. the official national language of Somalia, rather than one of the country's many tribal dialects.

As has been described above, none of the children from Somali-speaking families subscribe to an identity connected with one of Somalia's tribal factions. However, many of the children whose families originate from Somalia describe themselves as having a composite identity, such as being 'Somali ... and a little bit English', that expresses the dialectical nature of identity as anchored and transient, as well as individual and collective. Contrastingly, the children whose families have originated from Arabic-speaking countries typically describe themselves as 'being Libyan' or 'being Moroccan' etc. strongly adhering to an identity that is connected to their country of origin but not associated with their current country of residence.

In contrast to the permanent UK residency status of many Somali families, the majority of Arabic-speaking families at Sunnyside are only in the UK on a temporary basis while one or both parents complete a postgraduate course. Most plan to return to North Africa where their children will complete their education in an Arabic-speaking environment. Aziza contends that the temporary nature of their residency in the UK is the key reason why most Arabic-speaking families encourage their children to continue using Arabic alongside learning English at school. During the conversation above, it's important to note that Aziza was also quick to point out that not all families conform to these generalisations.

The valuing of linguistic capital for different communities can help to explain Fariido's reaction to her classmates talking in Arabic. As Fariido comes from a community that values and promotes the use of the English language, it is interesting to note that she not only admonishes her Somali-speaking classmates if they speak in Somali—which she does on other occasions—but also her Arabic-speaking classmates for speaking in Arabic. It is also significant that Fariido is often asked, when a bilingual support worker is not available, to act as a translator between her mother—who has a limited knowledge of English—and classroom staff. Fariido is embarrassed to do this in front of her peers and more often than not becomes very dismissive of her mother, speaking to her in a derogatory tone. Orellana et al.'s (2003) research with Spanish speaking migrants in the USA reveals how this role of translator can impact on power relations within families as children are granted an inordinate position within decision-making processes both inside and outside the family. This position can then have an impact on the way that children view and relate to their parents and in some cases, as with Fariido, can result in children devaluing the cultural capital that their parents possess.

After the January starters joined the class, classroom dynamics around the use of language changed. While a number of the September starters, such as Aafia and Mustafe, regularly spoke to each other in Arabic, they did not do this to actively exclude their non-Arabic speaking peers as when asked—and often when unasked—they would translate their conversation into English. Both Aafia and Mustafe also acted throughout the course of the year as translators for Kareem, actively including him in activities and games with their non-Arabic speaking peers. In contrast, some Arabic-speaking January starters actively used their linguistic capital to exclude their non-Arabic speaking peers. Consequently 'being Arabic' for some children starts to take on a new meaning, with language taking on symbolic value as it forms an intrinsic part of an Arabic identity. This is juxtaposed against Amir's definition of 'being Arabic' as primarily representing his religious identity.

> In early May, I am sitting at the writing table with Deka. Saida joins us. As she does she says to Deka, 'Deka, you're not my friend.' Deka doesn't respond so I ask Saida why. She explains to me that Sadira and Abia are her friends as they speak Arabic saying, 'Sadira and I speak in Arabic and with Abia too.' I ask her if she is friends with anyone who doesn't speak Arabic. She shakes her head at this. Deka continues to draw, appearing to ignore our conversation.

In January, all three girls (i.e. Saida, Abia and Sadira) speak little English. However, as the year progresses, Saida and Abia—who are both confident and outspoken—quickly soak up and reproduce the English language. While the shyer Sadira appears to understand more and more English every week, she does not use this newly-acquired knowledge to converse with her peers. As Drury (2007) and Bligh (2011) highlight, learning through the so-called silent or non verbal period, like this, is a common strategy amongst young new language learners (YNLL). These two different approaches to learning a new language, however, begin to impact on this group of girls' patterns of interaction. As the year progresses, Sadira begins to play more and more with Kareem and Lina—who like Sadira are quiet and reserved while at school—and then predominantly starts to play on her own becoming reluctant to talk to any of her peers. In early July, she tells her mother that she does not want to come to school, confiding in her that Abia and Saida have been telling her that she cannot play with them as she needs to spend time with Mary so that she can learn to speak English. Her mother talks to Mary making her aware of the situation. With Mary's encouragement, Lina takes Sadira under her wing and she begins to flourish again, interacting once more with the quieter Arabic-speaking children.

These instances highlight some important points relating to children's use of language amongst their peers. Saida's (attempted) conversation with Deka shows how she actively excludes non-Arabic speakers from her circle of friends. Conversations with staff reported that other Arabic-speaking children in the school also actively use Arabic in this way to deliberately exclude their peers, even when they can communicate with them in English. However, as the year progresses, Saida and Abia come to value the linguistic capital that speaking English affords them and actively exclude Sadira from their activities and games as she, in their eyes, does not hold the same status as they do in relation to their newly gained linguistic capital. Notably, Saida and Abia continue to exclude non-Arabic speakers after they also begin to value their English language capital. Rather than substituting one language for another, they appear to value the capital that being bilingual affords them. These instances also highlight the challenges that monolingual school staff face in countering bullying in situations where children, borrowing Russell's (2011) terminology, overtly and intentionally resist school rules by using a language to exclude others from their games and activities.

Bakhtin's (1981) theory of dialogism can help to shed light on Saida's and Abia's behaviour. Bakhtin contends that language is socially and culturally situated and that language consequently transmits social and cultural meaning. Choice of language, both within and across languages, allows an individual to convey personal meaning relating to their specific social environment. Bakhtin terms this process 'ventriloquation.' Within this process, an individual uses language to actively manage the impression that others have of them as they perform their identity on Goffman's (1959) stage. While Bakhtin developed his ideas within a monolingual social environment, Drury (2007) argues that this theory is also relevant in bilingual and multilingual contexts. Her work shows how YNLL actively employ language within specific social contexts as they (re) negotiate their identity. In doing this Saida and Abia use language as a material marker of identity which can both grant group membership and exclude others depending on the immediate social environment.

Crul's (2007) research additionally shows that language can also have an impact on a child's patterns of interaction outside school as parents are more likely to encourage their children to be friends with children from families who they can easily communicate with. Conversations with staff at Sunnyside show that they believe that language is key in the social networks that parents form and consequently the circles that their children move in outside school. My observations at the start and end of the school day also reveal that language is an important factor in enabling or inhibiting how parents interact with each other. This as we will see below can influence children's patterns of interaction outside school. Firstly, though, we will explore children's patterns of interaction at school, starting with Kareem.

Kareem's patterns of interaction at school

In September, two boys from Libya, Kareem and Gamal, arrive at Sunnyside with very little English, a few weeks after the start of the school year. By the time they arrive a number of the children in the class, most of whom were at nursery together, have started to regularly interact with their peers. Neither Kareem nor Gamal join one of the classes' established friendship groups, i.e. *the gang*. Both new boys speak a modern form of Arabic, though Gamal's dialect is markedly different from the dialects that the other Arabic-speaking children at Sunnyside use. Kareem, on the other hand, can communicate easily with a number of his Arabic-speaking peers.

As discussed in Chapter 3 Arabic is often erroneously thought of as being one language for collective identity purposes where as in reality modern Arabic dialects are often 'mutually unintelligible'. Further, classical Arabic and modern

Arabic dialects are linguistically understood to be distinct and separate entities (Heath, 1997). These varieties of classical and modern Arabic dialects make communication across different forms of Arabic difficult. Therefore, while Chapter 4 highlighted that learning to speak Arabic at Koranic school is an important part of Amir's self-defined identity, his new language does not enable him to communicate (in a version of) Arabic with his school peers, such as Kareem and/or Gamal. Additionally not all of the 'Arabic-speaking' children in the class are able to communicate with each other. While for some children in the class Arabic holds symbolic value, for Kareem and Gamal language appears to be primarily functional.

These two new boys have contrasting identity performances at school. Kareem is quiet and reserved while Gamal is loud and boisterous. Their identity performances guide the ways that they both respond to the challenges of being in a predominantly English speaking environment. Kareem quietly soaks up the new language that he is exposed to. In formal learning situations he watches and listens to Mary, Suzie and his peers, and tries hard to follow the material that is being covered. When he understands, he looks animated and smiles proudly to himself when he is praised for getting an answer right. Gamal, on the other hand, finds it difficult to concentrate in formal learning situations and quickly gets bored. At the start of the year, he regularly falls asleep during the afternoon free choice session, seemingly exhausted by the morning's events. It is unclear though if Gamal's tiredness is symptomatic of his learning approach, the cognitive load of the morning's activity, not going to bed until late or another reason.

Both boys also have different approaches to their peer interactions. During free choice sessions, Kareem typically prefers to choose activities that require little spoken communication and races to the computer or the interactive white board when restricted to the indoor learning area. When he can not choose either of these activities, he typically hovers at a nearby activity station, such as the role play or construction areas, until a place at the computer or interactive white board becomes free. Kareem's peers soon notice that these are his favourite activity stations and at times tease him about always using them. During a piece of topic work (in February) when Kareem is asked to write about what makes him happy at school, he chooses to write about playing on the computer.

Outside, Kareem's preferred activity is riding a bike, again a predominantly solo activity, or playing football, a game in which the players, for the most part (though not always!), agree on the rules and is therefore an activity that requires little verbal communication. If these options are not available, Kareem will work at an activity station where he can easily play on his own, such as at the maths area, doing a jigsaw puzzle or with the musical instruments. After watching the other children's chasing games in the outdoor play area for a number of weeks, and ascertaining the rules of play, Kareem begins to also join in with these games. When he does interact directly with his peers, this is chiefly with other (reserved) Arabic-speaking children. At the start of the year, Kareem's verbal interactions are conducted for the most part in Arabic and as the year progresses these interactions become interspersed with more and more English words and phrases. Unlike Saida and Abia above, language does not appear to be a strong marker of identity for Kareem but rather is primarily a communication tool with functional value.

Kareem soon learns to follow classroom rules and quickly responds to non-verbal cues such as Mary's use of the tambourine to signal tidy up time. He gets frustrated when the other children do not follow these rules and even more frustrated when they do not respond to his admonishments. It is, however, unclear if this frustration stems from Kareem's identity performance, and his almost constant wish to be 'star of the day',[10] or from his limited use of English and frustration when the other children who do speak English do not follow instructions despite understanding what is being asked of them. Either way Kareem's frustration with his peers relates to the second stage of Stones' (2005) quadripartite cycle of structuration, *internal structures* within the agent, as Kareem's actions conform to his internal disposition to follow the classroom rules.

While language clearly plays an important role in Kareem's patterns of interaction, ethnic diversity is also a factor revealing how macro contexts can play a part in the way in which micro contexts unfold. At the start of the school year, Kareem at times refuses to play with a black child though as the year progresses he begins to interact with children from different ethnic backgrounds than himself. As Kareem, in all aspects of his learning, seeks to please and be praised by school staff, he responds well—at least on the surface—to school anti-discriminatory initiatives and begins to play with black children when language is not a key factor in the game. As none of the black children in the class speak Arabic, it is not possible to ascertain how Kareem would interact

10. Each day one child in the class is awarded the status of 'star of the day' based on the work that they have done and their behaviour throughout the course of the day. Amongst the children this is a highly coveted status as the day after they have received their award 'the star' gets to sit on a special chair during formal learning sessions while the other children sit on the carpet.

with a black child with whom he shares a common tongue. However, it is unclear from Kareem's interactions if he starts to play with his black peers in an attempt to please staff, in line with Goffman's (1959) notion of impression management, or if the school's anti-discriminatory initiatives have begun to change Kareem's attitude towards his ethnic minority peers.

Kinship ties and family networks also impact on Kareem's patterns of interaction at school. Kareem's younger brother is in the nursery class during afternoon sessions. When both the nursery and reception classes are in the outdoor play area at the same time, Kareem, more often than not, will choose to play with his own and Lina's brother who also attends the nursery. This is reminiscent of Lareau's (2003) work which suggests that kinship ties can have an impact on children's peer interactions at school.

Unlike Kareem, Gamal's outgoing and boisterous nature allows him to interact freely with other children in the class from his first days at Sunnyside. Gamal regularly and enthusiastically chats with his Arabic-speaking peers despite only being able to communicate in a few words across their Arabic dialects. He also expressively tries to communicate with his English-speaking peers. He starts to speak in his newly-acquired English much earlier in the year than Kareem does and uses this newly-acquired language to play with the other children. Where there is a communication barrier, rather than withdrawing from the situation as Kareem does, Gamal physically shows the other children what he wants them to do by taking the object that he has asked for or barging into their game. The more reserved children in the class quickly give in to Gamal and let him have his way while the other outgoing children regularly stand up to his demands, objecting to Gamal snatching their toys away from them. This often causes an argument to erupt.

While these two boys moved to the UK at a similar time and started Sunnyside during the same week, their strategies for dealing with their dialects mean that they have two very different approaches to interacting with their peers. For Kareem, his patterns of interaction are for the most part with other Arabic-speaking children who also share his reserved identity performance at school, while Gamal actively involves himself in a range of tasks irrespective of the languages that the other children who are involved in the activity can speak.

A few weeks after the two boys have arrived at school, Gamal's arguments with the other children start to escalate. He also starts to get frustrated when a staff member asks him to stop playing and do something else, such as tidy up or take part in a formal learning activity. He starts to feign ignorance and pays no attention to the requests of his peers and staff members.

> At the end of September, I am in the outdoor play area with Suzie watching the two boys play. I comment to Suzie that the two boys seem to be coping in different ways to their new school and language environment. Suzie agrees with me saying that 'they are two very different boys with polar personalities'. She contends that Kareem's quiet nature is an important factor in his patterns of interaction, as well as language. As we watch Gamal play, she tells me 'he understands more than he lets on' before commenting that an incident that I had observed earlier that day when Gamal refused to tidy up is becoming a frequent occurrence. She then explains that 'you can tell when he understands and when he doesn't. He has a look in his eyes.' This, she continues, is in stark contrast to Kareem who tries to please staff members and do what is expected of him.

On other occasions, Mary explains Gamal's behaviour in a similar way. As trained professionals, both Suzie and Mary interpret the paralinguistic features of Gamal's behaviour, borrowing Russell's (2011) terminology, as intentional and overt resistance to conform to classroom rules. In this way, Gamal actively tries to manage the impression that others have of him. Using Goffman's (1959) imagery Gamal, at times, promotes his Arabic-speaking identity to school staff and peers as he actively tries to hide his emerging bilingual identity as a way of justifying breaking the classroom rules.

Kareem's interactions with his peers typically follow the patterns in the examples below where he tries to take part in one of his favourite activities and either withdraws when he cannot communicate with the other children or plays enthusiastically with them when Arabic is the dominant language. Brooker's (2001) work shows that some children with little English in her study likewise withdrew from peer activities to watch other children play.

In late March, a morning session in the outdoors play area highlights the typical way that Kareem interacts with his peers.

> There are no bikes out and Barak has the only football. Kareem watches him play with it, goes over to him but soon moves under the covered area where he flits from one activity station to the next, not settling in one place. Every now and then he looks over to where Barak and Ferran are playing with the football. Mustafe, who has been doing a guided activity inside, comes out. Kareem runs over to him and then comes to me and tells me that now that Mustafe is here they would like

to play football, asking me if there are any more balls to play with. I look for one but can't find any. The previous week, the outdoor area was broken into and a lot of the foundation stage resources were stolen. I explain to him that I can't find any and suggest that they ask Barak if they can play with him. Kareem tells me that Barak has said that he can't play. I decide to intervene and go and ask Barak if Kareem and Mustafe can play with him. He agrees that they can. Barak then gives both Mustafe and Kareem a number of instructions in English in quick succession.

Despite speaking Arabic at home, Barak chooses to only speak English at school positioning himself amongst his peers by his choice of language or as Bakhtin (1981) describes the process of 'ventriloquation.'

Mustafe runs over to the goal while Kareem stands on the pitch next to Barak. They begin to play but Kareem has not understood what Barak wants him to do and cannot grasp the follow up instructions that Barak shouts to him. As Mustafe is in the goal at the other end of the playground, he is not close enough to easily translate Barak's ongoing instructions to Kareem. Kareem looking perplexed soon leaves, gets a book from the reading corner and sits next to me at the maths area. We read the book together.

When we go outside during the afternoon session, Kareem races to get to the football before the other children. He plays with his brother, Lina's brother and Mustafe. When they have finished he runs over to me smiling and tells me that his team scored three goals while Mustafe's team only scored two. He punches the air in celebration. As we are talking, Lina's brother picks up the football and asks Kareem and me to play catch with him. After a few minutes Harit comes over and asks to join in so I let him have my place and sit back down on the steps. Harit wants to change the rules of the game. Kareem, though, struggles to understand him and soon gets frustrated. He asks me to mediate. I slowly explain to him the changes that Harit wants to make. They continue to play but again, with more new changes to the rules, Kareem gets frustrated. As soon as a bike becomes free, Kareem leaves the game and runs to get it before another child does. He rides round the playground on his bike smiling at me as he passes.

A little while later, Mustafe and Mansur get the football back after some of the other boys have finished playing their game. Mustafe asks Kareem and his brother, in Arabic, to play with them. All four of these boys shout instructions to each other in Arabic. Kareem and his brother form a team as do Mustafe and Mansur. Mustafe's team starts off with the ball and head towards the goal where Kareem is

> the goalkeeper. They score a goal and all of the boys run to the middle of the pitch. Kareem and his brother now kick off and head towards the goal where Mustafe is the goalkeeper. Each team takes it in turns to score a goal before swapping over. Throughout the game, Kareem enthusiastically calls to the other boys in Arabic.

Being able to communicate effectively with his peers is a key dimension of Kareem's patterns of interaction. When language is a barrier Kareem often becomes frustrated and withdraws from the game or activity to play on his own or with other Arabic-speaking children. Language for Kareem, therefore embodies an *external structure*, as defined by Stones, which stipulates his interactions with his peers. Structural factors relating to language appear to be dominant for Kareem and in most situations, render the efficacy of his social agency to interact with his peers in non-verbal ways as mute.

Unlike the other focus children whose patterns of interaction are predominantly gender segregated, Kareem regularly plays with both girls and boys (almost all of whom speak Arabic), and is the only male focus child who openly states that he likes (to play with) girls. In contrast to Kareem's apparent powerlessness to challenge the linguistic structures that influence his patterns of interaction, he is as Stones describes an *active agent* in challenging dominant structural discourses relating to gender. In this way Kareem regularly challenges his peers' stereotypes of what they consider to be acceptable behaviour for a boy as he engages in activities that are thought of as being part of the girl's domain, such as doing household chores and taking care of the baby. Kareem's mother was pregnant and gave birth to a baby girl during the course of the school year. As the due date looms on the horizon, Kareem starts to play more and more with the dolls at school, continuing to do so after his sister was born. During research activities, he excitedly talks about his sister, telling me that he likes to help his mother look after her.

While he interacts with Mustafe and Aafia—who act as his peer translators—for extended periods of time on a daily basis, he does not regularly interact with any other children in the class. Alternatively, his patterns of interaction tend to be relatively fluid where he interacts sporadically with a number of Arabic-speaking white children who, for the most part, share his reserved identity performance at school. When playing football with Mustafe, he at times plays with *the gang*. In their successful interactions, Mustafe acts as a mediator and translator, facilitating the game as Kareem appears to be unable to negotiate on his own with this group of boys. During the afternoons, when the nursery children are also in the outdoor area, Kareem almost always plays with his own and Lina's brother. If the nursery children arrive when reception are already outside, Kareem more often than not will drop the activity that he is doing to run over and greet these two younger boys. All three will then start a new activity together. Below we discuss how Kareem's family spends a lot of time with Lina's family outside school. Similarly to the children in Lareau's (2003) study, Kareem's collective family identity and associated family practices influence his patterns of interaction at, as well as outside, school.

In summary, language (on a functional level), ethnic diversity and kinship ties all influence how Kareem interacts with his school peers. Macro structures relating to social norms in Kareem's home country of Libya also seep into the ways in which he does this. When he is unable to verbally communicate with his peers Kareem withdraws from the group activity to play on his own.

The gang's patterns of interaction at school

The other two male focus children, Amir and Daud, unlike Kareem, have very fixed friendships at school. They, with Mubarak, are the core members of *the gang*. As has been previously mentioned *the gang* had strong patterns of interaction even at the start of the school year. All three original members of *the gang*—Amir, Daud and Mubarak—were at nursery together and reportedly interacted with each other regularly during this time. In the first term, these three boys regularly choose to play together as a group occasionally involving one of the other boys such as Barak, Ferran or Jabir, in their activities. The two key exceptions to this are in the outdoor play area when they play football with Mustafe and Kareem or chase *the older girls*. After the Christmas break, the arrival of the January starters begins to change the dynamics of this group of boys.

The two final members of *the gang*, Barak and Ferran, were also at nursery with the other boys. At the start of the year, they sometimes interact with *the gang* but also play regularly together and with Jabir. After Christmas, when the January starters arrive, they both begin to form closer ties with *the gang* and, by the February half term, the girls in the class also refer to them when they discuss this group of boys. In contrast, Jabir becomes friendly with some of the new, younger children in the class. As Barak and Ferran start to regularly interact with Amir, Daud and Mubarak and join in their collective games, the three original gang members create an inner gang membership for themselves, whilst also giving Barak and Ferran an outer membership of the group. They, for example, have secrets that they only share between themselves and more often than not create the rules for their collective games. Barak and Ferran accept this and seem proud to be included in *the gang's* activities, while at the same time retaining close ties, mirroring the inner circle's secret telling by confiding in each other. After the Easter break, Ferran's younger brother starts coming to nursery in the mornings. When the Reception class is in the outdoor play area with the nursery children, Ferran and Barak regularly play with Ferran's brother, again changing the dynamics of *the gang's* patterns of interaction. Kinship ties, as for Kareem (above) and Deka (below), consequently impact on the class' internal peer interactions.

At the start of the school day the inner gang members almost always look pleased to see each other. As they arrive at school, they seek each other out and share a story, a book or a toy that they have brought to school with them. They also habitually move their name cards so that they can sit near each other. Where possible these three boys play together as a collective group. When one of the boys is required to do a guided activity with a member of staff, he often keeps half an eye on the other boys while doing this and, as soon as he is free to choose, makes a bee-line for the others. If only one of the three boys is able to choose, he more often than not wanders aimlessly round the learning area, flitting from one activity station to another without settling to any given task, until his 'best friends' return.

Throughout the school day at every opportunity they get, these boys can be found playing together. At times this requires the boys all to be at the same activity station, for example when they are all making model cars. However, on other occasions the boys may be working at different areas of the classroom while still all playing together in what Corsaro et al. (2003: 290) term 'interlaced collective patterns of interaction' where children's role play incorporates complex and at times apparently disparate activities within a collective game. When the boys' games require a number of different components, the boys will decide amongst themselves who will prepare the objects they are going to play with. For example, in late November, when being ninjas, the boys all go to the creative area and make 'ninja hats' (i.e. headbands).

> As I am sitting at the creative table, they ask me to help them measure their heads and stick the ends of their headbands together before they go their separate ways. Amir stays at the creative table and makes some 'ninja sticks', Mubarak goes to the maths area and makes sashes out of the chain link pieces while Daud reorganises the furniture in the role play area, turning it into the ninjas' secret meeting place.

> While at first glance it may appear to the casual observer that the three boys are engaging in separate activities, when the boys themselves are asked, they clearly articulate how what they are doing relates to the other gang members' actions. Once the preparations are complete, the boys all congregate in the role play area to enact their game.

While the current example occurred in one free choice session, at times the boys are not able to complete their preparations in one session but will store the items that they have been making, hiding them behind a piece of furniture or in a drawer, and regroup when they are next given the opportunity to do so, to either continue their preparations or enact their game.

All three inner members of *the gang* were born in England and regularly talk among themselves, and with me, about aspects of popular global culture that they like to engage with, for example the games that they like to play on their Playstations and the TV programmes and films (i.e. about ninjas) that they like to watch at home. All three boys actively incorporate aspects of their religious identities into their role play at school and in doing so, at times, articulate which aspects of popular culture they consider to be *haram*. The ways in which these boys negotiate 'being Muslim' and growing up in a Western culture form an active part of their identity (re)negotiation at Sunnyside. Identity for these boys is operationalised as *performative, situated and dialectical*. Within the boys' conversations and actions, identity is revealed as a process of interaction where aspects of identity are transient. Within this, the boys negotiate amongst themselves how they can incorporate features of popular culture into other aspects of their identity. However, certain criteria are non-negotiable as the boys also adhere to relatively fixed notions of what is *haram*. By using my newly coined term *relative fixity* (Chapter 3 p. 66), it is possible to theorise how these boys conceptualise and operationalise their identities as and as a collective group.

The three boys also regularly get into trouble together when one of their games becomes 'too' boisterous or they play out with the classroom rules. When asked to explain their actions, the boys' normal excuse is 'But Daud and Mubarak did it' or 'But Amir and Daud were doing it' and so on. Mary and Suzie both admonish these boys for this type of behaviour, telling them that they 'don't have to do everything that the others do.' Occasionally, *the gang's* disputes with some of the other older boys in the class spill over into fights where Amir and Mubarak will unite against one or more of the other boys. While these fights are not common place, when they do occur Amir and Mubarak always back each other up. Typically Daud takes a more passive role in these encounters though, if specifically called upon by Amir or Mubarak, also joins in to defend his friends. *The gang* have formed a relatively fixed friendship group, where their collective identity is defined both by their relationships to each other within the group and their relationships with their peers who are outside the group.

The gang members almost never argue amongst themselves though occasionally their role playing becomes too rough for one of them, for example when they are playing cops and robbers and put each other in gaol, or when they are taxis stuck in traffic and start to get road rage when playing on the bikes in the outdoor play area. If this 'roughness' results in one of the boys getting hurt, this can lead to an argument, with one of the boys walking off, shouting 'I'm not friends with you!' When this happens, the other gang members are quick to respond and reaffirm their group's friendship ties. Unless someone's injuries require First Aid, *the gang* do not actively involve an adult in these interactions but swiftly resolve the argument on their own. When *the gang* are playing with limited resources, they collectively work out a strategy for sharing them and incorporate this into their role play. For example, in early January, there is only one bike free in the outdoor play area. The boys decide to play cops and robbers where the cop is on the bike chasing the robbers round the playground. During the course of the game they each take a turn being the cop on the bike. While *the gang* effectively share resources amongst themselves, they are reluctant to let another child in the class be part of these negotiations.

Although Daud is an active member of *the gang* he also likes to spend time with adults—including myself—and regularly tries to engage the attention of one of the staff members when Amir and Mubarak are doing a guided activity. This is in contrast to the other boys who will play with another of their peers, while flitting from one activity station to the next, when their 'best friends' are otherwise detained. Daud can also at times be found wandering round the learning area with his hands in his pockets, deep in thought. When asked what he is thinking about, he will reply saying that he is thinking about how something works, such as how a rocket can get to the moon or why we can see through glass. In the outdoor play area, Daud often slowly cycles round on a bike watching the other children play, thinking, and sharing with me, similar weighty thoughts.

Whilst these boys don't talk as often as *the older girls* about 'being friends', they do at times comment on their friendships to their peers and to me.

> In January, we are putting our jackets on to go to the outdoor play area when Amir says to me, 'I had a dream about Daud.' 'What happened?' I ask. 'We were hugging.' Daud, who is standing behind him chips in, 'we are friends.' I smile at this and help some of the other children zip up their jackets. As we are lining up, I look to the back of the line where Amir and Daud are standing arm in arm. 'Look!' Amir calls over to me. As I do, Daud shouts to me, 'we are friends.' Amir then puts his left hand on his hip and continues, 'and Mubarak here', before also linking arms with Mubarak. All three boys grin at me as they march outside arm in arm.

In early May, I begin to observe Daud and Callum sometimes playing on their own together. This new friendship begins to change the dynamics of *the gang* as well as prompting Amir to assert that 'being Muslim' is a requirement for gang membership as a way of excluding Callum from *the gang's* activities. While Daud continues to regularly play with *the gang*, he also starts to interact more and more with Callum. Notably, at times Daud will leave a game that *the gang* are involved in to do something else with Callum. Callum, however, never joins in *the gang's* games though very sporadically Daud will be drafted in to be a son in Deka's family games, where he dutifully plays his role alongside Callum. While working with Amir and Daud—they elected to do this simultaneously—on their PATs in late June, Daud tells me 'Callum is my new best friend.' Amir looks up from his drawing as Daud says this and retorts, 'He's *haram*', before going on to tell Daud that he can't be friends with Callum. Daud tells Amir that he and Callum both like to do things together and are therefore friends. Amir doesn't comment on this but tells me that he isn't friends with Callum. It is not possible to tell from this conversation if Amir's objection to Callum purely stems from Callum not 'being Muslim' or if Amir also reacts in this way as he is upset that Daud has called him his 'new best friend', the status that Amir and Mubarak previously jointly held. It is also important to note here that Amir at times does interact with Callum, for example when he helps Callum to write a letter to his father. In this instance, Amir has a skill that Callum does not yet possess, i.e. being able to form his letters and phonetically spell words, and relishes the roll of scribing for the other children. In this example, Amir treats Callum in the same way as his Muslim peers.

At other points in the year, the inner gang members do clearly tell me that you have to be Muslim to be in *the gang*. As seen in Chapter 5, 'being Muslim' was important for these three boys as it unites them in a special brotherhood, forging their fictive kinship ties. Interestingly, the boys often tell me this as they are asking me to play with them negotiating amongst themselves my entry into their game. In doing this they afford me a liminal position in their activity making it clear to me that I do not meet their membership requirements on three accounts; of 'being a girl', a non-muslim and an adult. As Turner (1967) advocates, in his broadening interpretation of van Gennep's (1908) concept of liminality, the boys temporarily suspend the social rules pertaining to gang membership while requiring me to temporarily dissolve aspects of my identity, as a girl, non-Muslim and an adult—that would normally be considered as taboo—thereby allowing me to access their game. In this way the boys' *active agency*, to bend their own rules (i.e. *internal structures*), comes to the fore as we collaboratively negotiate my participation in their activity.

For these children, their religious identities coupled with their gendered identities, are instrumental in defining what it means to be a member of *the gang*. 'Being Muslim' and 'being a boy' are important and intersecting aspects of their identities that they regularly talk about. Research by both Connolly (1994) and MacNaughton (1996) show a similar pattern in children's intersecting identities and illustrates how it becomes an important factor in interactional behaviours. The boys' identity of being a member of *the gang* is also important to them, with the fictive kinship status that gang membership affords. This impacts on how they interact with each other and their classroom peers. For Amir, *the gang* and his 'best friends' are influential in his actions at school. Daud, however, at times enthusiastically throws himself into *the gang's* activities and clearly articulates that the other gang members are important to him—while at other times he removes himself from *the gang's* games to be by himself, voluntarily interacting with an adult, or as the year progresses to play with Callum. If Callum had been granted gang membership, Daud most likely would have not distanced himself so frequently from *the gang's* activities.

In summary, *the gang* have very fixed friendships, though contact with younger siblings in the nursery did have an impact on group dynamics. 'Being a boy' and 'being Muslim' is essential for gang membership with the boys creating *fictive kinship* ties as 'Muslim brothers' between themselves and actively excluding other children who do not fit their membership criteria.

The older girls' patterns of interaction at school

The three female focus children, Nasra, Deka and Annakiya, are likewise part of a fairly fixed group of friends, who call themselves *the older girls*. Unlike *the gang*, *the older girls* do not often play as a collective group but rather two or three of these girls will do an activity together while another two or three girls will do another separate activity together. Within this group, however, Nasra and Fariido do not interact with each other to the same level as with the other girls. During the course of a free choice session, each of these seven girls will repeatedly change the small group of older girls who they are playing with. Goffman's (1963) imagery of the 'cocktail party', where small groups of party goers—who normally know each other—may be partially engaged in a number of different conversations or activities simultaneously, is paralleled in *the older girls* interactions. While Goffman's work focused exclusively on adult interactions deliberately excluding children as 'nonpersons', Corsaro's (1979) work with young children reveals that they too engage in a similar practice. *The older girls* at Sunnyside engaged in a similar process of peer interaction.

This 'cocktail party' behaviour is in contrast to *the gang* who, where possible, will all play together. At times, however, when *the older girls* are outside, they will all engage in a collective role-play game. More often than not, these games are initiated and developed by Deka, with the other girls being assigned different roles to play. The two games that Deka repeatedly creates are Eid Parties and Muslim Families, where she plays the role of either the party's hostess or 'being the mum'. Interestingly, as has been mentioned in Chapter 5, Annakiya as a non-Muslim is allowed to the girl's Eid parties while the Muslim boys are not, with the girls specifically stating that 'dads, brothers and boys can't come'. These role plays appear to serve a similar function to the role play games that the girls in Connolly's (1998) study engage in. Connolly interprets these games as being primarily associated with the exploration of 'being a girl' within the context of heterosexual relationships. Similarly *the older girls* in their games discuss and act out 'being a girl' in relation, and at times as a direct reaction, to their perceptions of binary opposing male identities. Even though boys are not allowed to the girls' Eid parties, oppositional, antithetical gendered identities and normalised heterosexual relationships between family members are played out in these situations.

After the January starters arrive, Deka soon becomes friends with Callum and coerces him to be the father in the girls' family games. Callum is the only boy who is regularly included in these role-plays. Callum, like many boys in other studies (e.g. Davies, 2003), only engages in the girls' games on their terms, taking on the gendered role that he has been ascribed. The girls' gendered identities form a key part of their patterns of interaction with the boys in the class. The only other instances that this group of girls collectively interacts with the boys is within the context of chasing games, where most children take on gender segregated roles, maintaining a boundary between the two genders (Chapters 3 and 5). As Thorne's (1993) research shows, this kind of 'borderwork' is common in young children's chasing games and is often used by children to reinforce stereotypical gender roles and behaviours. Annakiya is the only girl who challenges these stereotypical roles in the classes' games.

The older girls often talk about being friends (or not) with each other, doing so on a more regular basis than other children in the class. In early January, as we are tidying the indoor play area, Nasra, Deka, Fazia, Aniso and Fariido start discussing who is friends with who. They all tell each other who their friends are before starting to squabble over who is best friends with who. This type of interaction occurs on an almost daily basis. Fariido is often instrumental in initiating these arguments and is often the first of the girls to say 'I'm not friends with you' and walk away from the group pouting. She is also more often than not the first of the group who tries to get an adult to intervene in an argument—though all of *the older girls* are prone to doing this. This is in stark contrast to *the gang* who only involve an adult in their arguments if someone has been physically hurt in a scuffle. As a result, Fariido is often the 'divider' within the group and instrumental in causing a temporary group split. Early in the school year, staff members begin to refer to *the older girls'* arguments as 'girls being girls' or 'just girls arguing' highlighting the frequent nature of the group's disputes and reconciliations. Deka often takes on the role of 'reconciler' and after a staff member has intervened, can be seen organising a game involving all of the girls while saying something like, 'Now you are friends, right?' as she encourages everyone to participate.

Additionally, it is important to note that in these conversations about 'being friends', the girls only ever talk about being friends with other girls and, when specifically asked, say things like 'all of my friends are girls not boys'. Even Deka who regularly plays with Callum and actively incorporates him into her games doesn't mention him when reciting her list of friends to her peers. She does, however during research activities, mention to me that she is friends with Callum, while also adamantly articulating that she is not friends with any of the other boys. Connolly's (1998) work also shows that the girls and boys in his study likewise articulated that friendships were gendered. Interestingly, while the boys in his study strongly declared that they were not friends with girls, they at the same time stated that they had girlfriends in the class. For these boys the only legitimate relationship that they could have with their female peers appeared to take a sexualised form. Neither the girls nor the boys at Sunnyside openly engaged in such sexualised discourses, though both *the gang* and *the older girls* clearly and regularly stated amongst themselves, as well as to myself and their peers, that they could not be friends with member of the opposite sex. This, however, was not the case for Kareem and some of the other more reserved Arabic-speaking children who openly stated to each other and myself that boys and girls can be friends. They did not, though, reveal these views to their peers who disagreed with them.

While Nasra, like the other older girls, at times tries to involve an adult in her arguments, as the year progresses her strategies for dealing with these situations changes. After the Easter break, Nasra's predominant response when she has fallen out with one of the other children is to hide under a table, or, if we are in the outdoor play area, the climbing frame, and curl up in a ball, not only physically removing herself from the situation but also attempting to shut out the rest of the (social) world. When she does this, the other girls initially attempt to draw her out and then, if she insists on staying where she is, go back to their games. Staff members likewise encourage Nasra to come out from her hiding place.

As seen in previous chapters, 'being Muslim' or 'being Christian' form an important part of Deka's, Nasra's and Annakiya's identities. Wearing hijab to symbolise this is important for both Deka and Nasra, while Annakiya and Deka regularly discuss and at times argue about the differences between their two religious backgrounds. Chapter 5 revealed that ethnicity, most notably conceptualised in terms of skin colour, is important for these girls who collectively view 'being white as better than being dark.' This understanding frames the girls' places in a social hierarchy as evidenced in their discussions. Interestingly, this hierarchy does not appear to impact on who directs the groups' activities, as Deka who is described as being the darkest almost always takes charge of the girls' whole group games, as well as regularly directing the course of a splinter group's activities. Structure and agency are therefore intertwined in the development and maintenance of Deka's patterns of interaction at school. In the current example, relevant *external* structural factors take the form of wider racist discourses that impact on the girls' patterns of interaction, while Deka's social agency allows her to take charge of the girls' games and, in doing so, begin to counter this dominant discourse. It is interesting to note though that, in these games, Deka does not try to challenge dominant gender discourses prevalent amongst her peers but rather unquestioningly continues to take on the accepted role of 'being a girl.'

While the other girls often talk about their skin colours and rank each other, Deka does not contribute to these conversations but rather tries to withdraw unnoticed from the place where these conversations are taking place. When talking about her identity with her peers, she emphasises her religious identity of 'being Muslim' and does not discuss her ethnic identity. In the games that she directs, 'being Muslim' also comes to the fore—in the Eid parties that she organises or her family's excursions, which often visit a mosque, either in passing or as a final destination. In these games Deka always takes on the role of a Muslim matriarch, either as the Eid party's hostess or 'the bossy Muslim mum cause Muslim mum's are bossy!' Valentine and Sporton's (2009) research with Somali teenagers living in the UK similarly reveals that their respondents' experiences of racism caused them to distance themselves from having a black identity and, in doing so, solidified their Muslim identity. In actively asserting her Muslim identity and avoiding as far as possible reference to her skin colour, Deka's bossy demeanour in the games that she organises can be seen as the way in which she attempts to regain control of the group's patterns of interaction and tries to reassert her own value within the group's complex hierarchy.

Whilst regularly joining in group activities and games, Annakiya and Nasra both at times choose to play on their own. The girls explain their reasons for doing this during separate research activities. Annakiya explains that there are certain activities, such as riding a bike and reading that she prefers to do on her own, while Nasra explains that the other girls are sometimes 'too noisy for me.' During observations, Nasra can often be seen withdrawing to the writing table or reading areas when the girls' games get noisy and boisterous.

When doing formal learning sessions on the carpet, cousins Nasra and Deka almost always sit next to each other at the back of the group of children, surrounded by *the older girls*.

> In early May Deka is the 'star of the day' and therefore sits on the coveted 'star of the day' chair. During carpet sessions, Nasra repeatedly goes to sit next to Deka's chair. As they are chatting, rather than listening to Mary's lesson, Aziza the bilingual support worker tells Nasra to 'move back to where you normally sit at the back of the carpet.' As she moves, Nasra smiles cheekily at Deka. However, throughout the course of the day during subsequent carpet sessions, Nasra always sits next to Deka's chair rather than in her normal spot.

Their close relationship outside school and kinship networks are influential in their behaviour at school. Observations from the start and end of the school day reveal that both of their mothers promote this friendship, encouraging them to draw on each other for support. This will be explored in more detail in the next section.

To conclude, like *the gang, the older girls* engage in gendered play at school. In free choice sessions they regularly adopt what Goffman (1963) describes as cocktail party behaviour, splintering into smaller groups and fluidly moving between these sub-groups. Within their interactions skin colour forms an important way of stratifying the group as the girls' create a hierarchy that informs their peer interactions. Some of the girls though, through asserting their *active agency*, are able to subvert this hierarchy as they regain a higher social status through emphasising another aspect of their identity, such as 'being Muslim', that carries high cultural capital within the group.

Patterns of interaction outside school

As previous research has shown (e.g. Connolly, 1998; Brooker, 2002; Lareau, 2003) a child's microsystems outside school, such as the home, mosque or church, can influence their patterns of interaction within school, most notably via the social and cultural capital that each child brings with them and their family's collective identities and associated practices. I will now explore in more detail the different microsystems that are at play in the lives of my six focus children.

Kareem's patterns of interaction at school are largely influenced by language, with the vast majority of children he interacts with being Arabic speakers. While Kareem's parents both speak some English, as my conversations with them at the start and end of the school day revealed, their social networks, according to Kareem, are predominantly made up of other Libyan families in the UK on temporary student visas. Kareem and Lina both report that outside school their families spend a lot of time together, with the children often being collected from school by each other's parents. During the course of the year, Lina's younger brother also joins the nursery class and joins in with Kareem and his brother's games in the outdoor play area. Both Kareem and Lina talk regularly about the things that their two families do together outside school. Notably, whilst at school, Kareem regularly plays with his own and Lina's brother—though only occasionally plays with Lina. Despite this, he often talks about the games that he plays with Lina outside school, laughing as he recounts a particular activity that they did together.

School staff also believe that language is a key factor in determining which families mix outside school, noting that families appear to mix with other families with similar linguistic and cultural backgrounds to themselves. My observations at the start and end of the school day also show that language is a key factor in determining which parents interact with each other. Aziza largely attributes this behaviour to communication challenges but notes that, for some families from North Africa, maintaining a sense of racial segregation that they had experienced before coming to the UK is also important. She is, however, quick to point out that this is not true for all families.

As seen above, Kareem regularly plays with Mustafe at school, who also acts as his peer translator. When making his model identity, Kareem tells me that he lives near Mustafe and sometimes sees him in a local park, though these meetings appear to be accidental rather than by design. Neither Kareem nor Mustafe talk about visiting each other at home though both boys do regularly go to after school club where they like to play with each other.

In relation to ethnic diversity, Kareem's own patterns of interaction at school do appear to be influenced by the *external* structural discourses of the racially segregated microsystem that he experienced in Libya. Kareem's patterns of interaction outside school also appear to be limited to his own and other white Libyan families. While it is unclear the reasons for this—for example his family's prior social networks, the minority status of his family's cultural capital, a conscious decision to associate with other Libyan families—it is important to note that Kareem's family appear to have not made links with other families who are not from Libya.

Kinship ties are also important to Kareem. At home, he reportedly spends a lot of time playing with his brothers. At school, when he has an opportunity to do so, he almost always seeks his younger brother out. At home, his peer relationships are predominantly restricted to his brothers, baby sister—who Kareem says is too small to play with—Lina and her brothers. Although Kareem has other friends at school, he tells me that he does not see them outside school, apart from at the after school club. Likewise, he tells me that he doesn't get to play with his friends at the mosque outside of this setting. Without minimising the importance of young children's social agency, it is important to highlight that children, like Kareem and the other children in this study, are routinely dependent on their care-givers to facilitate access to their peers. As Corsaro (2003: 288-9) points out, 'because children often are constrained to nurture friendships in the places where they create and share joint activities ... [there are frequent] ... structural barriers to the maintenance of their friendships.' For Kareem, the lack of links between his microsystems creates a barrier to the maintenance of many of the friendships that he forms at school, the mosque and after school club.

While *the gang* are good friends at Sunnyside, they only occasionally see each other outside school. Mubarak occasionally goes to play at Amir's house where they like to play on Amir's Playstation. Daud, at times, sees Mubarak's older siblings at the mosque—though Mubarak himself doesn't go. When talking about the mosque amongst themselves, it is interesting to note, that Mubarak clearly asserts that he will start going to the mosque after his next birthday and will see his 'best friends there'. Daud and Mubarak do, however, at times see each other in their local park. This seems to be unintentional rather than by design.

As noted above, Daud at times tries to get the attention of an adult in the classroom. Daud's mother also mentions that Daud often does this at home. He lives with his mother, younger sister and teenage brother. His father lives close by with Daud's 'Auntie', i.e. his father's second wife, and sees Daud and his siblings on a daily basis. Rather than play with his sister, who he is closest to in age, Daud more often than not chooses to do jobs with his father, such as helping him do DIY in both his own and his 'Auntie's' house or fix his car.

One way of describing childhood in family contexts is to use an apprenticeship model. Brooker's (2001) research discovered that the Bangladeshi families that she worked with viewed children's roles within the household differently from the ways in which (using her term) the Anglo parents did. Brooker concludes that, while all children are apprenticed, they are apprenticed to different things. The Bangladeshi families apprenticed their children to 'the life of the family and community', while the Anglo families apprenticed their children to 'childhood, and to play' (Brooker, 2001: 51). Like Daud, the Bangladeshi children in Brooker's study did jobs round the house with older family members. While it is beyond the scope of this study to explore parents' views on childhood, such as how they conceptualise children's roles in the home, it is important to note that Daud's behaviour at home is mirrored in his interactions with peers at school, as he at times chooses to withdraw from peer company and seek out an adult's attention. It is unclear, though, if spending time around adults and doing 'proper jobs', learning about how things work, has prompted Daud's tendency for thinking weighty thoughts or if his natural curiosity about the world causes him to seek out adult company and what he calls 'adult work.'

Daud's father also regularly takes him to the mosque where he likes to 'pray, read [and] talk there' with his friends, including Mubarak's siblings. If his father is not around, Daud chooses to listen to his older brother's conversations with his friends and watch them play on the computer or watch TV with them. Lareau's (2003) work likewise reveals that older siblings can have a strong influence on younger sibling(s)' social development and peer interactions with some taking on the role of surrogate parent. Daud's elder brother habitually drops Daud off or picks him up from school. When he does so, Daud proudly shows his brother off to both Amir and Mubarak.

Daud's eldest sister also lives close by. She has a son who attends Sunnyside's nursery and is therefore close in age to Daud. Daud and his nephew regularly see each other outside school. While at school, Daud proudly tells his friends that his nephew is in nursery and introduces him to them—though they rarely play together in this context. Daud's family have relatives in Birmingham who they visit at different points throughout the year. Daud enjoys going there and playing with his cousins. While he does not see these cousins on a regular basis, he often talks about them with his peers and me during research activities. Kinship ties are important to Daud and form the largest part of his patterns of interaction outside school.

Daud's family live close to Umar's family and reportedly spend a lot of time together. Umar proudly tells his classmates when Daud has been to his house and recites the games that they have played together. Daud, however does not volunteer this information to his peers though, if asked about it, does confirm that he sees Umar outside school. In school, the boys rarely interact. In this instance, Daud's *active agency* overrides his family's social capital (or wider structural factors) when choosing his school friends as, despite his mother's encouragement, Daud chooses not to play with Umar at school. As already seen in Chapter 3, Daud masterfully employs his social agency as he carefully manages the impression of himself that he performs when his various microsystems interact. Social environment is consequently important to how Daud operationalises his identity. Daud's actions show that he has learnt to conform to (some) wider social structures (both *external* and *internal*) that demand he behave in a certain way. However, his *active agency* in relation to his choice of school friends reveals that a 'strong structuration' framing of identity, as conceptualised by Stones (2005), is at play in Daud's patterns of interaction.

Amir likewise spends a lot of time with his family outside school. He has two older brothers and a number of half siblings who he sees regularly. He also regularly visits his maternal Grandmother. He also goes to Koranic school on a weekly basis where he sees Nasra and occasionally Jabir. While he enthusiastically talks to his peers about going to Koranic school, the activities that they do there, seeing Jabir and his other male friends, he rarely mentions that he sees Nasra. Nasra, on the other hand, happily tells her peers that she sees Amir at the mosque. Amir's and Nasra's mothers are also friends and regularly visit each other with their children. Amir, again, does not talk about going to Nasra's house with his peers, while Nasra happily informs her peers when she visits, or has been visited by, Amir and his family and in great detail describes the games that they play together. As Lareau (2003) points out, while young children often engage in gendered play, age can also be an important factor in their patterns of interaction. For example, when there are a limited number of children of the same age, boys and girls frequently play together. Based on Nasra's accounts of her interactions with Amir outside school, this appears to be the case, as the two youngest members of each family they often choose to play together rather than with their elder siblings.

While Amir's and Nasra's mothers' friendship influences their children's patterns of interaction outside school, at school these social networks (*external structures*) appear to cause Amir to keep his distance from Nasra more than from the other girls to avoid his friends teasing him about being friends with a girl. Consequently Amir's *active agency*, like Daud's, over-rides his family's social networks. A 'strong structuration' framing of identity likewise helps to explain Amir's patterns of interaction at school.

Going to the mosque in and of itself does, however, directly impact on the *way* that Amir interacts with his school peers, as he regularly teaches the other gang members what he has learnt at the mosque, such as Arabic writing or how to pray. He also instigates role plays of going to Arabic school in their games. Within *the gang*, Amir enacts the role of what Broadhead and Burt (2011) understand as being the 'master player' through recreating his life experiences in his peer interactions at school. In doing this, he creates a mesosystem to link his microsystems of Koranic school and religious learning at home with his Sunnyside microsystem. This practice allows Amir to explore aspects of his own identity with his peers and furthermore facilitates how *the gang* (re)negotiates their collective identity at school. Significantly the boundaries between home, school and other microsystems can be quite porous.

As well as seeing Amir outside school and attending Koranic school with her sisters, Nasra spends a lot of time with her nuclear and extended family. Her kinship networks appear to form the largest part of her peer interactions outside school. She likes to play with one of her sisters but finds the other boring as she does not like to play with dolls, fairies or do ballet but prefers to practice breakdancing. Nasra visits cousins on both sides of her family on a regular basis though rarely talks, in our activities, about her 'Christian cousins', who live nearby. She does, however, often discuss visiting her 'Somali cousins' who live in 'England ... higher than us' despite only seeing them occasionally. The family members who she talks about most, however, are her sisters, Deka and Deka's siblings. Outside school the two cousins spend a lot of time together, with both girls regularly telling their peers and myself that they went to the park together last night, had sleepovers at the weekend or went to their *Ayeeyo*'s (grandmother's) house together with their siblings. Nasra and Deka are also encouraged by their mothers to support and play with each other at school. Similarly to the working class children in Lareau's (2003) study, extended kinship ties are critically important to both Nasra and Deka as they form the basis of their patterns of interactions both at and outside school.

In Chapter 5, I discussed an incident, near the end of March, involving one of Deka and Annakiya's theological discussions that resulted in Deka being excluded from school for the remainder of the day. Continuing this story the next day the importance of extended kinship networks for the two cousins are revealed.

> I am sitting at the back of the carpet area as Mary is taking the class register. Deka arrives late—just after 9.15—and comes into the classroom. Her mother opens the door and lets her in. Deka goes to sit down on the carpet before turning to wave to her mother who beckons her back to the door and tells her something. I can't hear what is being said from where I am sitting. Nasra turns to look at them, smiles and waves to her aunt. Deka's mother leaves and Deka sits down on the carpet next to Nasra, saying to her, 'She says I have to play with you today.' Nasra looks at her, smiles and then emphatically asks 'With me?' 'Yes,' replies Deka smiling, 'I have to play with you.' Nasra smiles back at her and the two girls giggle.

While Deka's mother did not openly encourage her daughter to play with her cousin, Nasra, *every* school morning, she did so at different points throughout the school year when there was a particular situation that one of the two girls was struggling with. Throughout the school year Nasra's mother likewise on occasion encouraged Nasra to play with Deka at school so that the two girls could offer each other mutual support. After dropping their daughters off at Sunnyside on a morning, the two sisters-in-law often stay in the reception area chatting about different aspects of family life. Their reliance on this mutual support can be seen as influential in encouraging their daughters to also support each other at school and in doing so replicate their own social support networks.

While building their model identities the extent of Nasra's and Deka's relationship outside school is further uncovered. Deka chooses to depict the places that are important to her in the UK, while Nasra chooses to depict her imagined impressions of Somalia, where her father was born. As seen in Chapters 3 and 4, 'being Somali' is an important part of Nasra's identity.

Nasra and her family feature strongly in Deka's model. On the left hand side of her model, Deka builds two houses and places two female *Lego* pieces outside them. As she sits back on her heels and looks at her model she points to the *Lego* figure near the middle of the model and tells me that this is herself. She then points to the other figure and tells me that this is her cousin Nasra, 'who lives in the house next door.' She then goes on to tell me that while they live close to each other (in real life) and often see each other, they are not actual neighbours. Interestingly though, Deka chooses to represent her close relationship with her cousin by the use of space in her model.

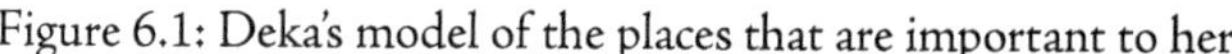
Figure 6.1: Deka's model of the places that are important to her

As mentioned above Lareau's (2003) research likewise reveals the importance of extended kinship networks and collective family identities on children's patterns of interaction. Notably, Lareau contends that these extended networks were more important for working class families than their middle class counterparts. In the current study, Daud, Amir, Nasra and Deka are all from working class backgrounds and all have strong ties to their extended families.

Kareem and Annakiya are the only two focus children from middle class backgrounds. As both families have recently arrived in the UK and have no extended family members here, it is not possible to ascertain if Lareau's findings would be replicated in the current study. Notably though, both Kareem and Annakiya talk about their cousins, who still live in their countries of origin, and tell me that they miss playing with them. Cultural values and practices relating to kinship ties and collective identities consequently appear to an important factor, alongside class values, in determining the extent to which families are tied to their extended kinship networks.

While their close kinship ties impact on both Nasra and Deka's patterns of interaction at school this does not exclude them from seeking additional friends amongst *the older girls*. Unlike Nasra, Deka does not reportedly see any other children from Sunnyside outside school. While 'being Muslim' for Deka is as important—if not more important due to dominant *external structures* that ascribe her a low ethnic social status amongst her peers—as it is for Nasra, Deka does not go to the mosque or Koranic school on a regular basis. Rather, her *Ayeeyo* spends time teaching Deka and her siblings about Islam. Outside school, Deka largely spends time with her siblings and her cousins. At school Deka regularly discusses her extended family and their collective identity. This for Deka links with her own individual identity in a dialectical relationship where both aspects inform the other. Her kinship ties, and her family's related collective identity, consequently influences her patterns of interaction both at and outside school.

Like Deka, Annakiya does not purposefully see any of her classmates outside school. Unlike Deka though, she lives in a different part of town to most of the other children. Annakiya has two older sisters who she likes to play with, though she prefers to play with her middle sister who, like Annakiya, likes to play with dolls. Her elder sister now thinks that she is too old to play with them and chooses to listen to music instead. On Saturdays, Annakiya goes to 'ballerina lessons' and on Sundays she and her family go to church, both in the morning and in the evening. She has friends that she likes to play with there. Some of her friends from church come to play at her house. She often talks about her friend, Lizzy, who goes to church with her and regularly comes to play at her house, describing her as 'helpful and beautiful'. Lizzy's father and Annakiya's father are friends. As with some of the other children, her parents' friendships influence the children that Annakiya interacts with outside school.

Annakiya also likes to play with Mark, who lives behind her house. She and her sisters play with Mark on their bikes and scooters. Mark is reportedly the same age as Annakiya. While gender forms an important part of Annakiya's patterns of interaction at school Lareau's (2003) work shows that, when there is a scarcity of children to play with, age can become a dominant factor in determining patterns of interaction.

As mentioned above, Annakiya at times talks about the friends and cousins she left behind when she moved to the UK. She misses them and during research activities reminisces about the games that they used to play together. This recent severing of extended kinship ties features more strongly in Annakiya's conversations than it does for Kareem whose family arrived in the UK at a similar time to Annakiya's family.

While some of the children at Sunnyside have wider family or social networks that overlap, predominantly connected to their parents' studies or Muslim activities, Annakiya's family networks are formed primarily based on their Christian beliefs and where they live. As a result of this Annakiya does not see any of her school peers as part of the activities that her family naturally engage in. Additionally, as has been mentioned in Chapter 2, her parents are uneasy with Annakiya attending a predominantly Muslim school. The networks that they have created for themselves and the peers that they encourage Annakiya to interact with outside school mostly seem to stem from their own religious identity. It is, however, unclear if these networks are a natural part of their family's everyday life or if they are placing more emphasis on Annakiya developing friendships with other Christian children because of the multi-religious make-up of her school or if both of these factors are influential.

In summary, children's social environments, kinship networks, religious identities and their parents' friendship groups can all play a part in the peer relationships that children form outside school. For some children, these intersect with their friendships at Sunnyside and, for some, these are separate. Children react differently to these social networks, with some patterns of interaction outside school actively encouraging friendships at Sunnyside. In other cases, patterns of interaction outside school actively cause children to distance themselves from certain peers at school.

Summarising children's interlaced collective patterns of interaction

As previously discussed, once the January starters arrived Barak and Ferran began to play more regularly with *the gang*.

> In early February, I am sitting at the writing table. Amir, Mubarak and Daud put some pieces of *Lego* into their pockets and congregate with Barak and Ferran in the toilets. Suzie soon chases them out and the boys split up. Amir comes and sits at the writing table and begins to draw a picture. Barak heads to the maths area where he makes a chain out of the chain link pieces. He comes over, swinging the chain in his hand before putting it on his shoulder. He laughs and tells me, 'it's a lady's handbag' before giving it to me. He puts it round my neck and leans next to where I am sitting watching Amir. After a few minutes he wanders up to the sandpit where Mubarak is playing. Daud comes over and says to Amir, 'Where are you?' 'Here', Amir replies. I ask Daud, 'Are you coming to write?' Yes, he replies, and Amir stands up and says, 'Here I'll move your picture to the writing table'. He goes over to the choose board and moves Daud's picture so that he is now 'officially' at the writing area. Barak comes back over to the writing table and says to Daud, 'Where were you? I was calling you.' Daud replies, 'In town', and gets the *Lego* pieces out from his pocket, puts it to his ear and shakes his head, whispering to me, 'He didn't leave a message.' He then wanders off to the role play area. Barak reaches into his own pocket and takes out a piece of *Lego* which he gives to Amir, telling him it's a phone. Amir talks into the phone before giving it back to Barak. Daud comes back over to us and tells Barak, 'My phone was broken. I'm not lost any more', in explanation for their earlier interaction. Daud and Barak walk around the room together talking on their phones. Barak comes back up to me and says, 'We are gangsters'. Mubarak who comes up behind Barak also tells me, 'I'm a gangster'. He then asks if he can have my necklace which Barak gave me earlier. I take it off and give it to him. Amir has been watching all of this. As the boys wander off again, talking on their phones, he turns back to his writing.

Similarly to Corsaro's (2003: 290) observations, many children's patterns of interaction at Sunnyside, as revealed by the boys' gangster role play are made up of a number of 'interlaced collective patterns of interaction' where children's role play incorporates complex and at times apparently disparate activities within a collective game. This type of play is often employed by members of *the gang*.

Patterns of interaction at Sunnyside are influenced by children's gendered, ethnic and religious identities where identity is operationalised as *performative, situated and dialectical*. For Kareem, language and skin colour impact on his choice of playmates. Additionally Kareem's kinship ties, most notably in the form of his younger brother, affects the extent to which he interacts with his peers at school. Family networks are also important to cousins Nasra and Deka and impact on their peer interactions at school. In contrast Annakiya's social networks outside school are completely separate from her peer interactions at school. For Amir and Daud, having a collective identity at school as a member of *the gang* is important for their peer interactions. 'Being Muslim' and 'being a boy' are also important to them both. Unlike *the older girls,* who engage in 'cocktail party-like' behaviour, *the gang* members predominantly all play together. For *the older girls,* religious and gender identities are also important. In addition to this, their ethnic identities also play a role in their patterns of interaction as they enact a complex hierarchy based on skin colour. This hierarchy can, however, be challenged as children emphasise another aspect of their identity that affords them higher social status.

Within the class, girls and boys tend to resolve their arguments using two different strategies. While the girls seek an adult's involvement in their squabbles and reconciliation, the boys prefer to resolve their arguments within their peer group.

The peer interactions of all children are strongly influenced by children's past and concurrent experiences, dominant structural discourses and the degree of *active agency* that children are able to exercise. In the next concluding chapter I will revisit the ways in which some children actively challenge structural discourses (both *external* and *internal*) at Sunnyside before raising some questions relating to how practice, policy and future research can respond to my key findings.

Chapter 7

The story so far: Summary and concluding thoughts

'No-one is born hating another person because of the colour of his skin, his background or his religion [sic]. People must learn to hate, and if they can learn to hate they can be taught to love, for love comes more naturally to the human heart than its opposite'

Nelson Mandela at his Inauguration as President of South Africa, 1994 [as quoted by Brown, 2007: 11].

Challenging dominant discourses

As discussed in earlier chapters, children at Sunnyside are not only aware of notions such as similarity and difference; self and 'the other' but are also aware of, actively perpetuate, and at times challenge, wider social discourses of discrimination and hierarchies of difference relating to gender, religious and ethnic identities.

The discourses that were most often challenged by children in the class related to gendered identities. Umar's drawing of a flower, which was discussed in Chapter 5, highlights the typical way that some children challenge, what Stones (2005) terms, dominant *external* and *internal* structural discourses.

> I am sitting with Deka and Annakiya at the writing table. They are both drawing a picture of a flower. Umar comes over and sits down with us. He reaches for a piece of paper and looks over at Deka's drawing. 'I'm making a flower', he tells us, to which Deka replies, 'But you're a boy.' Umar doesn't respond to this but begins to draw his flower appearing to be unperturbed by Deka's comment. After a few minutes, Amir comes over and asks if he can join us. I tell him that he can, and pass him a piece of paper. As he sits down Annakiya tells him, 'You have to draw a flower'. He turns his nose up at this, and tells me that, 'Boys don't draw flowers'. I tell him that he can stay and draw whatever he likes. He, however, decides to go and play elsewhere. As he leaves, Umar looks up from his drawing and says, 'But boys can draw flowers. Look!' as he shows us all his drawing.

Kareem, Ferran, and at times Barak also challenge discourses relating to gender showing, as Umar does above, that boys can draw flowers, play with dolls, be chased and so on depending on the game or activity that they are engaging in at the time. In contrast, Annakiya is the only girl who, at times, chooses not to conform to the classes' *internal* structural discourses pertaining to gender roles. She, though, is aware of her peer's criticisms of her when she does this, modifying her behaviour to hide her actions from *the older girls*. This is reminiscent of Brown's (2007) and Davies' (2003) work, which also highlights that more boys than girls challenge dominant gender discourses.

Children's *internal* structural discourses relating to gender mirror *external* gendered discourses promoted in wider society. In contrast, dominant *internal* discourses relating to religious identity that most children in the class promote, such as the importance of 'being Muslim', are not commonly shared by wider UK society, including most staff members at Sunnyside. In developing an alternative discourse, children at Sunnyside overtly and intentionally resist, borrowing Russell's (2011) terminology, wider social norms relating to Islamophobia, which some of the children have direct experience of. In this way, children's *internal structures*, by their very nature, begin to challenge wider social discourses of discrimination relating to religious identity. These dominant *internal structures* are not, however, shared by all children in the class. As seen in Chapters 5 and 6, Annakiya habitually exercises her *active agency* and challenges Deka, and less often her other peers, about these discourses. As well as prompting children to discuss their religious identities with each other and navigate their social interactions in light of these at times conflicting discourses, *internal structures* also impact more directly on some children's patterns of interaction. This is most notable for *the gang* where 'being Muslim' is part of the criteria for group membership, forging fictive kinship ties between members. Amir, as one of the leaders of *the gang*, habitually tells the other gang members that non-Muslims are *haram*, using this as a way to exclude Callum, who Daud has become friends with, from gang membership. As seen in Chapter 6, while functioning as a collective group *the gang* excludes Callum from their activities, Daud exercises his *active agency* by, sometimes, withdrawing from *the gang's* games to play with Callum, despite his friends' cautions.

The older girls and *the gang* respond differently to discourses relating to ethnic difference. As discussed in Chapter 5, gang members regularly discuss ethnic diversity and the differences between themselves based on their national and ethnic identities. 'Being Muslim', for these boys takes on the role of a 'superordinate identity', which is defined by Gaertner et al. (1999) as a collective salient identity that comes to the fore in diverse social situations as a way of promoting a sense of togetherness. This 'superordinate identity' takes on a fictive kinship role where the boys are united, irrespective of their ethnic background, as Muslim brothers. In creating this discourse, gang members generate a unifying *internal structure* relating to ethnic diversity that challenges the divisive *external structures* promoted by powerful factions in wider society.

While most of *the older girls* also self-define as 'being Muslim', they, unlike *the gang*, do not subscribe to Islam's assertion that all individuals are equally valued as part of the wider Muslim family irrespective of their ethnic background (Chapter 5). Skin colour, for these girls, relates to a hierarchy of difference which draws upon and perpetuates *external structural* discourses of discrimination. Ethnic diversity, therefore, features more strongly in *the older girls'* patterns of interaction than gang members' interactions. For other children at Sunnyside, such as Kareem, *external structures* concerning country of origin and segregated macro structures also impact on how they view ethnic difference. This also illustrates how children's collective experiences can and do link global (macro) and local (micro) contexts.

'Being different' in a strong structuration framework

'Being different' can also take other forms. In the current study, both Annakiya and Amir were put on the gifted and talented register early on in the year. Amir in particular soaked up formal learning opportunities and was almost always the first to master a new idea in all aspects of learning. As a result he often got bored and distracted, getting into trouble for misbehaving. On the other hand, Jabir, who flourished in social situations and was an engaging story teller, struggled to master basic aspects of literacy and numeracy that the other children were able to complete with relative ease. Both Amir and Jabir knew that they were 'different' with respect to their approaches to and mastery of formal learning activities. On separate occasions both boys confided in me that they felt that they did not really fit in because of this. 'Being different' can therefore take a variety of guises with children struggling to find their place and feel accepted if they do not, or are not able to, conform to the dominant social 'norm.'

This ethnography provides an in depth insight into the experiences of a diverse group of children who have come together via different life trajectories as part of the population flows that characterise globalisation in late modernity. The specific focus on the experiences of children from North and Sub-Saharan African countries who are constrained by social structures pertaining to racism, gender inequality, Islamophobia, 'the war on terror' and events in the Arab Spring are uncovered in striking detail. This focus fills a gap in the literature that has predominantly focused on children from South Asian families currently living in the UK. This study shows that children's everyday interactions are enabled and constrained by wider structural discourses as children (re)negotiate their identities against this complex backdrop. This study is also significant as it reveals how identities and interactions unfold over time. Dynamic local and global politics, the arrival of new classmates, changes in family structures and Koranic school attendance all influence children's everyday sense of self and are reflected in the development of peer relationships.

As seen throughout this study, young children conceptualise and operationalise a complex and dynamic understanding of *identity as performative, situated and dialectical* in their everyday lives. When these daily negotiations are interpreted within a 'strong structuration' framework, identity can be seen as salient in children's daily negotiations relating to diversity and inequality. The way in which children conceptualise and operationalise difference is consequently related to *the duality of structure*, the intersectionality between different aspects of identity and the links that children make between macro and micro social contexts. By unearthing a rich and nuanced account of young children's experiences of identity (re)negotiation this study uncovers the prevalence of identity in children's every day social interactions.

Children's discussions about difference and identity are not constructed in isolation from wider social discourses but, as this study shows, discourses and social structures that are dominant in both mainstream popular and minority cultures are foundational in children's own constructions of self and other. Consequently as Hall (2000: 4) points out, identities can be understood as being 'constructed within, not outside [of], discourse'. Discourses of difference, and particularly fear or disdain of the so-called other are prevalent in all aspects of life from classical children's stories, popular films and TV programmes, media advertising to local, national and international politics. As Lowles and Painter (2011) highlight, fear of difference when left to fester can quickly turn to hatred. While these discourses of fear, disdain and at times hatred are prominent across most, if not all, cultures and seem to pervade virtually all aspects of social life this need not be the case. As Nelson Mandela stated in his inauguration speech:

> People must learn to hate, and if they can learn to hate they can be taught to love, for love comes more naturally to the human heart than its opposite. (Mandela, 1994 as quoted by Brown, 2007: 11).

In our strive for social justice, we must all, therefore, counter these discourses on a daily basis and teach our youngest members of society to love, value and respect both themselves and others, to celebrate diversity and to fight for equality in all aspects of life.

Unlearning discrimination

While the aim of this study was to *uncover and improve understanding of how cultural minority children explore identity and social interaction in a multi-ethnic Early Years classroom*, it has at the same time highlighted the good practice that Sunnyside promotes around diversity and equality. Over the course of the year, Mary instigated project work that not only celebrated diversity, for example by exploring different religious festivals and cultural practices, but that also began to counter related discriminatory discourses. Work, such as the *Elmer* topic (McKee, 1989), as well as the class' work on *Balamory*,[11] moved beyond purely celebrating diversity to exploring issues surrounding difference and inequality. Children often discussed *Elmer* and *Balamory* amongst themselves after project work on the topic had finished. They also raised these topics with me during research activities. The story of *Elmer* seemed to particularly resonate with a number of children and pictures of *Elmer* featured habitually in children's drawings. While creating her PAT, Deka draws the picture below. As she is doing so tells me, 'This is *Elmer*. I love you *Elmer*, and your patchworks are beautiful.' She instructs me to write and continues by saying 'Everyone loves you in the whole wide world.' She then describes to me the colours that she is using to complete *Elmer*'s patchworks before telling me, 'If I see *Elmer* ... it's a girl ... I would say to her your colours are nice. You don't need to be like the other elephants.'

Topic work, like the class explorations of the story of *Elmer*, allows children to explore issues of difference and underlying structural discourses of inequality. However, a discussion with Annakiya, where she tells me, 'It's OK to be different, like *Elmer*, but really I wanna be like you' (Chapter 5), highlights that deep seated discourses of discrimination are difficult to change and need to be constantly challenged.

As this study shows, children often experience being stereotyped based on their gender, ethnicity, religion, ability, etc. and in turn have also stereotyped others. Therefore linking wider discussions around diversity and inequality to children's own experiences will be more effective in countering discrimination

11. *Balamory* is a Scottish television series on BBC television for pre-school children.

than simply telling children about diverse cultural practices. In doing this policy and practice need to go beyond multiculturalism and adopt an anti-discriminatory approach that facilitates the exploration and celebration of diversity in a safe environment, while also actively challenging *external* and *internal* structural discourses of inequality and social injustice.

Recent examples from around the world show that multi-ethnic schooling environments that celebrate diversity and attempt to counter discrimination and inequality can be foundational in children's experiences and actions later in life. Policy changes in Kenya in the 1980s, which led to the development of ethnically segregated Kenyan schools, is widely thought of as negatively contributing to increasing ethnic tensions in Kenya in recent years, as fear of 'the other' is perpetuated at all levels of society, while discourses challenging this fear are no longer given a voice (Wrong, 2009). Closer to home, in his autobiography *The Islamist*, Ed Hussain (2007) attributes his positive primary school experiences, which celebrated diversity and countered inequality, as being one of the influences that later in life brought him back from what he describes as the dangerous clutches of Islamic fundamentalism.

Nelson Mandela, on accepting his Nobel Peace Prize in 1993, as the oppressive system of apartheid in South Africa was in the final stages of being dismantled, also highlights the importance of enabling children to counter discourses of discrimination. In his speech he stated:

> the Southern tip of Africa, a rich reward is in the making ... an invaluable gift for those who suffered in the name of humanity when they sacrificed everything for liberty, peace and human fulfilment. [The reward is] not to be measured in money ... It must be measured in the happiness of children, the most valuable citizens in any society and the greatest of our treasures. [as quoted by Brown, 2007: 137]

Children, as 'the most valuable citizens in any society' and the future of our social world have the right to grow up in a world that values them for who they are, irrespective of their background. They should not be made to feel that they are inferior to others or that they cannot achieve their dreams because of their social attributes. Unfortunately, for some children in this study, this is not currently the case. Policy, practice and research all have a responsibility to counter this trend and show children that in Annakiya's words 'It is OK to be different', with no buts or conditions attached.

Moving Forward

In response to this, I will now raise questions for how policy, practice and research can respond to my study's findings.

Raising questions for policy

As Russell (2011) and Moss (2012) highlight, the current dominant narrative surrounding the purpose of education in many countries focuses on 'quality'. 'Quality' is narrowly defined within this discourse as improving formal educational outcomes, employment and earnings, while also reducing social problems and ensuring individual and national survival in a competitive world. In achieving this, education plays an important role in exploiting 'human capital', assuring high returns on 'social investment.' Current educational policy in the UK, as developed by past Labour and the current Coalition governments, has been firmly built on this narrative. Moss (2012) argues that this discourse is overly simplistic and reductionist, as it ignores the social context in which education operates and the complexities of social life. While this approach offers an economically cheap solution, it fails to recognise or respond to structural inequalities and social injustice, which this study has shown have a very real impact on the daily negotiations of children at Sunnyside. The incongruity of dominant educational narratives with the lived experiences of children today raises fundamental questions that policy makers need to consider: what is the purpose of education? Is the key function of education to ensure national survival in a global economy? Is it to develop responsible global citizens? Is it to address social injustice and begin to create a more equal society? Or does it have another purpose? In considering this, policy makers need to envision the kind of social world that they want for the future and the role that education can play in achieving this.

Our current educational system is built, as Russell (2011) and Moss (2012) point out, on systematic inequality, and is dependent on this for its survival. Maintaining the status quo is therefore one of the key functions of educational establishments. Consequently, it is important to question if it is possible for the current system to effectively challenge social injustice and inequality at a local and personal level, or if change needs to start at a more fundamental level with the system itself. At present, policy makers, while talking about diversity and the complexity of learning, appear to stifle this at every turn. For example, the new focus in the revised Early Years Foundation Stage framework on school readiness fails to take into account children's diverse backgrounds or the different ways in which children learn. We therefore need to consider how education can move beyond 'talking' about diversity to 'doing' diversity and effectively tackling deep seated issues of inequality.

To do this, it may be helpful to consider the concept of democracy as a quality of life, not purely as a political system (Jeffs and Smith, 2005). In drawing on democracy in this way, as a multi-dimensional concept that embodies a form of political governance, a way of life and model for interacting with others, we can begin to challenge *external* and *internal* structures of inequality and resist the dominant educational narrative, or what Unger (2005: 1) terms 'a dictatorship of no alternative.' As Wright (2010) suggests, when resisting dictatorship, we need to go beyond purely critiquing the current system to also strive to create 'real utopias' that bring about real change.

Bringing about this type of systematic change is a long term goal which must be achieved if education is to become an arena to effectively challenge social injustice and structural inequality. Hand-in-hand with striving for this, there are fundamental changes that policy makers can implement within the current system to start education on the road to achieving equality.

First, policy makers, when reviewing and revising curriculums and teacher training programmes, need to refer to the wealth of research that counters the prevalence of child development theories, which contend that young children are not aware of or able to employ abstract social concepts that relate to discrimination. Research, such as this study can be drawn upon to do this.

Second, policy makers can raise the profile of issues relating to diversity and inequality within the curriculum and provide clearer guidance to schools about good practice in implementing an anti-discriminatory approach in their everyday practices. Initial teacher training and continuing professional development programmes need to cover this as a core element of their syllabus.

Third, adequate funding needs to be directed to schools to allow them to purchase resources to allow them to effectively implement this part of the curriculum.

Fourth, policy makers need to take into account social theories of identity and use these to inform their training programmes. These theories reveal that *identity is performative, situated and dialectical.* Within the current framework, identity is also understood as being intrinsically linked to wider social structures. These theories counter asocial models of identity, which early years' policy and practice currently subscribes to.

Finally, additional funding needs to be made available to schools who are working in multilingual environments to enable them to employ adequate numbers of well-trained multilingual staff, which in turn will create greater access for children with little English. An increase in multilingual staff will not only allow children with little English to engage more fully with formal learning opportunities but will also facilitate peer interaction with children from different linguistic backgrounds and help to counter bullying (Chapter 6). It is also recommended that schools with a linguistically diverse population be encouraged to employ a multilingual receptionist or parent liaison officer who can facilitate communication between the school and parents, allowing support staff to function fully in their role with children.

Raising questions for practice

Connolly (2003), Brown (2004) and Brooker (2006) all contend that educational practitioners have a key role to play in countering discrimination. Despite this, Brooker (2006: 117) points out that in practice'educators, may serve to polarise children's identities' in stereotypical ways. While there were examples of good practice at Sunnyside in countering discrimination, some staff members also, when under pressure, perpetuated *external* structural discourses, most notably relating to gender by making comments such as'I know that pink is a girls colour' in response to a child's admonishment of their peers' actions. Educators need to be aware of the impact of their own actions, and prejudices, in perpetuating (and also in countering) social discourses of discrimination, particularly when they are under pressure or in exasperating circumstances.'Offering equality of opportunity ... and dismantling the prejudices of the wider society' (Brooker, 2006: 117) are central to the role that educators undertake and should consequently be paramount in their everyday practice. Questions surrounding how educators do this on a daily basis need to be carefully considered and reviewed in practice to ensure that they do not unwittingly perpetuate *external* structural discourses of inequality due to the high pressure demands of their jobs.

The dominance of child development theories in current teaching practice that contend that young children are not aware of or able to employ abstract social concepts relating to discrimination (Cole, 2011) further entrenches *external* structural discourses. If educators do not believe that young children are capable of understanding abstract social constructions until a later stage of their development, then they will also not likely see the relevance of adopting an anti-discriminatory approach in Early Years education. Until these perceptions are countered, purely advocating the importance of an anti-discriminatory approach is not enough. Challenging these developmental theories, therefore, needs to form a part of continuing professional development training for all staff members in preparation for further training about how educators can implement an anti-discriminatory curriculum in their own practice. Researchers also need to consider how they can best disseminate their research to practitioners in a way that is easily accessible and translatable into current practice.

As this study has shown, abstract concepts are prominent in young children's daily negotiations surrounding identity, diversity and inequality. Previous research by Connolly (2003), Brown (2004) and Brooker (2006) confirm that this is also the reality for children in different social contexts. The salience of these discourses mean that children need a safe environment in which they can explore these topics in an open and honest way, without feeling that they have to hide their true thoughts and feelings from school staff. Educators can, as Jeffs and Smith (2005: 50) highlight, play a key role in encouraging dialogue around these difficult issues in non-judgemental ways:

> Educators need to work so that people can be more comfortable with change and diversity; and to question exclusion ... we should not play down the pressures to conform or the difficulties of dealing with difference. ... One thing we can work out fairly easily is that if people are to enjoy a humane and common life then they must engage with each other—and allow each other to be different.

As Jeffs and Smith (2005) highlight, honest and open conversations about difference need to be carefully balanced within an anti-discriminatory framework that promotes inclusion and equality. In essence, young children need to be given the opportunity to 'dream' and the permission to aspire to be who they want to be, irrespective of their social background. They also need to be given the tools to fight for these dreams in an unjust world that will attempt to limit their life choices based on their gender, ethnicity, religious background or another social attribute. Educators, alongside family members and local communities, play a key role in facilitating this and need to draw on a wide range of resources to help them do so effectively.

Raising questions for future research

As has been seen in this study, *the duality of structure* is key to unlocking how young children make sense of and respond to their social worlds. Responding to Stones' (2005) call for more research to apply a 'strong structuration' framework to a range of empirical contexts this study contributes to and extends the growing body of work that explores structuration at the *ontic* level. However, more research is still needed in this area to develop the ongoing critique of this concept. In addition to Stones' general call for researchers to frame their work within 'strong structuration', I contend that further empirical work, exploring the nature of *identity as performative, situated and dialectical*, needs to be conducted within this framework. Additionally, given the prevalence of asocial interpretations of identity in early years policy and practice (Bath, 2009), research with young children needs to further unearth how young children conceptualise and operationalise *identity as performative, situated and dialectical*, whilst paying particular attention to how their research findings are disseminated and adopted by policy makers and practitioners to achieve the maximum impact.

This research adds to the growing body of literature, such as Connolly's (2003; 2008) work in Ireland, that explores how young children use material markers of difference to operationalise identity. Further ethnographic research that can uncover the detail and prominence of children's daily identity negotiations is needed in a range of cultural contexts to add to this growing body of research.

The current study is distinctive in its unearthing of nuanced accounts of a small group of children's daily negotiations about identity and diversity, revealing the salience of identity for young children. This in-depth ethnographic account provides one tile in the overall mosaic of young children's experiences of identity, diversity and inequality. When drawn together with other ethnographic tiles, such as Van Ausdale and Feagin's (1996, 2001) work in America, Brooker's (2002) research in England; Connolly's (1994, 2003) work in England and Ireland and Russell's (2011) work with teenagers in England and Australia, a fuller image of children's lived experiences begins to emerge. Further ethnographies need to be conducted with children from a range of social and cultural contexts to add to these tiles to complete the mosaic's image and further our understanding of young children's experiences from a diverse range of backgrounds.

Additionally, this study has highlighted gaps in the literature that this thesis has begun to fill but which need further exploration in other social contexts. These are summarised below:

The impact that kinship ties can have on children's peer interactions at school.

The influence of family structure and composition on children's imaginative play at school and the role that these aspects can have in perpetuating and challenging discourses of discrimination.

Further, the data in this study has thrown up additional areas of interest that were beyond the scope of this study but that warrant further exploration:

The complex forces and discourses of discrimination that cause children to exclude their peers from their games.

The challenges that monolingual school staff face, and the strategies that they employ, in countering bullying in situations where children use a language that staff members cannot speak to exclude others from their games and activities.

The impact of repeated (or in some cases continual) migration on young children's conceptualisation and operationalisation of identity.

Parents' roles in both perpetuating and countering discourses of discrimination and consequently children's views on difference.

How and why refugees conceptualise and operationalise collective family identities in a post-civil war transnational environment and the role that language plays within this process of identity (re)negotiation.

How, and to what extent, both girls and boys challenge *internal* and *external* structures pertaining to gendered identities and gender roles.

Young children's perspectives on learning about diversity and difference at school.

Furthermore, as Brooker (2006: 116) contends, research projects, such as the current study and areas for future research outlined above, are important as an end in themselves, as they can 'provide a rare opportunity for ... children to question and reflect on stereotypes' that are often taking for granted by wider structural discourses. When policy, practice and research all work to encourage children to challenge discourses of discrimination, and hierarchies of difference the process of unlearning discrimination may begin to become a reality rather than just a dream.

My future journey

The time I spent at Sunnyside listening to and sharing in children's stories were filled with laughter, fun and, at times, deep sadness as children shared with me their joys, dreams and pain. Discovering the deep seated derogatory views that some of the *older girls* have of themselves in relation to their ethnic identities continues to distress me.

In turn, this has invigorated me since completing this study to continue to work with the school in an advisory role to find ways to help these children fight against dominant structural discourse, enabling them to feel proud of who they are and encouraging them to strive for their dreams in the face of discrimination. It is my hope that this book will also help others to take up this fight against discriminatory social structures in their own communities.

Bibliography

Archer, M. S. (1995). *Realist social theory: The morphogenetic approach.* Cambridge, Cambridge University Press.

Arnold, C. (2010). Under*standing schemas and emotion in early childhood. London*, Sage.

Association of Social Anthropologists of the UK (ASA) (2011). *Ethical guidelines for good research practice.* [online], www.theasa.org/ethics/Ethical_guidelines.pdf [Accessed 21 November, 2013].

Bakhtin, M. (1981). *The dialogical imagination.* Austin, University of Texas.

Banks, M. (1995). Visual research methods. *Social research update,* [online] 11, sru.soc.surrey.ac.uk/SRU11/SRU11.html [Accessed 9 July, 2014].

Barker, M. (1981). *The new racism: Conservatives and the ideology of the tribe.* London, University Publications of America.

Barley, N. (1983). *The innocent anthropologist: Notes from a mud hut.* London, Penguin Books.

Barley, R. and Bath, C. (2014) The importance of familiarisation when doing research with young children. *Ethnography and Education,* 9(2): 182-195

Barth, F. (1969). *Ethnic groups and boundaries: The social organisation of culture difference.* London, Allen and Unwin.

Bath, C. (2009). *Learning to belong: Exploring young children's participation at the start of school.* London, Taylor and Francis.

Bauman, Z. (1996). From pilgrim to tourist—or a short history of identity, in Hall, S. (ed.). *Questions of Cultural Identity.* London, Sage, 21, 19-38.

Berg, B. (2009). *Qualitative research methods for the social sciences.* Boston, Pearson Education.

Bligh, C. (2011). Rights in Early Years settings and a young child's right to silence, in Jones, P., Richter, I. and Walker, G. (eds.). *Practical applications of children's rights: Theory and practice.* Sage, London, 95-108.

Blumer, H. (1962). *Symbolic Interactionism: Perspective and method.* Berkeley, California, University of California Press.

Bourdieu, P. (1977). Cultural reproduction and social reproduction, in Karabel, J. and Halsey, A. (eds.). *Power and ideology in education.* Oxford, Oxford University Press.

Bourdieu, P. (1990). *The logic of practice.* Cambridge, Polity Press.

Breglia, L. (2009). The 'work' of ethnographic fieldwork, in Faubion, J. and Marcus, G. (eds.). *Fieldwork is not what it used to be: Learning anthropology's method in a time of transition.* New York, Cornell University Press, 129-142.

Broadhead, P. and Burt, A. (2011). *Understanding young children's learning through play.* Florence, KY, Routledge.

Brooker, L. (2001). Researching children's perspectives. *British Educational Research Journal,* 27: (2): 226-227.

Brooker, L. (2002). *Starting school—young children learning cultures.* Buckingham, Open University Press.

Brooker, L. (2006). From home to the home corner: Observing children's identity-maintenance in early childhood settings. *Children and Society,* 20(2): 116-127.

Brown, B. (2007). *Unlearning discrimination in the early years.* Stoke-on-Trent, Trentham Books Ltd.

Burr, V. (1995). *An introduction to social constructionism.* London, Routledge.

Butler, J. (1990). *Gender trouble: Feminism and the subversion of identity.* London, Routledge.

Clark, A. (2004). The mosaic approach and research with young children, in Lewis, V. (ed.). *The reality of research with children and young people.* London, Sage, 142-161.

Clark, A. and Moss, P. (2001). *Listening to young children: The mosaic approach.* London, National Children's Bureau.

Coates, E. (2004). 'I forgot the sky!' Children's stories contained within their drawings, in Lewis, V. (ed.). *The reality of research with children and young people.* London, Sage, 5-26.

Cocks, A. J. (2006). The ethical maze: Finding an inclusive path towards gaining children's agreement to research participation. *Childhood,* 13(2): 247.

Cohen, A. (1985). *The symbolic construction of community.* London, Tavistock.

Cohen, A. (1994). *Self consciousness: An alternative anthropology of identity.* London, Routledge.

Cole, S. (2011). Situating children in the discourse of spirituality, in Wane, N., Maniymo, E. and Ritskes, E. (eds.). *Spirituality, education and society: An integrated approach.* Rotterdam, Sense Publishers, 1-14.

Collins, P. H. (2000). Gender, black feminism, and black political economy. *Annals of the American Academy of Political and Social Science,* 568, 41–53.

Connolly, P. (1994). All lads together?: Racism, masculinity and multicultural/anti-racist strategies in a primary school, *International Studies in Sociology of Education,* 4(2): 191-211.

Connolly, P. (1998). *Racism, gender identities and young children: Social relations in a multi-ethnic, inner-city primary school.* London, Routledge.

Connolly, P. (2003). The development of young children's ethnic identities: Implications for early years practice, in Vincent, C. (ed.). *Social Justice, Education and Identity.* London, Routledge, 166-184.

Connolly, P. (2008). Race, gender and critical reflexivity in research with young children, in Christensen, P. and James, A. (eds.). *Research with children: Perspectives and practices,* second ed., London, Routledge, 173-188.

Cooley, C. (1902). *Human nature and the social order.* New York, Schribner's.

Corsaro, W. A. (1979). 'We're friends, right?': Children's use of access rituals in a nursery school. *Language in Society,* 8(2-3): 315-336.

Corsaro, W. A. (2003). *We're friends, right?: Inside kids' cultures.* Washington D.C., Joseph Henry Press.

Corsaro, W. A., Molinari, L., Gold Hadley, K., and Sugioka, H., Keeping and Making Friends in Italian Children's Transition from Preschool to Elementary School, *Social Psychology Quarterly,* 66, 272-292, 2003.

Crenshaw, K. (1989). Demarginalizing the intersection of race and sex: A black feminist critique of antidiscrimination doctrine, feminist theory and antiracist politics. *University of Chicago Legal Forum*, 139-149.

Crul, M. (2007). *Pathways to success for the children of immigrants*. Washington, Migration policy institute.

Cummins, J. (2001). *Bilingual children's mother tongue: Why is it important for education.* [online]. inet.dpb.dpu.dk/infodok/sprogforum/Espr19/CumminsENG.pdf [Accessed 7 November/7 2013]

Davies, B. (2003). *Frogs and snails and feminist tales: Preschool children and gender.* New York, Hampton Press.

Davis, J. M. (1998). Understanding the meanings of children: A reflexive process. *Children and Society,* 12(5): 325-335.

Denzin, N. and Lincoln, Y. (2003). Methods of collecting and analyzing empirical materials, in Denzin, N. and Lincoln, Y. (eds.). *Collecting and interpreting qualitative materials.* London, Sage, 47-60.

Derman-Sparks, L. (ed.) (1989). *Anti-bias curriculum: Tools for empowering young children.* Washington, National Association for the Education of Young Children.

Devine, D. (2000). The exercise of power in children's experience of school. *Irish Educational Studies,* 19(1): 189-206.

DfE (2011). *Schools, pupils and their characteristics, January, 2012.* [online], www.education.gov.uk/rsgateway/DB/SFR/s001012/index.shtml [Accessed 16 August, 2013].

Drury, R. (2007). *Young bilingual learners at home and school: Researching multilingual voices.* Stoke on Trent, Trentham Books Ltd.

Durkheim, E. (1893). *The division of labor in society.* New York, Free Press.

Durkheim, E. (1912). *The elementary forms of religious life.* London, George Allen and Unwin.

Emond, R. (2005). Ethnographic research methods with children and young people, in Greene, S. and Hogan, D. (eds.). *Researching children's experience: Methods and approaches.* London, Sage, 123-139.

Engel, S. (2005). Narrative analysis of children's experiences In: Greene, S. and Hogan, D. (eds.). *Researching children's experience: Methods and approaches.* London, Sage, 119-216.

Entzinger, H. (2005). Changing the rules while the game is on; from multiculturalism to assimilation in the Netherlands, in Bodemann, Y. and Yurdakul, G. (eds.). *Migration citizenship, ethnos: Incorporation regimes in Germany, Western Europe and North America.* New York, Palgrave Macmillan, 121-144.

Eriksen, T. (2001). *Small places, large issues: An introduction to social and cultural anthropology.* London, Pluto Press.

Flewitt, R. (2005). Conducting research with young children: Some ethical considerations. *Early child development and care,* 175(6): 553-565.

Frith, S. (2000). Music and identity, in Hall, S. and Du Gay, P. (eds.). *Questions of cultural identity.* London, Sage, 108-127.

Furey, R. and Kay, J. (2010). Developing ethical guidelines for safeguarding children during social research. *Research Ethics Review,* 6(4): 120-127.

Gaertner, S. L., et al. (1999). Across cultural divides: The value of a superordinate identity, in Prentice, D. and Miller, T. (eds.). *Cultural divides: Understanding and overcoming group conflict.* New York, The Russell Sage Foundation, 173-212.

Gauntlett, D. (2007). *Creative explorations: New approaches to identities and audiences.* Oxon, Taylor and Francis.

Geertz, C. (1973). *The interpretation of cultures.* New York, Basic Books.

Giddens, A. (1984). *The constitution of society.* Cambridge, Polity Press.

Giddens, A. (1991). *Modernity and self-identity.* Cambridge, Polity Press.

Gillborn, D. And Youdell, D. (2000). *Rationing education: Policy, practice, reform and equity.* Florence: Routledge.

Gilroy, P. (1993). *The Black Atlantic: Modernity and double consciousness.* Cambridge, MA, Harvard University Press.

Glenn, E. N. (2008). Yearning for lightness transnational circuits in the marketing and consumption of skin lighteners. *Gender and Society,* 22(3): 281-302.

Goffman, E. (1959). *The presentation of self in everyday life.* New York, Double Day.

Goffman, E. (1963). *Behaviour in public places: Notes on the social order of gatherings.* New York, The Free Press.

Griffiths, M. (1995). *Feminisms and the self: The web of identity.* London, Routledge.

Gunaratnam, Y. (2003). *Researching race and ethnicity: Methods, knowledge and power.* London, Sage.

Hadj-Abdou, L. et al. (2011). Female Muslim Covering: An Opportunity for the Well-Being of Women?, in Bonvin, J. et al. (eds.) *Transforming gendered well-being in europe: The impact of social movements,* Farnham, Ashgate Publishing, 213-248.

Hall, S. (2000). Who needs 'identity'? In: Du Gay, P., Evans, J. and Redman, P. (eds.). *Identity: A reader.* London, Sage, 15-30.

Hammersley, M. and Atkinson, P. (2007). *Ethnography: Principles in practice.* London, Taylor and Francis.

Harro, B. (2000). The cycle of socialization, in Adams, M. (ed.). *Readings for diversity and social justice.* London, Routledge, 15-21.

Heath, J. (1997). Moroccan Arabic phonology. *Phonologies of Asia and Africa (including the Caucasus),* 205-217.

Hey, V. (1997). *The company she keeps: An ethnography of girls' friendships.* Buckingham, Open University Press.

Holland, D. and Lachicotte, W. (2007). Vygotsky, Mead, and the new sociocultural studies of identity, in Daniels, H., Cole, M. and Wertsch, J. (eds.). *The Cambridge companion to Vygotsky.* Cambridge, Cambridge University Press, 101-135.

Holmes, R. (1995). *How young children perceive race.* Thousand Oaks, Sage.

Hughes, E. (1945). Dilemmas and contradictions of status. *American Journal of Sociology,* 50(5): 353-359.

Hunt, S. (2011). *Master Status.* [online], www.blackwellreference.com/public/tocnode?id=g9781405124331_chunk_g978140512433119_ss1-44 [Accessed 7 February, 2014].

Hussain, E. (2007). *The Islamist.* London, Penguin Books.

James, A. (1997). How British is British food? in Caplan, P. (ed.). *Food, health and identity.* London, Routledge, 71-86.

James, A. (1998). Play in childhood: An anthropological perspective. *Child and Adolescent Mental Health,* 3(3): 104-109.

Jeffcoate, R. (1979). *Positive image: Towards a multicultural curriculum.* London, Writers and Readers Cooperative.

Jeffs, T. and Smith, M. (2005). *Informal education: Conversation, democracy and learning.* Nottingham, Educational Heretics Press.

Jenkins, R. (1996). *Social identity,* first ed., London, Routledge.

Jenkins, R. (2008). *Social identity,* second ed., London, Routledge.

Johnson, K. (2008). Teaching children to use visual research methods, in Thomson, P. (ed.). *Doing visual research with children and young people.* London, Taylor and Francis, 77-94.

Kay, J., Furey, R., Stiell, B., Shipton, L., Cripps, C., and Barley, R.. (2009). *Safeguarding children in research contexts.* Sheffield, Sheffield Hallam University.

Lareau, A. (2003). *Unequal childhoods: Class, race, and family life.* California, University of California Press.

LeCompte, M. and Schensul, J. (1999). *Analyzing and interpreting ethnographic data.* London, Altamira Press.

Lin, N. (2000). Inequality in social capital. *Contemporary Sociology,* 29: 785-795.

Locke, J. (1959). *An essay concerning human understanding.* Dover, Dover Publications.

Lowles, N. and Painter, A. (2011). *Fear and HOPE.* London, Searchlight Educational Trust.

MacNaughton, G. (2001). Beyond 'othering': Rethinking approaches to teaching young Anglo-Australian children about indigenous Australians. *Contemporary issues in early childhood,* 2(1): 83-93.

MacNaughton, G. and Smith, K. (2005). Transforming research ethics: The choices and challenges of researching with children, in Farrell, A. (ed.). *Ethical research with children.* Maidenhead, Open University Press, 112-123.

MacNaughton, G. and Smith, K. (2008). Children's rights in early childhood, in Kehily, M. (ed.). *An introduction to childhood studies,* second ed., Maidenhead, Open University Press, 161-176.

McKee, D. (1989) *Elmer.* London: Andersen Press.

Malaguzzi, L. (1993). The Hundred Languages of Children: The Reggio Emilia approach to early childhood education. Norwood: Ablex Publishers.

Malinowski, B. (1922). *Argonauts of the Western Pacific.* London, Routledge.

Mandell, N. (1988). The least-adult role in studying children. *Journal of Contemporary Ethnography,* 16(4): 433-467.

Marranci, G. (2006). *Jihad beyond Islam.* Oxford, Berg.

Marranci, G. (2008). *The anthropology of Islam.* Oxford, Berg.

Marx, K. and Engels, F. (1948). *The communist manifesto.* New York, International Publishers.

Mayall, B. (2008). Conversations with children, in Christensen, P. and James, A. (eds.). *Research with children: Perspectives and practices.* Abingdon, Routledge, 109-124.

McCall, G. and Simmons, J. (1978). Identities and interactions. New York: Free Press.

McCall, L. (2008). The complexity of intersectionality, in Cooper, D. (ed.). *Intersectionality and beyond: Law, power and politics of location.* Abingdon, Routledge, 49-68.

McGoldrick D. (2010). *Human rights and religion: The Islamic headscarf debate in Europe.* Oxford, Hart Publishing.

Mead, G. (1934). *Mind, self, and society: From the standpoint of a social behaviorist.* Chicago, University of Chicago Press.

Mills, C. W. (1959). *The sociological imagination.* Oxford, Oxford University Press.

Milstein, D. (2010). Children as co-researchers in anthropological narratives in education. *Ethnography and Education,* 5(1): 1-15.

Modood, T. (2007). *Multiculturalism: A civic idea.* Cambridge, Polity Press.

Modood, T. (2010). From multiculturalism to multifaithism? *Studies in ethnicity and nationalism,* 10(2): 307-309.

Morphy, H. and Banks, M. (1997). Introduction: Rethinking visual anthropology, in Banks, M. (ed.). *Rethinking visual anthropology.* London, Yale University Press, 1-35.

Moss, P. (2012). Respecting the singularity of the child, resisting the society of control. *The Centre for the Study of Childhood and Youth 4th International Conference, 10th July, 2012,* Sheffield.

Moss, P., Dillon, J. and Statham, J. (2000). The 'child in need' and 'the rich child': Discourses, constructions and practice. *Critical Social Policy,* 20(2): 233-254.

Mouzelis, N. (2000). The subjectivist-objectivist divide: Against transcendence. *Sociology,* 34(4): 741-762.

Mumford, S. (1990). *Himalayan dialogue: Tibetan Lamas and Gurung shamans in Nepal.* Kathmandu, Printing Support PVT Ltd.

Nayak, A. (2009). Race, ethnicity and young people, in Montgomery, H. and Kellett, M. (eds.). *Children and young people's world: Developing frameworks for integrated practice.* Bristol, The Policy Press, 91-108.

Nazroo, J. (ed.) (2006). *Health and social research in multiethnic societies.* Abingdon, Routledge.

Orellana, M. F., Dorner, L. and Pulido, L. (2003). Accessing assets: Immigrant youth's work as family translators or "para-phrasers". *Social Problems,* 50(4): 505-524.

Paley, V. G. (1993). *You can't say you can't play.* Cambridge, Harvard University Press.

Phoenix, A. (2011a) Theorising ethnicity. *ESRC Methodological Innovations Network Researching Ethnicity: What, why and how?, 13th March, 2011*, Manchester.

Phoenix, A. (2011b). Psychosocial interventions: Contextualising the accounts of adults who grew up in visibly ethnically different households, in Lutz, H., Vivar, M. and Supik, L. (eds.). *Framing intersectionality: Debates on a multi-faceted concept in gender studies.* Farnham, Ashgate Publishing, 137-152.

Pryor, J. and Ampiah, J. G. (2004). Listening to voices in the village: Collaborating through data chains, in Mutua, K. and Swadener, B. (eds.) *Decolonizing research in cross-cultural contexts: Critical personal narratives*, 159–78.

Punch, S. (2002). Research with children: The same or different from research with adults? *Childhood,* 9(3): 321-341.

Rice, L. (2011) Informal/peripheral production, in *Architectural Humanities Research Conference*, 27th - 29th October, Belfast, eprints.uwe.ac.uk.

Raj, D. (2003). *Where are you from?: Middle-class migrants in the modern world.* London, University of California Press.

Rao, J. (2010). The caste system: Effects on poverty in India, Nepal and Sri Lanka. *Global Majority E-journal,* 1(2): 97-106.

Russell, L. (2007). 'Visual methods in researching the arts and inclusion: possibilities and dilemmas' *Ethnography and Education,* 2(1): 39-55.

Russell, L. (2011). *Understanding pupil resistance: Integrating gender, ethnicity and class.* Stroud: Ethnography and Education Publishing.

Salway, S., Allmark, P. J., Barley, R., Higginbottom, G., Gerrish, K. and Ellison, G. (2009a). Researching ethnic inequalities. *Social Research Update,* [online] 58, sru.soc.surrey.ac.uk/SRU58.pdf [Accessed 9 July, 2014].

Salway, S., Allmark, P. J., Barley, R., Higginbottom, G., Gerrish, K. and Ellison, G. (2009b). Social research for a multiethnic population: Do the research ethics and standards guidelines of UK learned societies address this challenge? *Twenty-first Century Society,* 4(1): 53-81.

Seymour-Smith, C. (1986). *Palgrave dictionary of Anthropology.* Basingstoke, Palgrave Macmillan.

Sökefeld, M. (1999). *Debating self, identity and cultural anthropology,* Anthropology, 40(4): 417-47.

Spencer, S. (2006). *Race and ethnicity: Culture, identity and representation.* Abingdon, Routledge.

Spencer, S. (2011). *Visual research methods in the social sciences: Awakening visions.* London, Taylor and Francis.

Stones, R. (2005). *Structuration Theory.* Basingstoke, Palgrave Macmillan.

Tate, S. A. (2009). *Black beauty: Aesthetics, stylization, politics*, Farnham, Ashgate Publishing.

Taylor, G. and Spencer, S. (2004). Introduction, in Taylor, G. and Spencer, S. (eds.). *Social identities: Multidisciplinary perspectives.* Abingdon, Routledge, 1-13.

Thomas, N. and O'Kane, C. (1998). The ethics of participatory research with children. *Children and Society,* 12(5): 336-348.

Thompson, J. B. (1989). The theory of structuration, in Held, D. and Thompson, J. B. (eds.). *Social theory of modern societies: Anthony Giddens and his critics.* Cambridge, Cambridge University Press, 56-76.

Thorne, B. (1993). *Gender play: Girls and boys in school.* New Brunswick, Rutgers University Press.

Turner, V. (1967). Betwixt and between: The liminal period in rites of passage, in Turner, V. (ed.). *The forest of symbols.* Ithaca, NY, Cornell University Press, 3-19.

Unger, R. M. (2005). *What should the left propose?* London, Verso Books.

United Nations Human Rights Council (UNHCR) (2010). *Libya must end racism against Black African migrants and others.* Geneva, United Nations Human Rights Council.

Valentine, G. and Sporton, D. (2009). 'How other people see you, it's like nothing that's inside': The impact of processes of disidentification and disavowal on young people's subjectivities. *Sociology,* 43(4): 735-751.

Van Ausdale, D. and Feagin, J. (1996). Using racial and ethnic concepts: The critical case of very young children. *American Sociological Review,* 61(5): 779-793.

Van Ausdale, D. and Feagin, J. (2001). *The first R: How children learn race and racism.* Maryland, Rowman and Littlefield.

Van Gennep, A. (1908). *The rites of passage.* Chicago, University of Chicago Press.

Vandenbroeck, M. (1999). *The view of the yeti.* The Hague, Bernard van Leer Foundation.

Vertovec, S. (2007). Super-diversity and its implications. *Ethnic and Racial Studies,* 30(6): 1024-1054.

Walter, N. (2010). *Living dolls: The return of sexism.* London, Virago Press.

Weber, M. (1930). *The protestant ethic and the spirit of capitalism.* London: Penguin Books.

Wolcott, H. (1995). Making a study 'more ethnographic', in: Maanen, J. (ed.). *Representation in ethnography.* London, Sage, 79-111.

Wolcott, H. (1999). *Ethnography: A way of seeing.* London, Altamira Press.

Wright, E. O. (2010). *Envisioning real utopias.* London, Verso Books.

Wrong, M. (2009). *It's our turn to eat: The story of a Kenyan whistle-blower.* London, HarperCollins.

Index

Ethnography and Education publications

Titles in the series include›

Creative learning: European experiences, edited by Bob Jeffrey;

Researching education policy: Ethnographic experiences, Geoff Troman, Bob Jeffrey and Dennis Beach;

The commodification of teaching and learning, Dennis Beach and Marianne Dovemark;

Performing English with a postcolonial accent: Ethnographic narratives from Mexico, Angeles Clemente and Michael J. Higgins.

How to do Educational Ethnography edited by Geoffrey Walford

Ritual and Identity; The staging and performing of rituals in the lives of young people, Christoph Wulf et al.

Young people's influence and democratic education: Ethnographic studies in upper secondary schools, edited by Elisabet Öhrn, Lisbeth Lundahl and Dennis Beach

Learner biographies and learning cultures: Identity and apprenticeship in England and Germany, Michaela Brockmann

Learning care lessons: Literacy, love, care and solidarity, by Maggie Feeley

Further information available at

www.tufnellpress.co.uk

or

www.ethnographyandeducation.org

www.ingramcontent.com/pod-product-compliance
Ingram Content Group UK Ltd.
Pitfield, Milton Keynes, MK11 3LW, UK
UKHW020142250726
13967UKWH00002B/813

9 781872 767345